# LOVE ACROSS BORDERS

High rates of intermarriage, especially with Whites, have been viewed as an indicator that Asian Americans are successfully "assimilating," signaling acceptance by the White majority and their own desire to become part of the White mainstream. Comparing two types of Asian American intermarriage, interracial and interethnic, Kelly H. Chong disrupts these assumptions by showing that both types of intermarriages, in differing ways, are sites of complex struggles around racial/ethnic identity and cultural formations that reveal the salience of race in the lives of Asian Americans.

Drawing upon extensive qualitative data, Chong explores how interracial marriages, far from being an endpoint of assimilation, are a terrain of life-long negotiations over racial and ethnic identities, while interethnic (intra-Asian) unions and family-making illuminate Asian Americans' ongoing efforts to co-construct and sustain a common racial identity and panethnic culture despite interethnic differences and tensions. Chong also examines the pivotal role race and gender play in shaping both the romantic desires and desirability of Asian Americans, spotlighting the social construction of love and marital choices.

Through the lens of intermarriage, *Love Across Borders* offers critical insights into the often invisible racial struggles of this racially in-between "model minority" group – particularly its ambivalent negotiations with whiteness and white privilege – and on the group's social incorporation process and its implications for the redrawing of color boundaries in the U.S.

**Kelly H. Chong** is a Professor and Chairperson of Sociology at the University of Kansas. She is the award-winning author of *Deliverance and Submission: Evangelical Women and the Negotiation of Patriarchy in South Korea* (2008) and numerous journal articles. Her current areas of scholarship include race/ethnicity, gender, immigration, religion, Asian American studies, and Asian studies.

# LOVE ACROSS BORDERS

## Asian Americans, Race, and the Politics of Intermarriage and Family-Making

*Kelly H. Chong*

Routledge
Taylor & Francis Group

NEW YORK AND LONDON

First published 2021
by Routledge
52 Vanderbilt Avenue, New York, NY 10017

and by Routledge
2 Park Square, Milton Park, Abingdon, Oxon, OX14 4RN

*Routledge is an imprint of the Taylor & Francis Group, an informa business*

*Library of Congress Cataloging-in-Publication Data*
A catalog record for this book has been requested

ISBN: 978-1-138-21254-1 (hbk)
ISBN: 978-1-138-21255-8 (pbk)
ISBN: 978-1-315-45036-0 (ebk)

Typeset in Bembo
by Apex CoVantage, LLC

*For My Daughter Daria,*
*With Undying Love*

# CONTENTS

# ACKNOWLEDGMENTS

The making of this book was the result of a long, often arduous, journey. This book's completion would not have been possible without numerous colleagues, friends, and family members who supported me throughout the process of research and writing.

My deepest gratitude goes first to all of the individuals appearing in this book who have generously offered their time to talk with me. Although I cannot thank each of them by name, it goes without saying that were it not for their stories, this book would not exist. I especially thank those participants who went out of their way by making it their mission to help me make connections in the field and offering valuable insights along the way. I am grateful for their belief in the worthiness of this project.

I thank the former and current members of my home department at the University of Kansas Department of Sociology for their many years of professional and personal support. These friends and colleagues include Victor Agadjanian, Sandra Albrecht, Elif Andac, Bob Antonio, Lynn Davidman, Brian Donovan, David Ekerdt, Tanya Golash-Boza, Eric Hanley, Shirley Harkess, Shirley Hill, ChangHwan Kim, Meredith Kleykemp, Tracey LaPierre, Cecilia Menjivar, Joane Nagel, Mehranghiz Najafizadeh, Ebenezer Obadare, Emily Rauscher, Bill Staples, Jarron Saint Onge, David Smith, Joey Sprague, William Staples, Paul Stock, and Mary Zimmerman (Mary, you are my hero, and I would not have made it without you). I count my blessings for being able to be part of such a collegial department.

I am especially grateful to those who have taken the time to read and critique parts of this book; thank you, Bob, Brian, Cecilia, Joane, Lynn, and Mary. Special thanks are extended to fellow women chairs Cecile Accilien, Alesha Doan, Ani Kokobobo, and Faye Xiao at the University of Kansas (KU) for their friendship and encouragement. At KU, I also owe a debt of gratitude to Michael Doudoroff, Jennifer Duenas, Elaine Gerbert, D. A. Graham, Jennifer Hamer, Kyoim Yun, Mary Lee Hummert, Clarence Lang, Jennifer Ng, Ji-Yeon Lee, Carl Lejuez, Stanley Lombardo, Crystal Lumpkins, Marcy Quiason, Laurie Petty, Judy Roitman, and Akiko Takeyama. I must also thank sociology's marvelous staff members Beth Hoffman, Corinne Butler, and Melissa Wittner for their assistance on many fronts.

I am deeply appreciative of many colleagues and friends from all corners of the country and globe who have supported me in my scholarly endeavors: this list includes the late Nancy Abelmann, Angie Chung, Diana Lin, Jiannbin Hsiao, Nazli Kibria, Minjeong Kim, Nadia Y. Kim, the late Mary Ellen Konieczny, Loren Lybarger, Rebecca O'Riain, Jerry Park, Karen Pyke, Sharmilla Rudrappa, the late Martin Riesebrodt, Stephen Rosenberg, Leslie Salzinger, Miri Song, Paul Spickard, Jessica Vasquez-Tokos, Leslie Wang, and Jun Yoo. I also thank Jennah Bauswell, Scott Bloch, Tina Crawford, Rashmi DePaepe, the late Hilary Dunst, Carol Harrell, Susan Kraus, Leenor Lee, Moonsook Lee, Daniel Levy, Michele Longhurst, Addie Mehl, the late Anne O'Neill, Elena Vorontsova, Nina Yoo, and Kathryn Zimmerman. Your presence in my life has been a gift.

I thank the University of Kansas for its financial support for this project, particularly in the form of General Research Funds, grants through the Research Excellence Initiative, research leaves, and other forms of travel and research funds. I thank the American Philosophical Society for the Franklin Research Grant. I owe a special thanks to my editor Dean Birkenkamp at Routledge for his enthusiasm for and belief in this book and his guidance throughout the publication process.

On the personal front: I am profoundly sorrowful that my parents Dongyaw Kim and Hanchae Chong have not lived long enough to see this project to fruition. But they know they have my eternal gratitude. Stacy and Mark, I feel blessed to have you as my siblings. The last decade has been, in many ways, one of the most challenging of my life, especially for the many unexpected losses of those closest and dearest to me, including my parents, mentors, and closest friends. During these difficult times, my life partner, Tim DePaepe, has supported me in countless ways and unselfishly shared the burdens of parenthood. I also feel fortunate to have found in him a stupendous professional collaborator.

Last but not least, this book is dedicated to the teenager in my life in whose body and soul the wonders of the universe are wrapped, my daughter Daria. Daria, so many times I felt as though you were all but milking the life out of me, but when I look at you now, all I see is the flowering of love, goodness, generosity, and a spirit like no other. I cannot imagine never having met you nor lived a life without you.

# 1

# INTRODUCTION

When I was growing up in New York City, my family's mantra was "Marry your own kind. A nice Korean boy. Don't even think about doing otherwise." To me and my siblings, these admonitions were initially so obvious that they did not need to be questioned. Of course we must stick to our own kind. Of course we must preserve our cultural heritage. Koreans were, after all, a proud, homogeneous people with a unique culture and history, and we could not dare threaten that. National pride aside, I knew though that fear tinged my parents' ethnic and racial preservationist stance, a fear of the dominant majority White Americans whom they believed did not respect nor understand Asian people. My parents, and many other Asian immigrant parents we knew, viewed this as stemming from casual arrogance directed at immigrants by Whites, especially at immigrants of color, whom the dominant culture saw as racially and culturally inferior.

In most places around the globe, intermarriages, especially those involving imagined racial-mixing and boundary-crossing, elicit anxiety.[1] Even though interracial and other types of boundary-crossing unions (religious, ethnic, national, and so on) have long been a part of human history, the boundary-fixing constructs of race, ethnicity, nation, and religion continue to promote resistance to sexual or marital mixing. When sharp cultural, national, or racial inequalities exist among groups, interracial unions in particular face social condemnation and legal prohibition. In the United States, where racial conflict has historically occupied center focus, the sordid history of anti-miscegenation policies of the U.S. government targeted at mixing of "Whites" with people of color, such as with Blacks, Native-Americans, and Asians, is well known.[2] It was not until 1967 that the U.S. Supreme Court struck down anti-miscegenation laws in the landmark

*Loving vs. Virginia* decision. Since the 1960s, intermarriage rates have begun to climb for all major racial groups. Although intermarriage rates for Blacks still lag behind those of other racial groups,[3] the rates have risen significantly for other minority groups, including for Latinos and for Asian Americans.

Studies of intermarriage involving minority groups of color, however, especially those of African Americans and more recently of Latinos, challenge any benign or celebratory interpretations that a rise in, or acceptance of, intermarriages may signal a decline in racial prejudice, the breakdown of group barriers, or the majority group's acceptance of the minority group.[4] Many studies of racial minority intermarriages illustrate that despite the recent easing of opposition against intermarriages as a whole within the United States, marital boundary-crossings are still impacted by the issue of race; rather than simply being a sign of the breakdown of racial barriers or of assimilation, studies of intermarriage may exhibit how race still matters in the United States or "how racial borders still exist."[5] Furthermore, intermarital and romantic experiences of minority groups of color reveal that current colorblind discourses, which purport that people are marrying across racial borders and dismantling racial boundaries because people no longer see nor should see color, help disguise the centrality of race, color, and the system of racial hierarchy in the United States. Colorblind ideologies also make it palatable to gloss over the salience of race and color in interracial relationships, whether in how love and romantic desires are shaped or what role race may play in the dynamics of interracial relationships and marriages, identity negotiations, and family-making.

Despite the growing scholarship on intermarital unions, Asian American intermarriage has not been the subject of robust, in-depth qualitative scrutiny. Due to the popularized perception that Asian Americans are somehow more acceptable than darker-skinned minorities as marital partners for majority Whites, critical and nuanced analyses of the racial and gender dynamics of Asian American intermarriages have been limited. Like Latinos, persons of Asian descent occupy an ambiguous in-between space in the historically bifurcated Black-White racial divide in the United States. Although persons of Asian ancestry were negatively racialized, othered, excluded, and reviled throughout U.S. history, their current status is that of a "racial middle,"[6] and similar to Latinos, Asian Americans' position in the U.S. racial hierarchy appears more fluid and less fixed. Moreover, the stereotype of Asian Americans as a successful and cooperative model minority further complicates this ambiguous in-between position in the racial hierarchy, while encouraging Asian Americans' social invisibility. The underresearching of Asian American intermarital unions reflects the reality of this liminal position within the U.S. racial structure.

This book seeks to remedy this gap in the scholarship. Despite the easy-to-digest image of Asian Americans as a rapidly assimilating, socially acceptable group in an increasingly colorblind and multicultural society—a society striving toward a triumphant belief that racism may be losing its force—this book explores the personal meanings and social significance of intermarriage for contemporary Asian Americans. By qualitatively examining intermarriage and family-making from the perspective of this study's participants, this book will consider the inner dynamics of Asian American intermarriages; in particular, it will look at how issues of race, perceived social status of Asian Americans, and possible shifting racial boundaries in contemporary U.S. society affect these marriages.

This book will consider that similar to other racial minority groups, race is highly relevant to intermarriage and family-making of Asian Americans. Race matters in several salient, sometimes subtle and ambiguous, ways for the participants, including how romantic desires are formed, intermarital relationships forged, and child-raising negotiated. A study of intermarriage therefore reveals much about Asian Americans' racial struggles, their experiences as a racial minority group, and their process of social incorporation into U.S. society. Praised as "honorary Whites," though simultaneously othered racially and culturally through "forever foreigner" stereotypes,[7] it is easier to gloss over the racial struggles of Asian Americans because the problems they might be battling as the in-between racial minority are more difficult to discern than for other groups of color.

This book focuses on the politics and meanings of intermarital relationships among U.S.-born/-raised Asian Americans, primarily the second generation.[8] Although there has been a recent growth of rich, qualitative studies about cross-national, interracial marriages involving Asian-ethnics as a way of examining racial and gender politics of intermarital unions, particularly "marriage migrations" of Asian women to White men in the United States or Europe, investigating inter-marriages among U.S.-born/-raised Asian Americans is important for two reasons: 1) it throws into greater relief the significance of racial and gender politics of boundary-crossing unions since there is a tendency to assume that intermarriages of U.S.-born/-raised Asian Americans naturally occur due to assimilation or are purely motivated by love and individual choice; 2) it isolates the experiences of U.S.-born/-raised Asian Americans—a group more immersed in American culture and interracial dynamics than their foreign-born counterparts—enabling a more accurate gauge of the relationship of intermarriage to assimilation as well as a comparison to the assimilative experiences of European-ethnic groups.

Indeed, the rates of intermarriages, especially interracial marriages to Whites, rise in the second generation and later for most Asian American groups, leading many to believe that racial prejudice and barriers may diminish for each generation. However, if we do not begin with the assumption that this trend is an indicator of desired or inevitable assimilation for Asian Americans,[9] these intermarriages, and their internal dynamics and meanings, provide fertile soil for exploring the ongoing significance of racial politics in the lives of Asian Americans, the meaning and paths of their assimilation process, and the renegotiation and reworking of racial-ethnic identities and boundaries within the United States.

## Comparing Interracial and Interethnic Marriages

In this book, the term "intermarriage" refers to two types of boundary-crossing marriages among Asian Americans: interracial marriages and interethnic (intra-Asian) marriages, and this study compares these two types of marriages. Historically, the majority of Asian American intermarriages has been composed of interracial marriage to Whites; by 1980, this rate was as high as 90% of total Asian American intermarriages. Since then, however, there has been a notable growth of *interethnic* marriages, while interracial marriages have begun to decline, especially among the non-immigrant, U.S.-born/-raised generations.[10] As I will discuss in greater detail in Chapter 2, although interracial marriages are still higher in absolute numbers, the increase in Asian American interethnic marriages has begun to capture scholarly and media attention.

Comparing the intriguing phenomenon of interethnic marriages to interracial marriages, rather than studying interracial marriages alone, is important for a number of reasons.[11] First, investigating the respective reasons behind, and the internal dynamics within, the two types of marriages gives a better insight into the wider range of shifting experiences and identities of Asian Americans, especially related to racialized experiences. What motivates individuals to choose one type of union over another? More specifically, what prompts some individuals to traverse racial boundaries for marriage and others only ethnic boundaries? How are people's intimate desires and choices constructed in each case? Once married, what are the respective cultural and ethnic negotiations that occur between spouses, especially in the process of multiracial and multicultural family-making? What kinds of transformations do individuals' racial/ethnic identification and consciousness undergo over time in each type of union, and what kinds of identity-work are being engaged in by individuals? What do these reveal about the shifting racial politics and boundaries of U.S. society and the ability of individuals to exert agency in negotiating them?

Drawing attention to Asian American interethnic marriages leads to an exploration of panethnicity, more specifically, its post-1960s evolution and possible intensification.[12] Asian American panethnicity originally described a process of ethnogenesis primarily driven by political interests among Asian Americans of differing national origins in the 1960s. It now refers to a pan-Asian group identity based on a common racial and cultural identity. This book will examine to what extent the increase in intra-Asian marriages, particularly among the U.S.-born/-raised population, is related to a possible growth of pan-Asian racial identification in recent decades and what this identity signifies for the participants. Probing this issue is important because it raises key questions about the assimilation thesis, including the presumed likelihood of interracial marriage for immigrants down the generations, and about the evolution of racial and ethnic boundaries in the United States. Finally, addressing interethnic marriages allows us an exploration of a relatively neglected topic in the study of the Asian American community:

intra-Asian group dynamics and hierarchies. While panethnicity typically signals the construction of an Asian racial identity stemming from common experiences of racialization, this study of interethnic marriage not only affirms the diversity that exists along the lines of ethnicity, countries of origin, and economic status within the Asian American community but how this may precipitate a level of intra-Asian group hierarchy and interactional tensions, a hierarchy that at times manifests itself in terms of mutual stereotypes and power dynamics within marriages, including what Paul Spickard refers to as "hierarchies of intermarriage preferences" among Asian-ethnic groups.[13]

In sum, examining the two types of intermarriages gives rise to a complex picture of Asian American intermarriages. For both interracially and interethnically married couples, intermarriage, rather than being a barometer of assimilation, is an arena of ongoing ethnic identity and cultural struggles, although negotiated differently by the two groups. In both cases, this book shows the powerful effect of global and U.S. racial and gender politics on the participants. These racial and gender structures create a backdrop against which the participants' identity struggles are revealed in their ethnic and cultural negotiations with each other, as well as in their struggles over the retention, modification, and transmission of ethnic cultures and identities within the context of multiracial or multiethnic family-making. The Asian Americans in the two intermarital groups often have differing perceptions of themselves as individuals or as couples within the U.S. racial hierarchy and therefore negotiate their respective cultures and racial/ethnic identities within their marriages in different ways, but they also reveal commonalities in their ongoing efforts to construct a meaningful sense of group identity.

## Asian American Intermarriage and the Global, National, and Local Politics of Race

Historically, the study of U.S. immigrants and ethnic or racial issues have been territorially bounded within the United States as the host, or the receiving, country. Inspired in part by revitalization in studies of empires and post-colonialism,[14] a surge of immigration and race/ethnic relations scholarship brings a global and transnational framework to examining the experiences of U.S. immigrants, particularly related to the immigrants' experiences of race relations and incorporation into U.S. society.[15] Moving beyond immigrant experiences as shaped primarily by their social/racial location within the United States, these studies describe how inter-state power relations affect the social and subject positions of immigrants in the United States; that is, how immigrant experiences are shaped "by the positions of their home country within the global racial order."[16]

Situating Asian American immigrant experiences within this inter-state power context underscores the particular importance the global racial order has upon

U.S. racial politics and how instrumental this order is in determining the immigrants' social location, experiences, and self-understandings. The formation of the present global racial order is rooted in the rise of European and, subsequently, American "empires" in the past few centuries that have established Western dominance. Although the importance of military and economic might in securing Western global dominance cannot be overstated, Western imperialist hegemony has also expanded through cultural and ideological means, for instance, through culture-ideology of capitalism and enlightenment liberalism.[17]

A major instrument of Western cultural-ideological dominance is the propagation of White supremacist racial ideology. Although the West historically used cultural weapons such as religion to subjugate non-Western parts of the world, the claim of White racial superiority was central to legitimizing Western dominance, especially with the advent of "scientific racism."[18] Drawing upon the legitimacy of "scientific" evidence, scientific racism established a hierarchy of "races" in which the Negroes or mongoloids (Asians) were considered inferior to and fit for subjugation by the Whites. In relation to Asians, scholars have abundantly documented the ways in which imperialist, colonizing Euro-American nations constructed "Orientalist" discourses, representing Asians as an inferior, exotic, feminine other, in order to justify imperialist ventures in Asia.[19]

Especially since the decline of the Cold War, the United States has emerged as a virtually uncontested world power that continues to assert itself globally through various interconnected channels—economic, military, political, and cultural—shaping not only economic relations around the world but also cultural understandings and imaginings. Despite the recent rise of multiculturalist discourses, the cultural framework of White-supremacist racial hierarchy continues to retain its force and legitimacy, reflecting the hegemonic strength of the contemporary American cultural reach. Eduardo Bonilla-Silva refers to this post-imperialist, post-colonial dominance as "informal imperialism" or "dominance without empire" that binds Western nations together under a common ideology of "new racism," a form of contemporary racist discourse that asserts Western racial superiority in terms of cultural superiority and distinctiveness.[20] Closely connected to political and military might and disseminated through controlling images and discourses, current Euro-American racial ideologies, building upon Western colonial ventures over the past several centuries, continue to powerfully influence the conceptualization of racial order and social/racial positioning of minority and immigrant groups in the United States.

One effort to explain the U.S.-dominated system of racial order appears in recent scholarship on global racism.[21] Although rooted in the particularities of White racism that arose to justify Western colonialist capitalist expansion in the seventeenth century, global racism refers to the extension of racist principles, most centrally White racism, on a global scale. Bonilla-Silva states that the new international order has "led to the globalization of race and racial relations and the intensification and diversification of the numbers of racial Others in the Western world."[22] According to Batur-VanderLippe and Feagin, "Thus what makes racism global are the bridges connecting the particularities imposed by White racism, to the universality of racist concepts and actions, maintained globally by prejudice, discrimination, violence, genocide and total destruction, since the expansion of capitalism."[23]

One manifestation of the current globalized racism is that the system of White-dominated racial hierarchy of Western origins has now been propagated and adopted by the majority of the world population who have learned to situate others, and themselves, within this global racial hierarchy. In a study examining this among contemporary Korean immigrants in the United States, Nadia Kim traces how the immigrants' understanding of U.S. race relations and the meaning of race was already shaped by the hegemonic reach of U.S. racial ideology in Korea since WWII, especially through U.S. military presence in Korea, and how this affected the immigrants' engagement with racial politics and racial self-positioning in the United States.[24] Inderpal Grewal's study focusing on middle-class Asian Indians similarly analyzes how ideas about "Americanness"—imaginaries about America and the American dream which includes both a particular understanding of global racial hierarchy and "a search for a future which the desire for consumption, for liberal citizenship, and for work came together to produce a specific subject of migration"—is constructed within and outside the United States through transnational networks of knowledge and communication: "America produced subjects outside its territorial boundaries through its ability to disseminate neoliberal technologies through multiple channels."[25]

Although such recent studies have situated the race-related experiences of immigrants within the context of global and inter-state power structures, few studies of intermarriage within the U.S. borders utilize critically informed global racial frameworks. A study of Asian American intermarriages, however, must use global politics of race as a lens to analyze the dynamics of these unions, since global racial ideologies shape the racial dynamics of group and individual interactions, including intimate and marital relations. That is, one must situate such studies of intimacy within a theoretical framework that attends to "positions within power hierarchies created through historical, political, economic, geographic, kinship-based and other socially stratifying factors"[26] to help understand how such global and local power structures manifest in migrants' lives, including in romantic choices and self-understandings.

Recent studies on international cross-border marriages—unions that involve marriage migration across national boundaries, including military brides, picture brides, mail-order brides, or internet relationships[27]—have used global race frameworks to analyze the politics of intimacy and romance. In cross-border international marriages, the embeddedness of romantic choices and desires within international and global power hierarchies can appear more stark, which recent investigations of marriage migrations have highlighted. Referred to by Nicole Constable as a "global hypergamy,"[28] some of these relationships denote situations in which marriage migrants, often women from less economically developed parts of the world, attempt to strategically enhance their personal and economic opportunities by "marrying up" racially and/or economically to a spouse in a wealthier, more powerful country, giving rise to complicated and unequal inter-personal dynamics. Constable's study of cross-border marriages of Filipina and Chinese women to American men, for example, has demonstrated that the erotic and romantic desires between American men and Filipina and Chinese women have been configured by the gendered and racialized imaginings produced through the history of U.S. imperialism in the Asian-Pacific region. Although such mar-riage migrations, as noted, historically have involved women of color from less developed countries to mostly White men of Western nations, marriage destina-tion countries have recently begun to include newly developed and wealthy non-White nations, such as Japan, South Korea, and Taiwan. Sealing Cheng's recent study of Filipina migrant entertainers in South Korea calls such erotic imaginings and yearnings as being constructed by the "political economy of desires," and that "Through such an optic we may also come to understand how intimate longing and relationships with the Other can also be critical commentaries on gender and regional hierarchies within the larger political economy."[29]

When cross-racial marriages occur within the host society between racial minority individuals and those in the dominant racial group, or even between members of different ethnic or racial minority groups, it is more difficult to view these intimate encounters in global racial power contexts because it is easy to confine the analysis of such encounters within the context of domestic racial politics or deny the relevance of race in intimate relations altogether. Indeed, particularly in this moment of both multiculturalist and colorblind discourses, the tendency is to depoliticize and normalize these intimate interactions among people of diverse racial and ethnic backgrounds as being motivated by individual choice. When viewed through a global and international lens, however, one can discern how the dynamics of such intimate encounters and unions are informed by the disparities of inter-state economic and racial inequalities that have driven global migration flows in particular directions in the first place, historically from the developing to developed countries, and how these disparities profoundly shape the racial and gendered self-understandings and positioning of individuals within the racial dynamics of the country of settlement. Intermarriage is a fertile arena of global interconnectivities that play out in individual lives and in localized cultural contexts.

Although anchoring the analysis within the context of global inequalities remains central, the experiences and maneuvering of participants in this book, however, are also about negotiating the powerful cultural imperatives of various local, cross-cutting cultural/ideological domains within the United States, par-ticularly those of ethnic and panethnic communities. That is, while the individu-als in the study are inserted unquestionably into the global-level power dynamics of inequality, their experiences, subjectivities, and desires are an outcome of their efforts to simultaneously negotiate global, national, and local structures of power, with the local here signifying the ideologies of race/gender specific to various Asian-ethnic communities or the larger Asian American community. For example, a person's choice of interracial or interethnic marriage is a result of her/his negotiation of the particular expectations or pressures from her/his family and ethnic communities regarding who is appropriate to marry, balanced against the opportunities and limitations regarding cross-racial unions provided to members of racial minority groups by the larger society. A person's decision regarding what or how much of ethnic cultural elements to retain or transmit within an interracial or interethnic marital context is similarly an outcome of her or his negotiation of the pressures from, or resources provided by, the ethnic or the panethnic community for ethnic/racial assertion, weighed against the opportunities (or the lack thereof) provided by the larger society for social and cultural inclusion in that society.

In both cases, ethnic communities can serve as a source of resistance against larger structures of racial inequality—for example, through the panethnic construct of Asianness as identity and culture—at the same time that these communities can perpetuate their own system of social inequalities, such as patriarchal oppression against women. Furthermore, ethnic communities are not immune from trafficking in their own racist ideologies, particularly against fellow groups of color, that help to buttress the wider system of racial inequality. Indeed, the process of how ethnic, national, and global power structures simultaneously articulate in the participants' lives recalls the concept of "scattered hegemonies," a concept that captures the idea that while central aspects of West-centered hegemony may continue, hegemonic power may also be de-centered to the extent that it may multiply and disperse among various community and power structures. These multiple structures and sources of hegemony may include "global economic structures, patriarchal nationalisms, 'authentic' forms of tradition, local structures of domination, and legal-juridical oppression on multiple levels."[30]

## Love, Desire, and Ambivalence

Investigating the ways romantic desires, self-identities, and dynamics of intimate relations are constituted within the context of intermarital relations and family-making reveals the complex psychological ramifications of racial and gender power structures on Asian Americans that flow through global, national, and local ethnic channels.[31] Contemporary Euro-American cultures tend to view love as an individual, private affair, driven by personal emotions, especially of the romantic kind. A wide array of studies on gender and sexuality, not to mention cross-cultural studies of love, emotion, kinship, family, and marriage, have shown that love, desire, and emotions are profoundly social phenomena; they are produced and conditioned by society, "mediated by language and culture."[32] Not only is "love" defined differently across cultures (for example, is love sexual or non-sexual, action or feeling, commitment or passion?), but even as a feeling, love is experienced in different ways across socio-cultural milieus. The objects of love or desire are also socially constructed, determined by whom a person is allowed to view as appropriate to love (along the axes of gender, race, age, class, and so on). Love and desire are generated within this complex web of cultural meanings and rules. Inversely, the topic of love and intimacy is a highly fruitful lens for social analysis, "providing as it does a glimpse [in]to the complex interconnections between cultural, economic, interpersonal, and emotional realms of experience."[33]

Insofar as love can be viewed as generated from and contained within overlapping power structures, this emotion has been subject to a range of critical analysis for its potential as a source of both oppression and agency. One body of critical analyses, originating from feminist scholars, critiques love as a possible source of oppression of women. For example, love, particularly of romantic but also the maternal kind, has been seen as an "ideology" that enslaves women in exploitative heterosexual relationships, particularly as a powerful weapon in the service of institution of "compulsory heterosexuality." The institution of marriage is viewed in this context as a "beachhead of male dominance."[34] Chrys Ingraham writes:

> To begin, romance is ideology in action. Ideology manifests in words and images that establish and regulate meanings and beliefs justifying dominant interests. Ideologies naturalize our socially created world, replacing realistic perceptions with idealized notions of that world.[35]

In other words, romantic love as an ideology creates an illusion, and as an imaginary conceals the contradictions of inequalities created by institutions such as patriarchy and capitalism by enabling women to "reconcile" the reality of gender inequalities with the illusion or promise of plenitude, ecstasy, and well-being. However, from the perspective of feminists like Simone de Beauvoir,[36] love, though it can place women in situations of "self-annihilating dependence," can also be powerfully appealing to women as a kind of weapon of the weak. Or, as Stevi Jackson puts it, love, as linked as it is to women's search for positive identity in a society that devalues and marginalizes them, also "holds out the promise of power, of being the loved one. . . . It is perhaps the only way in which women can hope to have power over men."[37]

This dual aspect of love's power has been the ground upon which some recent scholars have conceptualized the social and intimate power of love in more agentic way, as a vehicle for self-realization,[38] often achieved through an intimate identification with the desired other. Kumiko Nemoto states:

> [d]esire and passion for other people is shaped socially and culturally, and often reflects a person's desire for self-realization and a social identity, and by extension a person's craving for certain social and cultural powers. The promise of self-realization can be seen fleetingly in one's identification

with another person, who is seen both as a source of pleasure to identify with, and as a power to possess. Intimacy is a cultural and social device of self-making.[39]

In short, romantic desires are expressive of one significant aspect of a self- and identity-making process, a pursuit of who one is or wants to be.[40]

Modern forms of romantic love (passionate, sexual love), linked closely to the rise of European modernity and ideology of individualism, are especially connected to this type of individualistic pursuit of self-making; romantic love is even viewed as a pathway to personal freedom. To wit, modern love is linked to individualism insofar as it denotes free choice of partners, but it is also individualistic in that it seeks exclusive recognition from the other as a unique being, expressing "the desire to be known, to come into being through the look of the Other."[41] But as pointed out, this self-making process through love has a two-sided relationship with power; while love and intimacy can hold the promise of self-fashioning and future-making for a person through the identification with the other, it can also serve as a vehicle of subordination insofar as the other has the structural advantage of being in a superior position in terms of race, gender, or class.

This double-sided perspective on love is directly pertinent to this study because the specific and shifting emotional configuration of love and desire on the part of the study's participants—connected to identification with the desired other—reflects a complex psychological topography of self-realization and identity formation for Asian Americans, especially along racial and ethnic lines. Similar to individuals belonging to other U.S. racial minority groups, central to understanding the self-making process of Asian Americans, of which the formation of romantic desire and love is an important part, is the relationship of Asian Americans' status as a racialized minority to the hegemonic ideals and discourses of whiteness and White middle-class culture. Whether interracially or interethnically married, the construction of romantic preferences is an outcome of complicated negotiations with whiteness and the participants' racialized subjectivities.

Sociological investigations of intimate relationships, including in-depth, qualitative exploration of racialized desires and their effects, are, however, sparse. As some sociologists have pointed out, this is not only because of the inherent difficulty of studying the psychic complexity of desires and subject-formations but also because of sociologists' general reluctance to confront the topic of racialized desires, including the sensitive issue of internalized racism among racialized minorities.[42] The reasons for this avoidance include tendencies in contemporary scholarship to "fetishize resistance," to deny the complicity of the subjugated in their own oppression because of the shame associated with it, and the concern that exposing internalized racism would embarrass racial minorities.[43]

Interrogating the question of racialized desires, including the issue of internalized racism, is, however, important because of their deep, inherent complexity. This book shows, for example, that the participants' romantic preferences rarely represent a one-dimensional case of internalized racism or mental colonization, revealing the profound intricacies of racialized desires. In this book, I describe the participants' identities and subjectivity-formations as fields of struggle, a state that is characterized by contradictions, ambivalences, and resistances in relation to both hegemonic whiteness and to imperatives of local ethnic identities and cultures. Situated at the nexus of two clashing forces—one, of U.S. society's social-cultural exclusion of the participants despite their U.S.-born status, and two, of pressures for conformity to the dominant White middle-class culture—the participants' lifelong identity struggles form the backdrop for the development of romantic desires and longings, whether in terms of desires for whiteness, repudiation of it, or both. Indeed, what is most pronounced about the negotiation with whiteness for Asian Americans in this study is not so much its occurrence but its deep ambivalence.

Indeed, post-colonial writers of color such as Franz Fanon and Albert Memmi have already written poignantly about the complex psychology of the colonial subject.[44] They have powerfully brought to light not only the reality of the internal colonization process that grips the colonial subject, particularly of self-denigration, but also the profoundly ambivalent love-hate relationship that the colonial subject develops with the colonizer, especially in the form of the simultaneous wish to mimic the identity and culture of the colonizer and to repudiate it. In *Black Skin, White Masks*, Frantz Fanon talks about this in terms of an interracial relationship; in dissecting the psychology of a Black man wishing to pursue intimacy with a White woman, Fanon refers to an intertwined desire "to be White" and to counterpoise the colonizing powers.[45] Within the discipline of sociology, W.E.B. Du Bois has proffered classic analyses of a similar psychological phenomenon from the perspective of American Blacks, a psychic phenomenon which he refers to as the "double consciousness."[46] This is a process whereby the devalued Black subject struggles with the societal ideal of the White personhood from which a person is excluded but to which he/she is expected to measure up: becoming "two warring ideals in one dark body," the American Black, like the colonized subject, internalizes racism and develops a fraught, ambivalent relationship with whiteness.

The understanding of psychic complexities in the formation of the racialized subject is aided also by pivotal insights from post-structuralist psychoanalytic and feminist theories that draw attention to the process of psychic division or splitting of the subject as a key moment in the identificatory process with the other.[47] The main insight here is that identificatory processes of human beings with a more powerful desired object—for example, an infant with the mother or adults with the desired love object—are inherently ambivalent because a perfect identification with the other, an imaginary ideal from which one seeks to form a self-image but to which one can never measure up, involves a partial self-loss/self-split.[48] A split self, "between that which one is, and that which is the other,"[49] can as well lead to a feeling of love-hate toward the emulated object and toward oneself, further bolstering the dynamic of emotional ambivalence. The relevance of these insights to sociological concepts like double consciousness in racialized minorities is obvious, where the desired identificatory object that can be a source of self-split and ambivalence is the racially and socially superior other.

Aside from spotlighting the issue of ambivalent identity formation, another key insight of these perspectives is that identity, or a sense of self, is therefore never whole but always in tension within itself. A fantasy of a whole, sealed subject or identity is only possible as an imaginary and is always in danger of being fragmented. Furthermore, scholars such as Judith Butler, although writing in relation to gender and sexuality, echo the insight that such imaginary "sutured" identity can only be achieved through a process of exclusion, an expulsion of the reviled other:

> The "abject" designates that which has been expelled from the body, discharged as excrement, literally rendered "Other." This appears as an expulsion of alien elements, but the alien is effectively established through this expulsion. The construction of the "not-me" as the abject establishes the boundaries of the body which are also the first contours of the subject.[50]

This analysis is applicable to how racialized identities form. From the perspective of the White dominant group or individuals, the abject "other" can be others or a part of oneself that are signified as non-White; from the perspective of the subjugated group, the reviled other can be an aspect of oneself that one wishes to deny and expel in order to identify with the dominant group. For individuals in both groups, however, an important insight is also that in this process, the disparaged "other" can never be completed refused as the other always remains within oneself, and the "attempt to expel the other to the other side of the universe is always compounded by the relationship of love and desire."[51]

In sum, these theoretical insights provide a great deal of purchase in understanding how the contradictory psychic processes generated by racial inequalities play out for Asian Americans, including the tension between internalized racism and ethnic/racial assertion, between love/desire and denial/refusal of the other, all within the context of the participants' efforts to negotiate and reconcile their racialized selves with the dominant other of whiteness. The racialized desire for whiteness and White privilege that is equated with Americanness, propelled by the still-powerful pressures for assimilation into the dominant White middle-class U.S. culture, appears at first glance to be more pronounced for those who choose the path of interracial marriage to Whites, but it is nonetheless a foundational dynamic that even the interethnically married individuals must negotiate. Each group, however, negotiates these racialized desires in differing ways throughout their growing-up and family-making processes. I argue in this book that for Asian Americans in this study, being a racially in-between group whose status alternates between inhabiting the alien, excluded other and the praised model minority renders the ambivalence with regard to whiteness particularly complex, subtle, and difficult to navigate. For many, the relationship with whiteness and the dominant culture is never straightforward; it is characterized by simultaneous and intertwined desires to accommodate, embrace, resist, and refuse and represents "love and hate that condition the mutual enmeshment of the 'dominant' and the 'disempowered.'"[52] However, insofar as identity is an ongoing, open-ended process, the arena of intimate relations, whether in the context of marital or family relations, may open up space for reconfiguring social conditions and dynamics, as well as ethnic and racial subjectivities, identities, and cultures.

## Constructing Hybridities: Negotiating Identities and Cultures

Identities and cultures are subject to ongoing processes of construction, re-creation, and even re-invention. Such constructionist views of ethnicity, race, and identity formation in general characterize situational or emergent perspectives on cultures and identities as adaptive responses to structural conditions or external forces (rather than arising from perceived inherited attributes), such as political or economic circumstances or social assignment of group identity.[53] Along with perspectives that consider race as a product of an ongoing constructed process,[54] this view is useful because it helps to clarify not only the fluidity and contingency of identity and cultural construction, which is how group identities and cultures emerge and change across time and place, but because it opens up space for considering individual and group agency. In this view, individuals are not passively formed by external forces, such as by the externally imposed racial or ethnic categories on a group, but exercise the ability to actively engage, and maneuver within, these discursive structures, shaping their own identities and cultures within the given constraints and opportunities: "Construction involves both the passive experience of being 'made' by external forces, including not only material circumstances but the claims that other persons or groups make about the group in question, and the active process by which the group 'makes' itself."[55]

The term "Asian American" is an interesting example. It emerged during the 1960s' civil rights struggle among young students of Asian descent as a self-formulated panethnic label as they forged a political movement for racial justice. In one sense, this term is a result and acceptance of racial lumping of diverse ethnic groups by the larger society. On the other hand, it can be viewed as a self-recuperative move by the students because the label rejected and replaced older stigmatizing terms like "Oriental" or "Asiatic" and allowed the students to define themselves on their own terms as a new panethnic, albeit racialized, collectivity united in common awareness and experiences of racism.[56] The term has now evolved into a cultural identity that is defined and redefined. In this book, the politics and construction of the panethnic Asian American identity and culture occupy a central place in the personal lives of the participants. To be specific, the book explores the ways in which the intermarried participants navigate hegemonic discourses at various levels—particularly at the interstices of the global, national, local-ethnic politics of race, ethnicity, and gender—which opens up space to challenge ideological structures in creating new identity forms and cultures, including attempts to reconfigure the term "Asian American." As a result, interracial and interethnic families exhibit emergent and novel forms of cultures and identities that engage both the dominant meanings, representations, and practices of the larger society as well as those of ethnic groups.

In analyzing the experiences and identity-making of the couples and families, this book utilizes the concept of "hybridity" to understand these emergent cultures. With origins in the field of biology, hybridity refers to the product of biological or plant species-intermixing, such as cross-fertilization in plants. Initially laden with negative connotations pertaining to contamination, perversion, and miscegenation that were rooted in the racist scientific discourses of the nineteenth century, it has recently become fruitful metaphor to describe or analyze intercultural mixing and transfers. In the last few decades, the term has been appropriated as a popular theoretical concept within both post-colonial and globalization studies[57] to refer to forms of "diverse linguistic, discursive, and cultural intermixtures" that arise as a result of cultural-social contact, whether through transnational circulation of cultures or through face-to-face group contact precipitated by direct colonial contact or voluntary, free migration.[58]

In this new incarnation of the term,[59] the notion of cultural hybridity, especially within post-colonial writings, has a political and ideological purpose; it calls attention to the cultural contact between groups with unequal power and the ways in which hybridity or hybridized cultures that emerge out of interaction between colonial and indigenous cultures can represent an alternative, resistant space against the dominant cultural powers. It is a space in which both the dominant group (for example, the colonizer) and the subjugated group (example.g., the colonized or the minoritized groups) are both transformed and transform each other in an ongoing way through the process of contact, challenging not only the modernist, essentialist fiction of a singular culture or identity but also binary logic (e.g., domination versus oppression), highlighting the possible agency of the subaltern. As Homi Bhabha puts it, "the 'hybrid' moment of political change . . . the transformational value of change lies in the re-articulation, or translation, of elements that are neither the One . . . nor the Other . . . but something else besides which contests the terms of territories of both."[60]

In recent discussions on globalization and late modernity, the hybridity concept has been used with similar connotations but presented as a cultural logic of globalization: that is, as representing the heterogenizing process against the homogenizing tendencies of the modern, West-dominated, globalizing world.[61] Stuart Hall writes: "Like the post-colonial, contemporary globalization is both novel and contradictory. Its economic, financial and cultural circuits are Western-driven and U.S.-dominated. . . . Ideologically, it is governed by a global neo-liberalism. . . . Its dominant tendency is homogenization."[62] However, contemporary globalization's movement toward this universalistic, U.S.-dominated culture and conception of the world, one that "always speaks English," is not the only trend; it invites at the same time countervailing, often unintended, forces that bring about resistance by generating differentiating effects within and between societies. One example is the intensification of localisms, particularisms, and pluralisms, or what Hall calls the "return of the local":[63] "what people do in the face of a particular form of modernity which confronts them in the form of globalization. . . . It is an effort of the margins coming into representation—in art, in painting, in film, in music, in literature . . . in politics, and in social life generally," and is a "most profound cultural revolution of the late twentieth century."[64]

Whether analyzed within the framework of post-colonialism or that of globalization, the central point is that these erupting forms of localisms, particularisms, or subaltern formations—whether ethnic, cultural, racial, religious, or national—comprise, and have given rise to, cultures of hybridity, or mutually transformed commingling of forms involving invention of traditions that often employ symbolic cultural elements:

> Everywhere, cultural identities are emerging which are not fixed, but poised, *in transition*, between different positions; which draw on different cultural traditions at the same time; and which are the product of those complicated cross-overs and cultural mixes which are increasingly common in a globalized world. It may be tempting to think of identity in the age of globalization as destined to end up in one place or another: either returning to its "roots" or disappearing through assimilation and homogenization. But this may be a false dilemma.[65]

Pertinent to this study is that cultural hybridization, both as a group and an individual phenomenon,[66] is generated by cultural encounters of one major type of global movement, in this case a mass movement of peoples that creates diasporic communities and cultures, or what Arjun Appadurai refers to as the "ethnoscape."[67] In diasporic communities, cultural intermixing and reconfigurations are "increasingly evident in the multicultural diasporas and other mixed and minority communities of the post-colonial world"; these include those communities made up of formerly colonized subjects who migrate from the "margins" to the "center (the formerly colonizing nations)" becoming "margins in the center"[68] like many Asian American and other immigrant communities within the United States or Western Europe. Utilizing the concept of cultural "translation," Hall writes:

> This [translation] describes those identity formations which cut across and intersect natural frontiers and which are composed of people who have been dispersed forever from their homelands. Such people retain strong

links with their places of origin and their traditions, but they are without
the illusion of a return to the past. They are obliged to come to terms with
the new cultures they inhabit, without simply assimilating to them and
losing their identities completely. They bear upon them the traces of the
particular cultures, traditions, languages and histories by which they were
shaped. The difference is that they are not and will never be unified in the
old sense, because they are irrevocably the product of several interlocking
histories and cultures, belong at one and the same time to several "homes"
(and to no one particular "home"). People belonging to such cultures of
hybridity have had to renounce the dream or ambition of rediscovering any
kind of "lost" cultural purity, or ethnic absolutism. They are irrevocably
*translated.*[69]

How does this inform this book's analysis of Asian American intermarriage
and identity/cultural politics? First, applying the concept of hybridity broadens
the vision and analysis of the American immigrant experience, especially as they
relate to intermarriage, beyond the U.S. borders, situating it within the framework of a modern U.S. imperialist and capitalist project. As mentioned, Asian
American immigration is part of the post-colonial diaspora, the spatial aspect
of the post-1965 late-capitalist economic transformation that has spurred the
movement of migrants, both legal and illegal, from the third world to the "core"
Western states; Asian migration, driven by a changing and expanding post-1965
system of global capitalism, is part of this post-colonial diaspora within the imperialist center of the United States.[70]

Within this imperialist center, the United States has tried to absorb continuous waves of immigrants into a homogenized brew, a process that has been
referred to as assimilation, especially of the classic Anglo-conformity kind. This
assimilative project and dynamics of intercultural/interracial contact that occur
within the United States are but the domestic face of the contemporary West-
centered globalization process that has resulted in myriad post-colonial cultural
and human encounters, the global spread of U.S. cultures, and the formation
of diasporic communities around the world. However, just as inequities among
nations are shaped by imperialism, the unequal positioning of national, ethnic,
and racial groups with respect to the United States configures their experiences
of incorporation within the U.S. citizenry, generating resistances and assertions
of local identities. Within this framework, one can begin to comprehend the
complexities inherent in contemporary Asian American identity struggles and
racial politics, including within the private realm of love, romance, marriage, and
family-making.

Much of what I explore in this book are the ways Asian Americans remake
and reconfigure their ethno-racial identity and culture in the form of emergent hybridized cultures as this occurs within intermarried families. Parallel

to ethno-cultural and ethno-identity constructions around the contemporary world, Asian American remaking of ethno-racial identities/cultures within U.S. Asian-ethnic communities and families betoken struggles carried out in relation to the dominant cultural logic of White superiority and the equation of whiteness with Americanness. In broad terms, the Asian American intermarried couples and families in this book, whether interracially or interethnically married, represent particularist assertion of identities in this post-colonial, globalizing world. At the level of personal identities, the participants are engaged in lifelong ethno-racial renegotiations in relation to global racial and gender politics; once married, these struggles take place via cultural and identity negotiations with their partners.

For interracially married couples, the hybrid cultural formations reflect the synthesizing of the Asian American partner's ethnic culture with that of the dominant White mainstream culture, while for interethnic couples, the hybridization process involves blending, selecting, and discarding elements of distinct Asian-ethnic cultures in dialogue with the mainstream culture. In the case of interracially married couples, the resulting cultural forms symbolize the struggle of the minority Asian-ethnic partner to achieve some sort of hybridized ethnic-cultural retention as a response to racism and potential cultural absorption by the dominant majority culture, with the level of success, as we will see, depending on such factors as the Asian-ethnic partner's cultural fluency and the cooperation of the non-Asian spouse. For interethnic couples, the culture-building efforts involve negotiations between minority cultures with greater sense of power parity and of solidarity, but contestations occur between spouses over how to craft and retain this panethnic culture and how to assert it against the dominant culture. Despite the ongoing dominance of White normativity for both groups, this book illustrates the ways in which the two intermarried groups are groping toward new forms of hybridized identities and cultural constructions that rearticulate ethnic, panethnic, and mainstream cultural elements, transforming all of them in the process.[71]

It is important to caution, however, that hybridity, despite its transformative possibilities, should not be treated as a celebratory concept simply to showcase the resistant possibilities of the subordinated. While it is important to recognize the empowering potential of hybridity, the dominant culture exerts power within hybrid spaces in reinscribed forms, even while such spaces are experienced as having independent cultural power.[72] One example of this is the seductive, powerful pull White privilege and culture has for the middle-class Asian American model minorities even while they attempt to craft and assert their ethnic identity/cultures; White middle-class culture remains the referential norm for the participants in this book even when the locus of hybrid cultures involve lateral intercultural negotiations with other minoritized groups.[73]

Furthermore, it is uncertain whether these hybridities, even if creative and empowering, pave the way for alternative cultures and ways of being that can feel dignified, equal, and distinctive in relation to the majority culture, or whether Asian-ethnics will remain subordinated to the White Euro-American culture that exercises dominance by harnessing and celebrating differences in the name of multiculturalism and diversity.[74] Additionally, insofar as hybridization is an ongoing, unsettling process of negotiating differences with others that guarantees no closure, it is important to recognize that hybridization generates deep dislocations, anxieties, and uncertainties, as is apparent in my participants' narratives. Indeed, any mode of social transformation "has deep and disabling 'costs' deriving from it multiple forms of dislocation and habituation," and such multiple forms of dislocation may include the "dissonances that have to be crossed despite proximate relations; the disjunction of power or positions that have to be contested; the values, ethical and aesthetics, that have to be 'translated' but will not seamlessly transcend the process of transfer."[75] The hybrid spaces inhabited by the participants in this study, therefore, are often experienced as one of uncertainty, lack of closure, and instability, yet also as a site of empowering possibilities.

## The Study

This book is based on in-depth, life history interviews of 100 U.S.-born/-raised individuals, comprising 78 self-identified, cisgender, heterosexual Asian American intermarried persons, in addition to 22 non-married and intra-married individuals. Of the 78 intermarried individuals, 72 were interviewed as couples—36 couples total—with six additional participants who were interviewed without their spouses. The fieldwork was carried out between 2009 and 2016. In this book, "U.S.-raised" refers to those who came to the United States at age 12 or younger, otherwise known as the 1.5 generation. In sociological parlance, it has become common practice to use the term "second generation" as encompassing both the U.S.-born and the 1.5 generation,[76] but this book uses the term "U.S.-born/or -raised" both because it is more precise and because my sample includes a few third and fourth generation individuals (four third generation and one fourth generation). The rest of the interviewees were U.S.-born/-raised second generation, and the vast majority, about 90% of this sample, were U.S.-born.

This book focuses on the U.S.-born/-raised because separating their experiences from the foreign-born is critical. First and foremost, because the second generation and later are exposed in comparable ways to the U.S. mainstream culture—the assimilation process and interracial dynamics are more similar to other U.S.-born groups than to their foreign-born counterparts—it is possible to ascertain with greater accuracy the meaning and patterns of intermarriage and its relationships to assimilation for this group and compare them to the experiences of other non-Asian groups. It is known, for instance, that interracial marriage of the U.S-born/-raised is related in different ways to assimilation from the foreign-born. That is, while interracial marriage for the U.S.-born/-raised is generally related to higher levels of acculturation, it is less so for the foreign-born, especially for foreign-born Asian-ethnic women, who display high rates of interracial marriage regardless of their levels of acculturation. For this and other reasons to be discussed more fully later in the book, decoupling the analysis of the U.S.- and foreign-born is therefore crucial in order to clarify the specificities of the U.S.-born/-raised group in relation to intermarriage and to enable a more accurate evaluation of the relationship between intermarriage and assimilation.[77]

Of the 36 couples, 19 couples were interracial and 17 couples were interethnic (72 individuals). Three additional interracially married persons and three additional interethnically married persons were interviewed without spouses (78 individuals total). The rest—22 individuals—consisted of six intra-married couples with one interviewed without the spouse (13 intra-married individuals) and nine single individuals (6 women and 3 men) who were interviewed to gain a comparative perspective on the intermarried participants. Although demographically the number of interracially married exceeds the number of interethnically married among the U.S.-born/-raised Asian Americans,[78] this study aimed for the number of interviewees from both marital groups to be as close as possible to obtain a robust comparative result. Interracially married couples are primarily Asian-White pairings. Since this book focuses on the comparison of interracial and interethnic marriages and is not a study of Asian interracial marriages along the lines of race, I controlled for race in interracial pairings, focusing mostly on those with White spouses; this enables the interracial-interethnic comparison more meaningful, in-depth, and manageable. Aside from the fact that Asian-ethnic/White unions still constitute the vast majority of Asian American interracial marriages, including Asian-ethnic/non-White pairings would have introduced race-related variables that would not have been wise nor feasible given the sample scope of this in-depth qualitative study. I look forward to other studies focusing on non-White/Asian unions, an important topic. Of the 19 interracially married couples, there are 12 Asian wife/White husband couples and five Asian husband/White wife couples,[79] one Asian wife/Black-mixed-race husband couple, and one Asian-White husband/White Hispanic couple where the husband identifies primarily as Asian American.[80] Two Asian-ethnic wives and one White wife were interviewed without spouses.

The interethnically married couples and participants are composed of individuals spanning a range of Asian-ethnic backgrounds, including Korean, Chinese, Japanese, Vietnamese, Filipino/a, Indian, Cambodian, and Laotian. All individuals were mono-ethnic except for two persons of mixed-Asian ethnicities and two Asian mixed-race individuals. Of the latter two, one was predominantly

Asian-ethnic in racial make-up and the other was Asian-White mixed-race; they both identified primarily as Asian-ethnic.[81] As qualitative studies on Asian Americans that compare the full spectrum of different Asian-ethnic/national origins are scarce, this study made a concerted effort to recruit those outside of Chinese, Japanese, and Korean heritages. Although Northeast Asians are still represented in greater numbers in this work, ethnic diversity, rather than proportional sampling reflecting each group's share of the demographics, was the primary goal given the limitations of the snowball sampling technique. Expanding the participant sample beyond Asians-ethnics of East Asian origin—typical of previous studies of interethnic marriages—also allowed an exploration of how interethnic dynamics across a larger number of groups might influence the negotiation of pan-Asian identity and culture. This study recognizes, however, that there are important differences in experiences across different Asian-ethnic groups and that the experiences of all Asian-ethnic groups, as a whole, cannot be homogenized. On the other hand, due to the limited sampling size in relation to each ethnic group, the aim of this study is not to assess interethnic variations in its results; this book has a more modest goal of being a study of middle-class Asian Americans whose shared experiences as the members of the professional middle class form the basis of analyses presented here.

The majority of interviewees were recruited from several large U.S. metropolitan areas with the largest Asian American populations in the United States, namely, Los Angeles, New York, San Francisco, Chicago, and Washington, D.C. Twelve participants are from small or mid-sized towns in a southern and a midwestern state. The participants were acquired mainly through snowball sampling in two ways: first, through initial contacts with key individuals associated with Asian American professional, political, and community organizations, particularly in Chicago and New York, which led to snowballing of participants in those and other cities, and second, through personal contacts that snowballed out to all of the cities mentioned above. Although the sampling strategy was not initially designed to target these particular cities, the majority of the interviewees ended up being recruited from cities with the largest Asian American populations in the United States.

Although most of my participants resided in urban areas, many were urban transplants; they did not necessarily all grow up in urban areas, but in smaller towns or suburbs, often with White-dominated homogeneous populations. A few grew up in even more racially diverse areas than where they now reside. Thus, the self-understandings and perceptions of my participants are informed by their life experiences in different types of environments at various stages of their lives, not only by their current location. For this reason, this study cannot and does not make comparative generalizations of differences among cities or regions represented in this book regarding identity development or the evolution of romantic and marital preferences, although it does consider the possible effects of certain types of demographic conditions (e.g., ethnic group size or neighborhood racial composition) on the evolution of racial and ethnic identity and marital/romantic preferences of the participants.

All the participants in my sample belong to the middle and professional class; all are college educated and some hold doctorates, and others Master of Arts degrees. The majority have professional degrees in fields like law, medicine, engineering, business, and education. In order to keep the interracial/ interethnic comparison meaningful and manageable, this study controlled for class and focused on middle-class participants only. Middle-class individuals, whether interethnically or interracially married, share similar kinds of integrative experiences that are associated with their socioeconomic status, including middle-class values, parental human and social capital, similar school and neighborhood contexts, and higher-education experiences, the latter being particularly central to Asian Americans' ethnic and racial identity formation— especially panethnic identity. Given these considerations, adding the variable of class would have introduced complexities related to socioeconomic status that would have confounded the focus of this study: the comparison between interethnically and interracially married. Moreover, given that middle-class Asian Americans, particularly as the model minority, are seen to be well positioned to assimilate into middle-class White America, focusing on the middle class with my limited sample size best situated this study to make any generalizable claims about whether such optimistic proposition might bear out. Because this is a study of middle- and professional-class couples, its findings therefore are not generalizable to the experiences of working-class couples, of which only a limited number of studies exist.[82] More studies that examine the intersection of race and class in Asian-ethnic intermarriages are needed. The ages for all married individuals ranged from 31 to 57.[83] Most couples had children under the age of 15; six couples were without children. Pseudonyms are used for all participants to safeguard confidentiality; in a number of cases, some identifying features have been altered to ensure anonymity (see Appendix A for list of participants). All spouses were interviewed individually and some together after individual interviews.

## A Note About Intersectionality

The key tenet of intersectionality theory is that the particular experiences, identities, and perspectives of individuals are structured by their location at the intersection of multiple social categories—including race, ethnicity, gender, class, nationality, sexual orientation, religion, and ability. In terms of understanding oppression, intersectionality theory addresses how a person's subordination arises from such interlocking systems of oppressions and "how race, gender, and class oppression are part of a single, historically created system."[84] Another related insight of this theory is that depending on a person's intersectional location, she or he can experience varying degrees of privilege or oppression, capable of being both the oppressor and oppressed. For example, White women have historically been in positions of subordination to White men but are situated in a position of privilege relative to Black men or other men of color. Wealthy, highly educated Asian-ethnic men may possess certain elements of class privilege over poor, under-educated White men and women, but they experience subordination in terms of race to both while being in a position of gender privilege to Asian-ethnic women.

Because this research controls for class and sexuality as it focuses on middle-class heterosexual individuals, the two major intersecting social categories in this book are race and gender. That is to say, insofar as Asian-ethnic women and men in this study are differentially situated in relation to race and gender, one must pay attention to their divergent intersectional experiences regarding romance, marriage, and assimilation. For instance, while both Asian-ethnic women and men are subordinate in terms of race to White women and men, Asian-ethnic women and men are not racially subordinated in the same way owing to imagined attributes the dominant culture attaches to Asian-ethnic masculinity (less desirable) and femininity (more desirable) that affects each gender's self-understandings and opportunities in romance and marriage. Along with this, the traditional privileges enjoyed by Asian-ethnic men over Asian-ethnic women within Asian-ethnic communities often provide incentives for outmarriage by Asian-ethnic women in pursuit of perceived greener romantic or marital pastures outside of the Asian-ethnic communities. A focused discussion of this important issue of intersectionality of race and gender, that is, the differences in experiences of men and women, is found in Chapter 7.

## Overview of the Book

In Chapter 2, this book reviews the history and current scholarship on Asian American intermarriage. This chapter overviews the ways in which marital and romantic boundaries for Asian-ethnics in the United States have been configured by state-sanctioned regulations of gender and sexuality of Asian-ethnics beginning in the mid-1800s, particularly by way of immigration policies, legal restrictions on marriages, and cultural imagery. Chapter 2 also examines key issues central to a study of Asian American intermarriage, especially how intermarriage is related to the matter of race and the process of assimilation.

Chapters 3 and 4 are devoted to a discussion of interracial marriage. Chapter 3 traces the development of racially transgressive romantic desires and marital choices of the interracially married Asian American participants; it focuses on the impact of the participants' coming-of-age experiences as racialized minorities on their self-understandings, identities, and romantic preferences.

This chapter also illuminates the ambivalences of identifying with the dominant other of whiteness and middle-class culture that give rise to racial consciousness and desires for greater ethnic reconnection in adulthood. Chapter 4 examines the politics of identity development and the dynamics of multiracial family-making in the context of interracial marriage, focusing particularly on the unexpected rekindling of interest in ethnic identification and culture on the part of Asian-ethnic spouses when children enter the picture. This chapter illustrates the ways in which the two key motivations for this stem from the fear of ethnic cultural erasure and the need for defense against racism. By drawing on interviews with White partners, the chapter also talks about the varying ways in which the White and Asian-ethnic partners simultaneously appropriate colorblind and race-conscious discursive frameworks in discussing themselves, their relationships, and children in the context of culturally hybrid family formation.

Chapters 5 and 6 focus on the experiences of interethnically married Asian Americans. Chapter 5 examines some of the reasons behind the development of interethnic romantic and marital preferences of the participants, a process shaped by a dialectic between parental/family expectations for same-race partnering and the development of pan-Asian identity centered on college experiences. After analyzing the romantic appeal of fellow Asian-ethnics, this chapter also considers the unexpected emotional complexities of being situated in racial-minority interethnic unions in a White-majority culture. Chapter 6 investigates the dynamics of interethnic family-making and cultural negotiations between partners, as participants attempt to construct hybridized Asian American culture and identities within their families. This chapter illustrates the ways in which the participants struggle to formulate "Asianness," an emergent concept and set of practices that are being constructed in the face of many participants' relative ethnic cultural incompetence and, in some cases, dearth of ethnic cultural resources. This chapter also describes the specific process of identity and cultural negotiations engaged in by the partners from divergent Asian-ethnic origins as they attempt to blend, co-construct, and pass down the hybridized Asian American culture within their families. It also looks at unexpected challenges related to power dynamics between the couples.

Chapter 7 directly tackles the issue of intersectionality; it examines the differences between Asian-ethnic women and men in regard to how they are positioned relative to the romantic and marital market. This chapter focuses on the shifting contemporary images of Asian Americans, especially in popular media, and how this affects the self-perceptions, experiences, and romantic desirability of Asian American women and men in divergent ways, particularly in their differing statuses as sexual model minorities. Chapter 8, the Conclusion, ties the main arguments together and pursues a preliminary comparison of Asian Americans and Latinos in regard to intermarriage.

# Notes

1. Blau 1977; DaCosta 2007; Hodes 1999, 90–91; Koshy 2004; Moran 2001; Root 2001; Kennedy 2003; Spickard 1989b; Yu 1999.
2. In a number of states, Asian or Asian Pacific Islander groups targeted under anti-miscegenation laws included groups termed "mongoloids," "yellow," "Asiatic Indian," or "Malay."
3. Racial intermarriage patterns show the greatest cleavage between blacks and non-blacks, supporting Yancey's (2003) "Black alienation thesis," though over time black/White intermarriages have continued to increase (Kalmijn 1993; Qian 1997).
4. Childs 2005; Dalmage 2000; Kalmijn 1993; Rosenblatt et al. 1995; Romano 2003; Steinbugler 2012; Yancey and Lewis 2009;. Jiménez 2010b; Telles and Ortiz 2008; Vasquez 2011a; 2011b.
5. Childs 2005, 3.
6. Abelmann and Lie 1995; Kim 1999; Kitano and Daniels 1988; Manalansan 2000; O'Brien 2008; Palumbo-Liu 1999; Vo and Bonus 2002.
7. Tuan 1998.
8. In this book, "U.S.-raised" refers to those who came to the U.S. at age 12 or younger, the "1.5" generation. Thus "U.S.-raised" is equivalent to the term "second generation" that scholars often use to include the "1.5" generation (see Kim 2004, fn1).
9. Gordon 1964.
10. Lee and Fernandez 1998; Shinagawa and Pang 1996.
11. There are very few studies explicitly comparing Asian American interracial and interethnic marriages at the national level, qualitative or quantitative. See Qian et al. 2001, 558.
12. See Espiritu 1992; Kibria 1997, 2002; Okamoto 2003; Shinagawa and Pang 1996; Tuan 1998.
13. Spickard 1989, 9.
14. For example, see Ashcroft et al. 2006; Gandhi 1998; Goldberg and Quayson 2002; Hardt and Negri 2000; Harvey 2003; Williams and Christman 1994.
15. Glick Schiller 1999; Grewal 2005; Kim 2008; Lowe 1996.
16. Espiritu 2003, 210. Also see Glenn 2011; Ong 1996, 1999; Volpp 2007.
17. Axtmann 1995; Sklair 1991; Smith 1990.
18. Doane 2003; Outlaw 1990.
19. Lowe 1996; Said 1978.
20. Bonilla-Silva 1999, 92.
21. Bhattacharyya et al. 2002; Batur-VanderLippe and Feagin 1999; Bonilla-Silva 1999; Goldberg 1990, 2002; Smedley 1993; Winant 2001; Hardt and Negri 2000.
22. Bonilla-Silva 1999, 90.
23. Batur-VanderLippe and Feagan 1999, 9.
24. Kim 2008.
25. Grewal 2005, 3.
26. Mahler and Pessar 2001, 445–46. This definition is part of what Mahler and Pessar refer to as "gendered geographies of power."
27. Cheng 2010; Constable 2005, 1995; Faier 2009; Kelsky 2006 [2001]; Padilla et al. 2007; Palriwala and Uberoi 2008; Sandel 2015; Williams 2010.
28. Constable 2005.
29. Cheng 2010, 10.
30. Grewal and Kaplan 1994, 17.
31. Exploring the dynamics of intimacy and love traverses the deeply psychological terrain of subjectivity and subject-making. Subjectivity, which I define here as the entire condition of being a subject/person—including self-awareness, thoughts, feelings, desires, and fantasies that are positioned in relation to particular practices and

discourses—is a key link between structure and agency and the psychic field in which individuals become subjectivated as raced/gendered beings.

32. Jackson 1993, 209. See also Hochschild (2003) on "feeling rules." Also see Abu-Lughod and Lutz 1990; Beall and Sternberg 1995; Cancian 1990; Harding and Pribram 2009; Hochschild 2003; Luhmann 1986; Rofel 2007, 14; Rosaldo 1984.
33. Padilla et al. 2007, xi.
34. Rich 1980, 633. See also Benjamin 1988; Firestone 1970.
35. Ingraham 2008, 123.
36. Beauvoir 1971.
37. Jackson 1993, 212, 205.
38. Cheng 2010, 6.
39. Nemoto 2009, 1.
40. Lisa Rofel thus observes that the "social field of desire" as a whole can be the "most explosive and powerful realm" for constructing the self (2007, 2).
41. Butler 1987, 137.
42. Nemoto 2009; Pyke and Dang 2003; Pyke 2007.
43. See Anzaldua 2007; Chou and Feagin 2015; Collins 1990; Osajima 1993. Pyke (2007) observes that when the topic of internalized racism is avoided, it is White racism that benefits the most, as such avoidance discourages the development of strategies to combat identification with whiteness and White privilege (109).
44. Fanon 1967, 2004; Memmi 1965, 2000.
45. Fanon quotes from a novel he is analyzing: "The majority of them, including those of lighter skin who often to the extreme of denying both their countries and their mothers, tend to marry in Europe not so much out of love as for the satisfaction of being the master of a European woman" (1967, 14).
46. Du Bois 1990.
47. These theories rely heavily on Lacan (1977) and Freud ([1921] 2000).
48. Hall states (1996a) "The mirror stage is not the beginning of something, but the interruption—the loss, the lack, the division—which initiates the process that 'founds' the sexually differentiated subject . . . the very image which places the child divides its identity into two" (9).
49. Hall 1991, 48.
50. Butler 1990, 133.
51. Hall 1991, 48.
52. Cheng 2001, 25.
53. Cornell and Hartmann 1998; Nagel 1994, 1996; Yancey et al. 1976; Roozens 1989.
54. Omi and Winant 1994. "Race" is a constructed social category in which a group of people are considered similar based on physical appearance or characteristics. In contrast to race, "ethnicity" refers to a belief in group distinction and peoplehood based culture, national origin, food, language, religion, customs, etc. It is worth noting that ethnicity and nationality are technically not identical—as people can share the same nationality but belong to different ethnic group and people can share the same ethnicity but be of different nationalities—but the two can overlap. As national and ethnic origins are viewed as overlapping for all participants in this study, I use the two terms interchangeably throughout the book.
55. Cornell and Hartmann 1998, 80.
56. Espiritu 1992; Lowe 1996.
57. For example, Bhabha 1994; Canclini 1995; Gilroy 1993; Hall 1992.
58. Raab and Butler 2008.
59. Similar terms include creolization, transculturation, or syncretism.
60. Bhabha, quoted in Hsu 2008, 312.

61. Indeed, the issue of the tensions between cultural homogenization and heterogenization has been central to the recent debates on globalization. See Nederveen Pieterse 2004; Tomlinson 1999.
62. Hall 2000, 215.
63. Hall 1991, 33. Hall also refers to this as the "subaltern" proliferation of "difference" (2000, 215). According to Axtmann (1995): "cultural globalization, similar to economic globalization, is more likely to result in generating and upholding heterogeneity as a feature as much inherent in its logic as homogenization" (37).
64. Hall 1991, 34. Such re-assertions are connected, of course, not only to the globalization process but to the dynamics of the post-colonial world, which incited the emergence of various forms of particularisms, such as ethnicities, nationalisms, and other kinds of identities/cultural assertions around the globe. Examples include the emergence of defensive-type localized group assertions and identity politics around the world and within the United States—from religious movements (like fundamentalisms) to assertions of ethno-national identities—to other even more localized, marginalized identities encompassing "new subjects, new genders, new ethnicities, new regions, new communities, hitherto excluded from the major forms of cultural representation (Hall 1991, 34)."
65. Hall et al. 1992, 310.
66. "Hybridity, a processual quality, and a resistance to (one-sided) definitions characterize not only national, cultural or ethnic group identities but also the identity of individuals" (Raab and Butler 2008, 6).
67. Appadurai 2004, 102–3. Ethnoscape is a "landscape of persons who constitute the shifting world in which we live: tourists, immigrants, refugees, exiles, guest workers, and other moving groups and individuals" that constitute an essential feature of the world characterized by the "realities of having to move or the fantasies of wanting to move" on a large scale." Appadurai identifies ethnoscape as one of the five of interrelated but disjunctive cultural flows of the new global cultural economy.
68. Hall 2000, 226–27.
69. Hall et al. 1992, 310. See also Bhabha 1994.
70. Lowe 1996.
71. In this sense, it is not useful to conceptualize hybridity in binary terms as a resistant or an oppressive space, but to interrogate how "hegemony-hybridity" operates in each case: "Hence hybridity raises the question of the terms of mixture, the conditions of mixing and mélange (Nederveen Pieterse 1995, 57, quoted in Tomlinson 1999, 147).
72. Tomlinson 1999, 146; Anzaldua 1987.
73. Cf. Kasinitz et al. 2004, 16.
74. Another way of looking at this is that while globalization is "structured in dominance," globalization cannot "control or saturate everything within its orbit: Indeed, it produces as one of its unintended effects subaltern formations and emergent tendencies which it cannot control but must try to 'hegemonize' or 'harness' to its wider purposes. It is a system for conforming differences, rather than a convenient synonym for obliteration of difference" (Hall 2000, 215).
75. Bhabha 1997 quoted in Hall 2000, 226.
76. See Kim 2004, fn1.
77. See Fu and Hatfield 2008, 254–55; Jacobs and Labov 2002; Alba and Nee 2003, 264.
78. Le 2013. See also Pew Research Center (2013b, 106) for statistics on interracial versus interethnically-married U.S. Asians.
79. There was one Asian-ethnic husband who was mixed-ethnic but identified primarily as Chinese American.

80. According to the 2000 U.S. Census, 76.6% of Asian American men who intermarried (13.4% of the total Asian American population) were interracially married, and 89.1% of Asian American women who intermarried (24.7% of total Asian American population) were interracially married, so the gender mix of this study's sampling (more outmarried Asian-ethnic women than men) is somewhat representative of the larger demographic pattern (See Okamoto 2007).
81. This research honors the racial/ethnic self-identification of individual participants.
82. There are only a small number of studies on working-class Asian Americans and their intermarriage patterns, and the results are contradictory, with some showing that working-class Asian Americans have a weaker sense of ethnic identity and tend to marry across racial boundaries, and others suggesting the opposite. See Lee's (2004) and Louie's (2004) studies on working-class Korean Americans and Chinese Americans respectively.
83. There were four single individuals in their mid-20s.
84. Collins 1990, 225.

# 2

# ASIAN AMERICAN
# INTERMARRIAGE

In this chapter, I briefly review the history of intermarriage among Asian-ethnics in the United States and discuss key issues in existing scholarship on Asian American intermarriage. I examine Asian American intermarriage particularly in terms of how it has been theorized in relation to sociological theories of race and assimilation.

## Regulation of Asian American Gender and Sexuality in U.S. History

Anti-miscegenation statutes, laws that prohibited sexual relationships and marriages between "Whites" and those considered "non-Whites," were not struck down by the U.S. federal courts until 1967, in the landmark *Loving vs. Virginia Supreme Court* decision. The "non-Whites" mentioned in these statutes first designated Blacks but was later extended to "Indians" (Native-Americans),[1] "Mongolians" (a category that included Chinese, Japanese, and Koreans), "Hindus/Asiatic Indians" (then the official term for South Asians), and to "Malays" (Filipinos). State-based anti-miscegenation laws go back as early as the 1600s and were legal in the majority of the U.S. until 1967, although a number of states voluntarily repealed these laws before WWII and some between 1948 and 1967. These statutes first went into effect in the South and lasted the longest there, but it was in the Western states where Asian Americans were added to the prohibited groups.[2] Because these laws were enacted on a state-by-state basis, a small number of interracial marriages existed before 1967, especially in states that legally allowed them. This includes White-Black marriages, but also a limited number of White-Asian marriages, especially between Asian men and White women, given the dearth of women of Asian descent in the U.S. before the mid-twentieth century.

The rates of intermarriages among Asian-ethnics, however, were small until WWII. This was by design stemming from race-based immigration policies of the U.S. government that systematically controlled the entry of individuals from Asian-Pacific Rim countries starting the mid-1800s, which combined with the restrictive laws regarding intermarriages to create particular demographic configurations of Asian American communities. Even though the existence of small Asian communities traces back to as early as the 1700s in the United States, Asians did not begin arriving in sizable numbers until the 1850s. The first immigrants arrived mainly as cheap physical laborers to work in the agricultural sector.[3] This first wave of laborers was recruited from countries such as China, Japan, Korea, and the Philippines by the U.S. government to work in Hawaiian sugar cane fields. Laborers, mostly men, arrived to the U.S. mainland as well; one main group was Chinese laborers recruited to build transpacific railroads and work in gold mining in the Western states, and workers from other Asian nations, including Japan and India, came to toil as agricultural workers in West Coast states. These laborers, working under unimaginably difficult circumstances and for extremely low pay (many under indentured servitude), fulfilled the needs of an expanding U.S. capitalist economy that depended on the importation of cheap, mobile labor force. Their contribution to the building of the American economy and nation, though significant, went unrecognized for decades.[4]

As the labor needs of the U.S. economy expanded and contracted throughout the late nineteenth and early twentieth centuries, immigration policies altered to accommodate these changing needs. The country opened up the borders when it needed labor and closed them when it did not. Racially discriminatory immigration legislation was introduced to restrict or even ban immigration of specific groups, in this case, immigrants from the Asian-Pacific Rim countries. One of the first such laws is the now infamous Chinese Exclusion Act of 1882, which completely prohibited immigration from China in response to a surge in nativistic and racist sentiments against Chinese laborers.[5] This piece of legislation—the first in U.S. history to exclude an entire category of immigrants on the basis of national origin alone—was followed by a series of immigration laws passed by Congress that banned immigration from the "barred zones." This included the "Asiatic Barred-Zones Act" of 1917, which prohibited immigration from East Asia, Pacific Islands, Mongolia, the Indian subcontinent, and the Middle East.

Asian immigrants were also placed in the category of "aliens ineligible for citizenship," a status that prohibited them from many privileges granted to citizens, such as owning land and entering professional occupations.[6] Of all the Asian-origin groups, the Japanese fared best because of the political and military leverage the Japanese government used to protect Japanese citizens into the early 1920s,[7] but even the Japanese were finally prohibited from entering the country in 1924 with the passing of the National Origins Act. This Act not only imposed a general yearly quota of 150,000 on all immigrants globally but specifically enacted bans on immigrants historically "ineligible" for citizenship, which included the Japanese. Filipinos, who were considered "nationals" as they were subjects of a U.S. territory after the United States colonized the Philippines following the Spanish-American War of 1898, were not banned at this time, but even they were finally restricted from immigrating via the 1934 Tydings-McDuffie Act.[8]

Racially motivated immigration restrictions significantly impacted the formation and growth of Asian American communities. Throughout the first half of the twentieth century, Asian American communities experienced little growth on the mainland because these immigrant policies were designed to allow only male workers into the U.S. while actively discouraging the entry of women. Except in Hawaii, which allowed female immigration and the establishment of families, these policies, working in tandem with anti-miscegenation laws against Asians, were deliberately designed to limit the formation of families and the growth of Asian American communities whose members could lay claim to American citizenship:

> Unlike other forms of miscegenation regulation, anti-miscegenation laws directed at Asian Americans were shaped by a need to police the sexuality of a primarily male immigrant labor force; the laws worked to impede their incorporation into America through marriage or through the creation of a subsequent generation of American-born citizens.[9]

Another piece of anti-miscegenation legislation directed exclusively against Asian men stripped citizenship from White women who married men of Asian descent, which further deterred interracial marriage.[10]

One of the main effects of this gender imbalance was the creation of "bachelor societies" in various Chinatowns in U.S. urban areas and dispersed Filipino enclaves.[11] Although a number of the heterosexual men in these enclaves were already married before immigrating and supported their families back in their home countries in the form of "split" households, most men lived out the rest of their lives without access to legitimate forms of female companionship or marriage. These men were also subject to widespread negative images depicting them as amoral, dangerous, filthy, and criminal—for example, as opium or gambling addicts and as sexually predatory (especially of White women)—further reinforcing their unfitness for citizenship. At the same time, these immigration laws, which essentially served as a mechanism to control the sexuality of Asian men that threatened the White power structure, buttressed White hegemonic masculinity by spreading images of Asian men as asexual and impotent. In reality, however, the men in these bachelor societies had to forge kinship with one another: "Institutionally barred from normative (hetero)sexual reproduction and nuclear family formations," many of these men had to create supportive networks with each other to "sustain themselves in a hostile society often by redefining and extending the concept of 'family' to include new forms of 'queer domesticity' . . . that counters normative expectations of 'respectable, middle-class, heterosexual marriage'."[12]

During this time, the few Chinese women who were allowed in the U.S. worked primarily as prostitutes, but to assure the stigmatization of these women as amoral, disease-carrying inciters of vice and corruption, the Page Act was enacted in 1875 to further reduce the number of Asian women; this Act specifically barred the entry of Chinese and other "Mongolian" prostitutes, and also felons and contract laborers.[13] Thus, from early on, Asian women's sexuality was viewed as deviant and different from White women's sexuality, further reinforcing the idea of "Oriental degeneracy" and legitimizing White-Asian segregation. Following the enactment of this law, the sex ratio within these Asian American communities became even more skewed; within the Chinese American community, for example, the sex ratio in 1870 was about 13 men to 1 woman, but by 1890, the sex ratio was 27 men to 1 woman.[14] Susan Koshy notes, "What is ironic is that while the system of slavery provided incentives for Black men and women to reproduce, the capitalist regime of the late nineteenth century benefited from the sexual subordination of Asian workers by passing on the costs of their social and sexual reproduction to their households in their homelands and profiting from their dependence on commercialized intimacies."[15]

As mentioned earlier, the only Asian American community that was able to somewhat escape this plight was the Japanese American community, notwithstanding their later internment experience during WWII, because the 1907 "Gentlemen's Agreement" with Japan allowed the entry of wives, children, and parents of Japanese residents until 1924, although it essentially terminated all Japanese labor immigration. By 1920, 46% of the Japanese in Hawaii and 34.5% of the Japanese on the mainland were women.[16] For the men of the other Asian-ethnic groups, the majority remained without access to marriage, but some interracial marriages did occur, especially with women of other racial minority groups. Although such outmarriages were uncommon for Chinese and Japanese men, some Asian Indians and Filipinos outmarried with White women as well as with Mexicans and Native American women (and a smaller number of Black women), especially in California.[17]

Interracial marriage rates for Asian Americans spiked after WWII, especially between non-Asian U.S. male citizens and Asian women, as tens of thousands of women from the Asian-Pacific Rim entered the United States as wives of U.S. servicemen. Some of these women entered the country when the War Brides Act was enacted in 1945, designed to allow American servicemen to bring their "alien" spouses and children into the United States. In 1947, the Act was also amended to include veterans with Asian ancestry, enabling Asian American servicemen to bring their Asian spouses during a three-year period. The Chinese Exclusion Act was finally repealed in 1943. Further liberalization of immigration laws in the post-WWII period and during the Korean War allowed more spouses of U.S. citizens to enter the United States as non-quota immigrants. During the 1950s, 80% of more than 45,000 Japanese immigrants were women, and almost all were wives of non-Asian U.S. servicemen who met during the post-WWII U.S. occupation of Japan. Between 1950 and 1964, more than 15,000 Korean women were allowed admission into the U.S., and almost 40% came as wives of non-Asian U.S. servicemen. A large number of Filipino women, about 16,000, and almost all wives of non-Asian U.S. servicemen, entered the country. Chinese women also came in sizable numbers, mostly as wives of Chinese male U.S. citizens or as wives of Chinese American GIs. Between 1945 and 1953, more than 12,000 Chinese immigrants entered the U.S., 89% of them female.[18]

The influx of female immigrants during this period, largely as wives of G.I.s, not only had an impact on intermarriage rates but also had important consequences for Asian American communities. The entry of post-WWII Asian female immigrants, especially the wives of G.I.s of Asian descent, began to correct the long-standing gender imbalance within Asian American communities and rejuvenate these communities by enabling the formation of families. Starting in the early 1950s, there was also a wave of so-called "intellectual" migration of middle- and upper-class immigrants from East and South Asia who came to the United States to seek graduate degrees or professional occupations. These immigrants also contributed to the growth of Asian American families and communities. Of the post-WWII Asian female immigrants who were admitted as intermarried spouses of non-Asian servicemen, many contributed to the growth of Asian American communities by constituting the initial core of chain migration activated by the 1965 Immigration and Naturalization Act (1965 Hart-Celler Act) that finally ended legal bans on immigrants from the Eastern Hemisphere.[19] Many post-1965 Asian immigrants entered the U.S. under the "Family Reunification" policy of the 1965 Immigrant and Naturalization Act, with many of these women serving as sponsors for relatives and as the originators of "chain migration."

Indeed, the 1965 Immigration and Naturalization Act was a key piece of immigrant legislation that opened the floodgates to immigrants from Asian-Pacific Rim nations to the U.S. for the first time. With the influx of Asian immigrants from a spectrum of nations—China, South Korea, the Philippines, India, and Vietnam being some of the largest sending nations—the Asian American population increased from about 1.5 million in 1970 to 11.9 million in 2000. Aside from the sheer increase in size of the U.S. Asian American population, this post-1965 "new" immigrant population was distinct from the earlier Asian immigrants in three key ways. First, unlike the low-skilled, low-wage laborers that made up the majority of pre-1965 immigrants, a large number of post-1965 immigrants were middle-class, college-educated, white-collar professionals, although there was a wave of lower-class refugee immigrants from Southeast Asian nations later on, such as from war-torn Vietnam, Laos, and Cambodia. This new middle-class immigrant profile was driven by the U.S. labor market need for educated, professional workers, which stemmed from a rapid growth in capital-intensive, high-tech industries and service sectors in the U.S. economy.[20] Despite the economic and cultural challenges many of these immigrants faced in the United States, especially due to downward social and economic mobility, the educational status and cultural capital these immigrants brought from their home-lands played a significant role in how these families acculturated into the U.S. middle-class society, feeding the creation of the contemporary, mythic "model minority" image of Asian Americans. Second, the majority of the post-1965 immigrants, even the later refugee immigrants, arrived as families rather than as single male sojourners, intending to settle permanently. Third, the majority of the post-1965 immigrants were female.[21]

According to the 2010 U.S. census count, Asian Americans make up about 5.6% of the U.S. population and have become increasingly diverse ethnically and socioeconomically, with Chinese Americans being the largest group, followed by Indian, Filipino, Vietnamese, Korean, and Japanese Americans. Other siz-able groups include Pakistani, Cambodian, Hmong, Thai, Laotian, Taiwanese, Bangladeshi, and Burmese. The majority of each of these groups is foreign-born except for the Japanese Americans; Japanese Americans have sizable third and fourth generations.

## Asian American Intermarriage in the Present

After the 1967 *Loving* decision, intermarriages began increasing among Asian Americans overall, primarily with the White population.[22] But the contributions of the war brides notwithstanding, intermarriage for Asian Americans overall remained low until about the 1980s. With the wave of "new" post-1965 immi-gration, the picture of intermarriage among Asian Americans began to change. Although intermarriages, both interracial and interethnic, are still a minority of all marriages for all minority groups in the United States, Asian Americans, by the 1980s, came to possess one of the highest rates of intermarriage among all U.S. minority groups, raising some interesting questions.

In 1980, the exogamous marriage rate (both interracial and interethnic) for Asian Americans was about 25.4%, whereas it was 12.7% for Hispanics, 2.2% for Blacks (and 1% for non-Hispanic Whites). By 1990, the intermarriage rate for Asian Americans was about 21%, 18.6% for Hispanics, and 5.8% for Blacks.[23] In 2000, the intermarriage rates were about 32% for Asian Americans, 20% for Hispanics, about 10% for Blacks (and less than 5% for non-Hispanic Whites).[24] An analysis of the latest census figures, from the 2010 census, estimates Asian American intermarriage (both interracial and interethnic) to be about 35%.[25] Looking at the overall numbers since the 1980s, what is clear is that intermarriage rates among Asian Americans are one of the highest for racial minority groups[26] and that the intermarriage rates are consistently lowest for African Americans, though their numbers have increased over the last few decades.

In most studies of Asian American intermarriages, some interesting phenom-ena have also been consistently noted. The first is that for Asian Americans, intermarriage patterns, as mentioned earlier, have always been strongly gendered; higher rates of intermarriage among Asian American women have been consistent over time. In 1980, 31.5% of women married out, while only 16.6% of men did; in 1990, about 27.1% of women intermarried while 14.1% of men did.[27] As recently as 2008, this ratio, almost 2 (women): 1 (men), has held more or less constant.[28] The second important aspect of Asian American intermarriage is the racial dimension; the majority of intermarriages by Asian Americans have been interracial, mostly to White spouses, although this trend is reversing, as will be discussed next. In 1980, 89.3% of all Asian American intermarriages were interracial marriages, 76.6% to Whites; in 1990, 78.8% were interracial marriages, and 61.4% to Whites.[29] Third, there have been some internal variations and exceptions among different Asian national groups in relation to intermarriage statistics, although the rates for different groups are undergoing changes; for example, Filipino and Japanese Americans have historically had the highest intermarriage rates compared to other Asian–ethnic groups, and Asian Indians are the most endogamous (marrying within one's national group). Another exception to the prevailing intermarital gender pattern, in this case in terms of gender, is that Asian Indian men consistently out-married at higher rates than Asian Indian women.[30]

Finally, for the purposes of this book, another important pattern to note is the difference in intermarriage rates by nativity, that is, between native-born Asians (born in the United States) and foreign-born Asians. All studies on Asian American intermarriage show that intermarriage rates are much higher among U.S.-born Asians than those who are not born in the U.S.[31] In 1980, for example, the breakdown along this dimension was intermarriage rates of 24.7% for native-born and 22.3% for foreign-born, and in 1990, 40.1% for native-born and 17.4% for foreign-born.[32] Using 2010–2012 data, the rate is about 23% for second generation (31% for third generation) and about 10% for the immigration generation.[33] Looking at newlyweds, a 2010 Pew Report finds that close to half (46%) of native-born out-married to a non-Asian person, as opposed to only 26% of foreign-born.[34] The other interesting aspect of this native-born/foreign-born difference is that native-born men are much more likely to intermarry than foreign-born men. Lee and Fernandez report that in 1980, native-born Asian American men were three times as likely to intermarry as foreign-born Asian-ethnic men, and in 1990, this gap grew to four times as likely.[35] Between 2010 and 2012, according to Pew Report data, this generational intermarriage gap among men continued (19% for second-generation men versus 5% for first-generation men out marrying).[36] The native-born/foreign-born gap is not nearly as great for women; however, native-born Asian-ethnic women still intermarry at higher rates than native-born men.[37]

## Interracial Versus Interethnic Marriages

As the term "intermarriage" is typically used to denote both interracial and interethnic marriages, it is important to unpack the differences between the two marital type trends because there are divergences in rates and patterns. As mentioned earlier, most intermarriages among Asian Americans, historically, have been interracial marriages, primarily to Whites. The first noteworthy recent trend is that since the 1980s, interracial marriages began to decline while interethnic marriages began to rise.

According to Sharon Lee and Marilyn Fernandez, between 1980 and 1990, the total intermarriage rate—interracial and interethnic together—declined for Asian Americans from 25.4% to 21.2%, but within this total, the proportion of interracial marriages declined from 89.3% to 78.8%, while interethnic marriages increased from 10.7% in 1980 to 21.2% in 1990.[38] Other studies have documented similar trends. Larry Shinagawa and Gin Yong Pang, using their own national data analysis, also show that the proportion of Asian American interethnic marriages rose about 400–500% between 1980 and 1990 while interracial marriages decreased significantly for both men and women.[39] They note that in specific regions with high numbers of Asians, interethnic marriages were the dominant forms of intermarriages, regardless of nativity. They also observed that younger age cohorts display an increasing proclivity toward interethnic marriage as opposed to minority-majority marriages.[40]

There are a couple of interesting features to note about the interracial versus interethnic marriage trends. First, even though interracial marriages have been and still are the predominant form of intermarriage in absolute numbers for Asian Americans, when controlling for the size of the group, Asian Americans, especially East Asians, are actually *more likely* to marry a member of another Asian-ethnic group than a White American, regardless of gender.[41] The second important feature to note concerns nativity; as mentioned earlier, while all studies point to higher rates of interracial marriages in the second generation and later as compared to the immigrant generation, it turns out that *interethnic* marriage rates are much higher than expected in the U.S.-born Asian American groups, and much higher than among immigrants, a counterintuitive trend if one assumes a greater level of assimilation among the U.S.-born.[42] For example, marriages between U.S.-born Japanese and Chinese Americans and between Japanese and Korean Americans are, respectively, 2.9 times and 2.7 times more likely for native-born couples than for mixed-nativity couples.[43] Indeed, an analysis of some of the most recent available national census data focusing on U.S.-born/-raised Asian Americans shows that during 2006–2010, rates of intermarriages, especially those involving Asian Americans and Whites, have declined overall, while rates of interethnic marriages have increased notably. Between 2006 and 2010, pan-Asian marriages among U.S.-born/-raised increased universally among all six ethnic groups (Asian Indian, Chinese, Filipino, Japanese, Korean, Vietnamese) for both genders.[44]

To explain rising rates in interethnic marriages in general, a number of quantitative studies have honed in on the possible effects of increased group sizes due to immigration replenishment, showing that ongoing immigration for a group leads both to increased endogamy, as well as to interethnic unions, while suppressing interracial marriage.[45] Although immigrant expansion and group size on intermarriage patterns may have some effects for the Asian American community on the whole, the impact of these factors, especially when broken down by generations, is not as clear cut. Numerous studies show that regardless of ethnic community size or immigrant replenishment, the tendency toward Asian marital panethnicity increases in the second generation and beyond[46] and that Asian American marital panethnicity is stronger down the generations than would be predicted by the size of the ethnic group. Zhenchao Qian states, "Interethnic marriage is frequent among American-born Asians despite small group sizes and limited opportunities for contact" in many areas.[47] Michael Rosenfeld has also shown that Asian Americans, especially the second generation, marry interethnically in certain geographic locations more often than predicted patterns. This is especially notable when compared to other ethnic/racial groups that have experienced immigrant replenishment, for example, Latinos, whose marital panethnicity tends to erode down the generations:[48] "Asian panethnicity is just as strong as Hispanic panethnicity among the foreign-born, but much stronger among those born in the United States."[49]

Other studies support these findings. One study that focuses only on the U.S.-born found that controlling for population composition, Asians marry members of other Asian groups 2.60 times as often as they marry Whites, 4.16 times as often as they marry Latinos, and 18.7 times as often as they marry Blacks, suggesting that boundaries between Asians and non-Asians are stronger than among Asian groups and also supporting the thesis of weaker Latino marital panethnicity.[50] Another study, again looking specifically only at U.S.-born Asian couples, shows that although U.S.-born Asians have lower endogamy rates than their foreign-born counterparts, an unsurprising finding, U.S.-born Asians have much higher endogamy rates when compared to U.S.-born Latinos as a whole.[51]

Although there is no doubt that marital decisions and preferences are shaped within the context of structural realities, there are clearly other forces at work than demographic-type structural factors such as ethnic group size when it comes to the interethnic marital choices of U.S.-born/-raised Asians. Focusing on the U.S.-raised/-born group, I aim in this book to tease out some key cultural and ideological factors, informed by subjective viewpoints, which play a role in shaping romantic desires and marital choices of these Asian Americans. Moreover, this study will focus on the nature of panethnic cultures and identities being constructed within these marriages and families in relation to the dominant American ideological and racial structures, and will discuss its implications for the incorporative process of Asian Americans.

## Intermarriage, Race, and Assimilation

### *Intermarriage and Race*

How have previous studies analyzed and theorized the phenomenon of Asian American intermarriage? There are two major issues addressed in the studies of Asian American intermarriage: first, factors that inform intermarriage, and second, how intermarriage connects to assimilation, an issue that relates to both the causes and consequences of intermarriage. First, as discussed, assessing what leads to intermarriage would require a consideration of both structural factors—factors that shape meeting and mating opportunities—and cultural factors, such as norms, identities, societal images, and group preferences, or the interplay thereof.[52] At the macro-level, scholars have vigorously debated the extent to which structural factors and cultural factors are comparatively relevant to the formation of these individual-level desires and choices.[53] However, because the former are more easily measured and described, a wider range of studies—mostly quantitative—exist that investigate the effects of structural factors on intermarriage and intermarriage patterns over time.[54] Discussions of structural factors affecting intermarriage have focused especially on matters such as group size, and, relatedly, regional concentration of groups or the presence of ethnic enclaves (ethnic segregation). The dominant view is that the larger the group size or the greater the concentration of an ethnic population in an area, the greater likelihood of propinquity and other "supply-side" factors such as robust existence of ethnic institutions and infrastructures. This leads to greater opportunities for people to meet members of their own group and develop a "taste" for them, leading to the likelihood of in-group marriage/endogamy.[55]

Studies, especially qualitative ones, that focus on cultural factors—and the more elusive issues of personal preferences/desires that are shaped by cultural factors—are more sparse. Moreover, of those qualitative studies, a greater number exists on interracial marriages than interethnic marriages because the latter is a comparably new phenomenon. According to Paul Spickard "intermarriage patterns, particularly gender patterns, are not just functions of social structure. They depend in large part on the images that people of the various ethnic groups have of each other and of themselves."[56] In line with this observation, even quantitatively oriented scholars have pointed out the importance of investigating cultural factors, in tandem with structural factors, in studying intermarriage. In fact, Matthijs Kalmijn and Frank Van Tubergen conclude that cultural forces may be even more important than structural forces in determining marital selection.[57]

Although cultural forces encompass a wide number of factors—larger social ideologies intersecting with different ethnic group features such as religion, endogamous norms, and even language fluency—recent studies of intermarriages have highlighted the significance of race as a contributor to intermarriage patterns in the United States Central to this analysis is how larger society's perceptions of particular ethnic groups affect their acceptability as marital partners to the dominant group and how romantic desires and spousal choices of the minority group members themselves, often expressed as personal preferences, are shaped by the larger societal racial ideological context. Analyses focusing on race have been especially pivotal to helping explain the variations in intermarriage rates along a number of fronts, including differing intermarriage rates across ethnic/national groups and variability in intermarriage rates by gender.

Numerous studies have made clear, for example, that race is particularly central to understanding the historical and continued low rates of intermarriage between Blacks and Whites as compared to other racial minority groups[58] and, conversely, that the United States' racial structure explains the rapid intergenerational assimilation of most "White" European immigrant groups by way of intermarriage. Race also helps to understand the effects of color (as opposed to simply race but related to race) in the likelihood of intermarriage among Hispanics.[59] Furthermore, macro-level structural explanations cannot fully explain gender dimensions to intermarriage, for example, why Black men marry White women at higher rates than vice versa, while this gender pattern holds opposite for Asian Americans. In the next section, I briefly trace the history and development of racialized images of Asian-ethnic men and women in the United States that provide context for understanding the role of race in Asian American intermarriage.

## Racialized Constructions of Asian American Femininity and Masculinity

Because racialized images and stereotypes of Asian Americans, or what Patricia Hill Collins calls "controlling images,"[60] are critical to understanding the construction of romantic desires and marital boundary-crossings, it is useful to briefly examine the social construction of Asian American femininity and masculinity. Throughout U.S. history, women and men of Asian descent have been divergently caricaturized and stereotyped, reflecting the ways in which the axes of race and gender intersect to produce differential ideological consequences for women and men. One can argue that throughout U.S. history, stereotypes of Asian women have been more consistent than those of Asian men, although images of Asian women have not been static. As discussed earlier, there were efforts in the mid-1800s, around the time of the enactment of the Page Law, to depict Asian women in negatively sexualized ways, as prostitutes or temptresses who were conduits of social vice and diseases. Susan Koshy argues that while this was the case within the United States, the imagined "Oriental licentiousness" of Asian women heightened their allure as sex objects in extranational locales around the world, especially in islands in the Pacific, treaty ports, and colonized lands, which led to the formation of the "White man-Asian woman dyad."[61]

Around and after WWII, sexual contact between White men and Asian women overseas was further encouraged by sexual license afforded to White men as part of occupying forces in Asia. Ironically, post-WWII immigration laws that enabled these extra-territorial interracial marriages to continue in the United States (as soldiers brought their Asian wives home) served as a "mechanism of selective incorporation of interracial sexual relationships" and normalization of White-Asian interracial intimacy, and, subsequently, these laws played an important role in "reconstructing images of Asian femininity from sexually licentious to domestically feminine; the recontextualization of White-Asian intimacy within marriage also increased the sexual capital of Asian American women."[62]

This history provides the context for some of the controlling images of Asian females that consist of simultaneous and contradictory construction of them as submissive, docile, self-sacrificing, compliant "lotus blossom/china doll/geisha girl," and as the ferocious, cunning, treacherous "dragon lady" and various incarnations thereof. Through the inter-war years, these contradictory and fantasized images of Asian women that were beamed from Hollywood films and other media outlets were substantially responsible for popularizing such racialized images of Asian women. In either case, what is common to the two polar images is that the Asian woman is constructed as the exotic and mysterious "other" with special sexual powers over and against the normative, respectable middle-class White femininity, whatever form that might take in a particular historical period—chaste/dependable, or feminist/liberated. Central to this exotified image of Asian-ethnic women was the implicit and explicit sexual availability of Asian women to White men; during and after WWII, these stereotypes become solidified in the figure of the war bride and the Asian prostitute (epitomized in operas like Madam Butterfly and Broadway shows like Miss Saigon). Both types of the Asian female were literally the material spoils of war and U.S. military plunder. This now globalized imagery of the submissive but hyper-sexual "Oriental" female becomes central to the formation of interracial desires throughout the twentieth century, particularly on the part of Western men for Asian women.

Although Asian females are commonly imagined to be a desirable and even marriageable commodity to White men as servile/submissive yet hypersexual sex objects, it is important to bear in mind that this commodification of Asian "femininity" makes it inferior to that of the normative middle-class White femininity.[63] That is, while Asian femininity may be the fetishized embodiment of Western womanhood and pitted against the "emancipated" (read: demanding, emasculating, promiscuous) White women—it remains an inferior femininity.[64] In fact, the seeming inclusion of Asian women into the category of White middle-class femininity by glorifying them as the embodiment of the "perfect" womanhood is "part of the broader program of hegemonic recuperation, a program that has as its main focus the reconstruction of White masculine power."[65] Indeed, Karen Pyke and Denise Johnson formulate a concept of "subordinated femininities" with regard to women of color as opposed to the notion of "hegemonic femininity" enjoyed by White women.[66] According to this conceptual formulation, even though Asian females (or other minority females) may be viewed as desirable by some White men, they are considered desirable insofar as they are substitutes for, or alternatives to, normative White femininity over which some of these men may feel they have less control and to which they have lack of access. Often, Asian women, along with (spicy) Latinas or (over-sexed) Black women, are endowed with "excess" femininity or womanhood by popular culture, which simultaneously hyper-sexualizes them and denigrates their sexuality as "slutty (read: abnormal)" or "submissive."[67] This internalization of inferior messages about the "essential" Asian womanhood (submissive, passive, quiet, and so on) is one of the reasons, as we will see throughout this book, why even interracially married Asian American women struggle with issues of problematic self-image.[68]

While the stereotypes of hyper-sexualized but docile/passive Asian American women have remained stable over time and have served as objects of Western male fantasies, stereotypes of Asian men underwent more perceptible changes over the course of U.S. history. In the nineteenth and into the early twentieth centuries, Asian men were primarily caricaturized, much like Black men, as deviant, dangerous, and sexually threatening, with special appetites for White women; the racist depictions of Asian men as "lascivious and predatory" were particularly prominent when nativistic sentiments/movements ran strong against Asians at the turn of the twentieth century. These stereotypes, however, reversed as "bachelor societies" began to form and Asian men began to be "feminized" and excluded from the hegemonic constructions of masculinity; Asian masculinity transformed from hypersexual to asexual, even homosexual.[69] Reflecting the reality of women-less Asian men who were increasingly being shut out of mainstream occupations and relegated to low-status, service-oriented "women's work," for example, as houseboys, laundrymen, or servants, feminization became "a crucial issue that plagued Asian American male subjectivity throughout the nineteenth and twentieth centuries."[70]

Thereafter, Asian American men, similarly to Asian American women, were subject to two-sided, contradictory images, each image rearing its ugly head when the social circumstances demanded it; one side was the sexually predatory, villainous, treacherous, overly clever incarnation of the "yellow peril," and on the other side, the nerdy, sexually undesirable geek. One early- to mid-twentieth century mass media character who embodied such dual stereotypes was the figure of the Fu Manchu, a sinister but brilliant villain who plots to destroy Western civilization. While clever and villainously powerful, Fu Manchu was also notable for his inscrutable "Oriental" ways and lack of any conventional masculinity; he behaved lasciviously but with homoerotic suggestiveness with his long dresses, batting eyelashes, and long fingernails, serving to undercut Asian American virility.[71] To this day, the two alternating mass media/Hollywood stereotypes of the Asian male are embodied, on the one hand, in various incarnations of the sexless houseboy characters, geeks, and sidekicks and, on the other hand, of the kung-fu, ninja-assassin villains.

These enduring stereotypes, which parallel the feminization of the "Oriental" nations as objects of the "masculine" Western imperial conquests, became ongoing psychic burdens on Asian men throughout the twentieth century and beyond, contributing to gender differences in Asian American intermarriage rates. That is, whether they are portrayed as a passive, sexually unappealing geek—recently bolstered by the rise of the "model minority" image—or as a kung-fu artist/villain, the Asian male is still robbed of acceptable mainstream manhood that would make him sexually and romantically desirable; indeed, as Frank Wu notes, even martial artists are targeted for denigration and mocking.[72] Furthermore, the invidious, double-edged "model minority" stereotype reinforces for both men and women the "otherness" of Asians as "unassimilable" and "foreign." For men in particular, "the contemporary model-minority stereotype further emasculates Asian American men as passive and malleable. . . . Disseminated and perpetuated through popular media, these stereotypes of the emasculated Asian male construct a reality in which social and economic discrimination against these men appears defensible."[73] In sum, as Elaine Kim analyzes, Asian women's hyper-sexuality and Asian men's asexuality both exist for the same reason: "to define the White man's virility and the White man's superiority."[74]

## Studies of Asian American Intermarriage and Race

One of the earliest full-length qualitative treatments of Asian American intermarriage (interracial and interethnic combined) is by Betty Sung, a study which focuses on Chinese Americans in New York City.[75] In terms of interracial marriages more specifically, more recent studies by Coleen Fong/Judy Yung and Sue Chow, which focus on Japanese and Chinese American interracial marriages, were one of the first to seriously attend to the cultural issues of racial and gender power in interracial marriages, moving beyond structural factors.[76] Both studies underscore the issue of racial inequality in America, pointing out how American racial structures that value Euro-American standards for attractiveness and culture carry powerful influences on the subjectivities of Asian Americans, often inciting desires for whiteness and negative perceptions of fellow Asian-ethnics.

Most recently, a book by Kumiko Nemoto looks at interracially married and single Asian American men and women of a wider range of national origins and differing nativity status, delving similarly into the racialized desires of these individuals and how these desires interact with larger ideologies along the lines of gender, class, and nation.[77] Nemoto's book is distinctive in that she analyzes men and women separately, highlighting and explicitly problematizing the gender differences in interracial marriage rates and highlighting the intersection of race and gender in interracial romance and marriage.

Although less attention has been paid thus far in terms of in-depth, qualitative investigations of interethnically married Asian Americans, this topic has not gone entirely unaddressed. Among recent works, Mia Tuan was one of the first to address the topic of Asian American interethnic marriage. In her book, *Forever Foreigners or Honorary Whites*, she devotes a small section to intermarriage, focusing particularly on the phenomenon of the recent rise of Asian interethnic dating and marriage and what it might mean. Tuan considers whether Asian interethnic dating and marriage might be related to the growing strength of Asian panethnic consciousness and the identification of Asian Americans along racial, rather than ethnic, lines: "their openness to dating other Asian Americans can also be seen as an example of new and thriving racial salience. Increasingly, the issue is not whether they date co-ethnics but whether they date others within the same panethnic and racialized category as themselves."[78]

There are other qualitative studies that deal more directly with Asian American interethnic attraction and what it might mean, but, like Tuan's work, they are not full-fledged studies of interethnically *married* unions. Building on works like Tuan's, and on earlier quantitative studies that linked Asian interethnic marriages to the possible growing strength of panethnic identity and consciousness, scholars such as Nazli Kibria examined the phenomenon of Asian American "ethnogenesis" among certain segments of the second generation Asian American population—a development of pan-Asian identity that may be both politically driven and cultural in nature—and its possible relationship to interethnic relationships or marriage.[79] The article by Chow mentioned earlier also deals partly with the issue of interethnic attraction by exploring some of the subjective factors driving interethnic partner preference. Recently, popular media explanations for the rise of Asian interethnic marriages point to the fact that Asian Americans might be marrying each other because they are looking to tap into and maintain their ethnic roots[80] or that improvement of societal and media images of Asian Americans are removing the barriers to attraction among Asian Americans.[81]

In studies reviewed here of both interracial and interethnic marriages, the continued salience of race as a context within which individuals make their marital choices, for either type of marriage, is clear. In my analysis of both types of intermarriages, I build on the insights provided by these analyses but extend the inquiry further by doing several things. First, I focus on U.S.-born/-raised second and later generations, which enables me to compare ethnic-racial and intermarital experiences of Asian-descent Americans with the experiences of other groups of native-born Americans. Experiences and choices of foreign-born and native-born as they relate to intermarriage, assimilation, and racialization processes, as discussed in the last chapter, are of a different order and need to be decoupled. Second, focusing primarily on *married* couples, unlike most of the previous studies, allows me to more accurately ascertain the motivations for spousal and romantic preferences through evidence that moves past speculations of unmarried individuals. Furthermore, investigating already married couples, especially those with children, helps move beyond questions of what leads to romantic choices and provides us with the advantage of exploring the process of family-making and cultural/ethnic-racial dynamics between the couples within their marriages, contributing to the growing literature on intermarriages and multiracial/multicultural families in the United States.[82]

## Intermarriage and Assimilation

How have Asian American intermarriages been analyzed in relation to the issue of assimilation? With regard to Asian Americans, who, like Latinos, occupy a racially in-between position in America's traditional Black-White divide, much of the initial studies on intermarriages were concerned with the meaning of what appeared to be surprisingly high rates of interracial marriage of Asian Americans, particularly with Whites, and what this may indicate about the path and type of their social assimilation and acceptance into American society. While some studies on Asian Americans optimistically perceive interracial marriage as a possible barometer of assimilation or some type of racial/ethnic boundary blurring,[83] a number of other studies have begun to show that interracial marriages among Asian Americans may not be the indicator of assimilation that some would like to believe.[84] To complicate this debate further, the recent uptick in the rates of Asian interethnic marriages has intensified attention to the question of whether Asian Americans are really on the way to assimilation as viewed from a classic "straight-line" assimilation perspective, or whether the increase signifies something more complex about the social position of Asian Americans, their group identity, and path of assimilation.

The assimilation paradigm has been abundantly criticized since it made its appearance in the mid-twentieth century. Although there have been variants of the early "straight-line" assimilation theory and subsequent attempts to complicate it, the core of its idea, that immigrant groups and their descendants would over time shed their ethnic and cultural distinctiveness to meld into the dominant White, Anglo-Saxon middle-class U.S. mainstream culture—the two central assumptions here being that the immigrants would *want* to shed their ethnicities and that mainstream society would *accept* them once they do—has been vigorously challenged.

Although the members of the Chicago School, such as Robert Park and E. W. Burgess, were among the first to define and popularize the term "assimilation,"[85] it is with W. Lloyd Warner and Leo Srole, based on their study of the residents of a Northeastern "Yankee City,"[86] that the idea of uni-directional assimilation by way of generations became clearly articulated, including the idea that all immigrant groups, although at different rates depending on their skin color and the like—for example, darker-skinned Southern Europeans and/or Jews versus the Northern Europeans—were moving toward a process of absorption into the mainstream culture (middle-class, Anglo-Saxon, Protestant White). According to them, this involved "unlearning" of their ethnic cultures deemed inferior by the host society and learning the ways of the dominant society to become fully accepted by it.[87]

In 1964, Milton Gordon, in his book, *Assimilation in American Life*, provided an influential theoretical synthesis of assimilation by making an important contribution; he sharpened the conceptualization of assimilation by breaking it into a multidimensional process involving seven different dimensions or stages— cultural, structural, marital, identificational (development of a sense of peoplehood), attitude receptional (absence of prejudice), behavior receptional (absence of discrimination), and civic assimilation. Gordon's conceptualization of assimilation was clearly more sophisticated than what had come before, enabling a view of assimilation as a more complicated process that involves multiple sub-processes or stages that may take place in varying degrees for any group or generation.[88]

Armed with this framework, Gordon underscored a major point that in the United States, at least up until the time of his writing, cultural/behavioral assimilation into the "core" culture of the dominant Anglo-Saxon Protestant middle class, or what he also referred to as "acculturation" (involving the members of the minority group learning the culture of the dominant group or adopting its cultural patterns such as language, customs, and values), did occur for most minority or immigrant groups, but that "structural assimilation" (the acceptance of the minority group into the "cliques, clubs, and institutions of host society on primary level") was more challenging. But once structural assimilation, the "keystone of the arch of assimilation" occurred—either at the same time or after acculturation—"all of the other types of assimilation will naturally follow;" this included marital assimilation or "amalgamation," the summit of primary-level group acceptance and an "inevitable by-product" of structural assimilation. Furthermore, he stated that although acculturation may not necessarily lead to structural assimilation ("acculturation without integration"), structural assimilation inevitably produces acculturation. By the same token, marital assimilation for Gordon meant that the "minority group loses its ethnic identity in the larger host or core society" and identificational assimilation subsequently takes place.[89]

Although Gordon is often thought of as a proponent of a simplistic view of Anglo-conformity-type assimilation, this is a misportrayal. Gordon astutely observed that although acculturation of the "Anglo-conformity" kind occurred on a large scale, structural assimilation has not happened and may not happen as easily for some minority groups. He also did not assume that all immigrants or minorities would necessarily *want* structural assimilation because some groups preferred to maintain a level of distinctive group life or ethnic identity because this provided them with benefits.[90] For other groups, full structural assimilation, even with acculturation, was not possible because of social barriers arising from the dominant group's refusal to accept them, as has been the case for African Americans. Nonetheless, precisely because Gordon understood the power imbalance between most minority groups and the dominant Anglo-Saxon majority, he posited that acculturation and a full assimilation process would signify a process of Anglo-conformity, contributing to the popular view of "assimilation" that was essentially a uni-directional adaptation to "middle-class cultural patterns of largely, white Protestant, Anglo-Saxon origins" and that eventual assimilation was a likely path for all groups.[91]

As the immigrant population became more racially and ethnically diverse after the mid-1960s, such assumptions of Anglo-conformity and assimilation into a White middle-class society were no longer tenable in describing the differing experiences of the "new immigrants" and their children in the United States, particularly those of immigrants of color. As these assumptions were mainly based on the assimilation experiences of European immigrants at the turn of the twentieth century who seemed to be roughly following the straight-line assimilation path into the White mainstream, these assimilation theories began to be criticized in the 1960s for neglecting important aspects of the "new" minority immigrant group experiences.

For one thing, these theories were critiqued for their presumptions about the inevitability of the assimilation process, particularly into the dominant White mainstream culture and society. This was accompanied by the critique of the assumption that all minorities or newly arrived groups desired to assimilate and "Whiten" as quickly as possible, and those who did not achieve this were viewed as incompletely assimilated, rather than perhaps being incorporated into the U.S. on a different basis. Related to this, some of these straight-line theories were taken to task for their thinly veiled Eurocentrism, the assumption of the superiority of the Anglo-American culture into which most minority or immigrant groups would blend, shedding their own ethnic cultures in the process. Furthermore, these theories, even when addressing older European immigrant groups, downplayed the contributions made by various ethnic groups in the construction of the larger American culture, and the cultural diversity and attachments that existed.[92]

In response to these criticisms, alternative models have emerged. One such model includes pluralistic theories of group relations that reject the inevitability or even desirability of assimilation or amalgamation, spotlighting instead the possible persistence of ethnic, racial, and cultural differences. Whether pursued out of need, for example due to racial barriers or discrimination, or more voluntarily to sustain cultural ties and ethnic identity, the pluralistic views envision a society composed of multiple ethnic/cultural groupings flourishing on an equal basis and without the assumption that ethnic identities and cultures would signal loss of mainstream advantages.[93] More recently, however, many immigrant and race/ethnicity scholars have addressed the fact that a simple pluralist model may not accurately describe the reality of U.S. society because many ethnic and racial minority groups face difficulties associated with racism, prejudice, and other social and class barriers to their full and equal incorporation. To better describe the possibly varied incorporative experiences of these newer immigrants of color and their descendants, these new theories have attempted to make sense of the unique assimilation experiences of minority groups such as Asians, Latinos, and other groups of color within the context of America's evolving racial hierarchy and discourses.[94]

One such theory is the influential "segmented assimilation" theory devised by Alejandro Portes and Min Zhou that envisions three different modes of immigrant incorporation, including the classic "straight-line assimilation" path followed by many light-skinned immigrant groups into the middle class (such as Miami Cubans) but also "downward" assimilation into the underclass as experienced by some recent immigrant groups of color (such as the Haitians in Miami). The "downward" assimilation model has received attention for being useful in explaining how the second generation and later members of a racially and economically disadvantaged immigrant group can still acculturate and integrate into U.S. society but not into the White, mainstream, middle-class sector.[95] The third mode of incorporation in this model is the "selective assimilation" process in which immigrants preserve and draw upon certain aspects of the immigrant community's values and solidarity as a means to gain upward economic mobility (one example would be Punjabi Sikhs Indians in Northern California).[96] The selective assimilation model has been viewed as useful for demonstrating how economic mobility and acculturation can be decoupled, that is, how certain immigrant groups of color, particularly their children, can achieve economic mobility without completely giving up their ethnic cultures and values; in fact, this model demonstrates the advantages of ethnic cultures, group life, and resources in possibly promoting economic and educational success, an insight missing in classic assimilation theories.

In the past few years, other scholars have illustrated how the process of assimilation may be even more varied than described by theories such as the segmented assimilation theory. Recent works, especially on Latinos, challenge both the straight-line assimilation and the segmented assimilation theories by highlighting an even greater level of diversity in the incorporative paths of immigrants of color and their children—diversity along the lines of racial status, color, class, and gender that may exist even within a single ethnic group.[97] In terms of the impact of race, one useful concept associated with this research has been "racialized assimilation," a process whereby racialized individuals, regardless of social status, "assimilate" into U.S. society but without being able to fully identify themselves as "un-hyphenated" Americans because of social and cultural exclusion and discrimination based on race and/or ethnicity.[98] Other studies have made use of Herbert Gan's concept of the "bumpy-line" assimilation theory which views assimilation as non-linear, with "bumps representing various kinds of adaptation to changing circumstances—and with the line having no predictable end."[99]

Especially by situating race at the center, these efforts to complicate the classic assimilation model have represented big steps forward in elevating the understanding of the incorporation process of recent immigrants of color. These theoretical advances also help us move toward an alternative way of thinking about the incorporation process of Asian Americans and what intermarriage may signify for them. Does interracial marriage for Asian Americans, for example, necessarily symbolize the culmination of larger society's acceptance of Asian-ethnics as a group? Does interracial marriage necessarily represent a desire to assimilate into the dominant culture and a wish to shed one's ethnic culture for the "American" one? If assimilation is defined as "the decline of an ethnic distinction and . . . cultural and social differences,"[100] as well as a decline in group social distance, does Asian American interracial marriage signify this process? Furthermore, what does the recent uptick in Asian American interethnic marriage mean for rethinking the assimilation process, and what are the meanings and dynamics of interethnic marriage for those who choose it? If Asian Americans are not necessarily following a traditional path to assimilation into the dominant culture, does interethnic marriage represent a different kind of incorporative process?

In answer to these questions, this book explores the ways in which interracial marriage and family-making do not simply represent a waystation to absorption into the White mainstream culture or "assimilation" in the sense of decline or disappearance of ethnic/racial identity, but that they betoken a terrain of identity struggles. For interracially married participants, intermarriage, rather than being an endpoint in a life-long journey toward assimilation, provokes an opportunity for serious reassessments and reworking of ethnic-racial identity. A particularly interesting finding is the participants' efforts to re-evaluate their early-life desires to distance from their ethnic/racial identity once children enter the picture, evincing the need to negotiate their yearning for mainstream acceptance and the need to affirm racial-ethnic identity.

For interethnic couples, although it might seem easier to interpret their preferences as a more visible case of repudiation of whiteness and/or assimilation, the issues of ethnic/racial identity, marital choices, and cultural negotiations in the process of family-making are complex for these participants as well. That is, the development of romantic desires, intermarriage, and family-construction for interethnic couples also represents a field of complex identity negotiations. This field is complex not only because identity-making involves negotiating multiple ethnic identities and cultures to form the amalgamated construct of the "Asian American"—a nebulous and oftentimes tension-riddled process—but because the making of the pan-Asian identity that is embraced by most of the interethnically married participants is itself negotiated in a conflicted, not simply oppositional, way in relation to whiteness and to the majority culture.

Much of this is shown, as we will see, by the extent to which the interethnically married participants struggle with a tension between their perceived right to claim "American" identity and their need to maintain ethnic identities/cultures in some form, especially in the shape of "Asianness."[101] This "Asianness," though re-invented and ill-defined is an actively negotiated construct that is central to signaling and performing group distinctiveness without rejecting the mainstream. Insofar as this is the case, Asian American interethnic marriages then can perhaps be seen as a tentative effort to navigate a path of integration into American society through an ethnically and racially based identity and/or culture.

## Notes

1. See Koshy (2004) for a more detailed comparison of the actual effects of anti-miscegenation regulations between Whites-Blacks versus White-Native Americans. For example, the mixed-race offspring of White-Native Americans (and White-Mexicans) were generally given restricted access to privileges of whiteness through Anglicization and assimilation, privileges that were withheld from the offspring of Whites and Blacks.
2. Koshy 2004.
3. Fong 2008.
4. Takaki 1979.
5. Merchants, teachers, students, and diplomats were exempted.
6. The Naturalization Act of 1790 restricted naturalization to "Whites" only. Persons of African ancestry were allowed to become citizens in 1870.
7. The treatment of different Asian groups shifted according to the changing international political relationship between the United States and specific Asian countries; for instance, Japan was viewed more favorably than China in the early 1900s, whereas during WWII, the perception was reversed.
8. Also called the Philippines Commonwealth and Independence Act, the Tydings-McDuffie Act was a U.S. statute that provided for the Philippines' independence after a ten-year period. The U.S. government took this opportunity to restrict the immigration of this soon-to-be independent country by applying the Asian-exclusion policy of the 1924 Immigration Act, which lowered Filipino immigration to a quota of 50 persons per year. As "nationals," Filipinos were not eligible for U.S. citizenship either in the U.S. or in the Philippines.
9. Koshy 2004, 7.
10. The Expatriation Act of 1907 took away citizenship from White women if they married foreigners, but due to protests, this law was scrapped in favor of The Cable Act in 1922. The Cable Act struck down the principle that women's citizenship was derivative of their husbands', except in cases where women married "aliens ineligible to citizenship," which is how Asians had been classified (Koshy 2004, 7).
11. Chou 2012; Espiritu 2003.
12. Espiritu 2008, 25–26.
13. Espiritu 2008, 22.
14. Okihiro 1994.
15. Koshy 2004, 8.
16. In contrast, until 1906, Chinese women were never more than 5% of the Chinese American population, while Korean women were only 20% of the adult Korean population in the United States. Just as skewed were gender ratios among the Filipino

and Asian Indian communities; in 1930, only 3.8% of the adult Filipino population was female, and by 1914 only 0.24% of the Asian-Indian population were women (Koshy 2004, 8).

17. Koshy 2004, 8.

18. Espiritu 2008, 63–65. Between 1943 and 1946, naturalized citizenship rights were finally granted to Asian-ethnic groups.

19. Despite their enormous contribution to the expansion of Asian American communities, the severe challenges undergone by these "war brides" have been chronicled (Yu 2002). These included difficulties of cultural adjustment, domestic abuse, and stigmatization as "loose women" and as military base prostitutes, the latter frequently by the members of their own ethnic/national communities.

20. Zhou and Gatewood (2000) point out that the shortage of skilled workers in the United States is not the only explanation for middle-class immigration from Asian countries, but "the global integration of higher education and advanced training in the United States in interaction with the opportunity structure in the homelands . . ." (10): that is, the lack of professional jobs in the Asian countries.

21. Espiritu 2008.

22. Shinagawa and Pang 1996, 136.

23. Lee and Fernandez 1998, 328–35. See also Shinagawa and Pang 1996, 131; Okamoto 2007, 1394.

24. Qian and Lichter 2007.

25. Pew Research Center 2013b, 106.

26. Native American intermarriage rates are the highest.

27. Lee and Fernandez 1998. See also Shinagawa and Pang 1988.

28. Pew Research Center 2010, 17; also see Le 2013.

29. Lee and Fernandez 1998. See also Pew Research Center 2010, 19; Hwang et al. 1997. Most studies also indicate that for Asian Americans, interracial marriages tend to occur most often among well-educated and professional Americans, regardless of nativity (see Qian and Lichter 2007; Fu and Hatfield 2008, 264). An exception to this finding is the study by Hwang et al which finds that intermarriage occurs more often among individuals of lower socioeconomic status (766).

30. Shinagawa and Pang 1980; Hwang et al. 1997.

31. See Okamoto 2007; Qian and Lichter 2007, 2005; Le 2013; Pew Research Center 2010, 2013a, 2013b.

32. Lee and Fernandez 1998.

33. Pew Research Center 2013a, 65.

34. Pew Research Center 2010.

35. Lee and Fernandez 1998.

36. Pew Research Center 2013a, 67.

37. See also Qian and Lichter 2007. Surprisingly, Korean Americans have the highest intermarriage rates for native-born (for both men and women), even more than Filipino native-born, which is also high.

38. Lee and Fernandez 1998.

39. Shinagawa and Pang 1996, 132.

40. Shinagawa and Pang, 140–43. Looking just at the state of California during the same ten-year time period, Shinagawa and Pang show this trend to be even more dramatic, with the rate of interethnic marriages surpassing the rate of interracial marriages for both women and men for some groups. The only exceptions to this trend were places with a high concentration of U.S. servicemen with Asian wives.

41. Shinagawa and Pang 1988, 101–3. According to Qian et al. (2001), "Of all exogamous marriages, marriages between Japanese- and Chinese-Americans are mostly

likely. They are about three times as likely as marriages between Japanese and White Americans and about six times as likely as marriages [between] Chinese- and White-Americans" (575). Japanese Americans are also more likely to be married to Filipino Americans than to White Americans, and Korean Americans are 46% more likely to be married to Japanese Americans than to White Americans, and so on (Qian et al. 2001, 575–76). Shinagawa and Pang (1988) state when one controls for group size, Asian Americans choose spouses in the following order: 1) members of their own ethnic groups; 2) other Asian Americans; 3) other Asian/Pacific Islanders; 4) Whites; 5) Hispanics and Blacks (103).

42. Qian et al. 2001; Shinagawa and Pang 1996; Le 2013.
43. Qian et al. 2001, 578; Shinagawa and Pang 1996; Le 2013.
44. Le 2013. One article that disputes this trend is by Min and Kim 2009.
45. Lee and Fernandez 1998; Okamoto 2007; Qian 2005; Qian and Lichter 2007; Pew Research Center 2010.
46. Feliciano 2001; Fu 2001; Fu and Hatfield 2008; Rosenfeld 2001.
47. Qian 2005, 37.
48. Rosenfeld 2001; Feliciano 2001; Qian and Lichter 2001.
49. Rosenfeld 2001, 169.
50. Fu 2001. Qian and Lichter (2001) also confirm that later-generation Latinos are much more likely than foreign-born Latinos to marry Whites, but this likelihood is stronger than for later-generation Asians, suggesting that White-Latino barriers to intermarriage are weaker than for White-Asian barriers. See also Okamoto 2007.
51. For example, U.S.-born Chinese and Japanese are 10 to 12 times more likely to marry each other than the national norm of exogamy would suggest (Fu and Hatfield 2008, 261). Studies also show that while U.S.-born Asians are highly likely to marry Asian co-ethnics, they have the least likelihood of marrying *foreign-born* Asians; that is, they are more likely to marry Whites than they are to marry foreign-born co-ethnics (see Feliciano 2001). By the same token, when immigrants marry U.S. natives, they are more likely to marry Whites than natives of their own ethnic group (Qian et al. 2001). At least one study shows, however, that recently, the Asian American immigrant and native co-ethnic combination may be increasing (Qian and Lichter 2007).
52. Kalmijn and Tubergen 2010; Fong and Yung 2000.
53. See Alba and Nee 2003, 99–100; Okamoto 2007.
54. Blau and his associates were one of the first to carry out a sustained investigation of structural factors in intermarriage (see Blau 1977; Blau and Schwartz 1984; Blau et al. 1982).
55. Hwang et al. 1997.
56. Spickard 1989, 19.
57. Kalmijin and Van Tubergen 2010, 476. Also see Hwang et al. 1997; Kitano et al. 1984.
58. See Childs 2005; Dalmage 2000; Yancey and Lewis 2009.
59. Alba and Nee 2003, 269–70; Qian 2002; Vasquez 2011b.
60. Collins 1990.
61. Koshy 2004.
62. Koshy 2004, 12.
63. Espiritu 2008, 110.
64. Tajima 1989.
65. Wiegman 1991, 320.
66. Pyke and Johnson 2003. Connell and Messerschmidt (2005) use the term "emphasized femininity" rather than "hegemonic femininity" to call attention to the subordinate

place of dominant femininity in a patriarchal gender order, that is, hegemonic femininity's "compliance to patriarchy."

67. Also see Espiritu 2008, 105.
68. These stereotypes also explain the recent explosion in demand for X-rated films or pornography featuring Asian-ethnic females, especially in bondage, as well as for sex workers and mail-order brides.
69. Espiritu 2008, 102. Also see Frankenberg 1993, 75–76.
70. Eng 2001, 210; Yu 2001; Zia 2000.
71. Chan 2001; Chin and Chan 1972; Lee 1999; Wong 1978; Wu 2003.
72. Wu 2003.
73. Espiritu 2008, 102.
74. Kim 1990, 70.
75. Sung 1990.
76. Fong and Yung 2000; Chow 2000.
77. Nemoto 2009.
78. Tuan 1999, 120.
79. Kibria 1997, 524. Qualitative works by such authors as Chou and Feagin (2015), Chang (2016), Dhingra (2007), and Song (2003) deal partially with issues of Asian American interethnic and interracial marriage.
80. Swarns 2012; Yip 1997.
81. Yang 2012; Song 2003, Chap. 6.
82. Also see Chang 2016; Song 2003, 2017.
83. Alba and Nee 2003; Lee and Bean 2004; Tinker 1982.
84. Chong 2013; Hwang et al. 1997; Olzak 1992; Song 2009.
85. Park and Burgess's (1924, 735) initial concept of assimilation, however, did not denote an inevitable homogenization into a mainstream Anglo culture nor the disappearance of all ethnic features; it was more suggestive of a coalescence of groups into a common culture. Nonetheless, the term "assimilation" came to be related most closely to Park's "race relations cycle" idea, which posited that assimilation was the endpoint of an irreversible cycle that began with contact, competition, accommodation, and eventual assimilation. See also Park 1950.
86. Warner and Srole 1945. See also Gans 1973.
87. Alba and Nee 2003.
88. By identifying various dimensions of immigrant adaptation, Gordon's model allowed the operationalization of a number of indicators with which to measure the degree of group and individual incorporation into the mainstream society.
89. Gordon 1964, 71–81.
90. Gordon 1964, 111.
91. Gordon also made no normative claims about the superiority or desirability of Anglo-conformity-type assimilation and even criticized "forced" Americanization efforts of the mid-twentieth century while arguing for the benefits of maintaining a degree of ethnic/cultural plurality.
92. Alba and Nee 2003, 2–5.
93. Alba and Nee (2003) explain that ethnic pluralism may be aided further by the new historical context of globalization and transnationalism, with advances in communication technology, market integration, and air transportation that make it feasible for immigrants and even their children to maintain ties to the countries of origin (6–7). See also Kitano et al. (1984).
94. Alba and Nee 2003, 7. These authors refer to experiences of contemporary immigrant groups of color as "incorporation associated with constricted opportunities."
95. Portes and Zhou 1993.
96. Gibson (1988) uses the term "accommodation without assimilation." See also Dhingra 2007; Zhou and Bankston 1998; Rumbaut 1997; Hurh and Kim 1984.

97. For example, Vallejo 2012; Vasquez 2010, 2011b.
98. Chaudhary 2015; Chong 2017; Flores-Gonzales 1999; Emeka and Vallejo 2011; Golash-Boza 2006; Vasquez 2011b.
99. Gans 1992, 44; Vasquez 2011a, 2011b.
100. Alba and Nee 2003, 11.
101. Also see Lowe 1996; Espiritu 1992.

# 3

# MARRYING-OUT

## Development of Racially Transgressive Desires

Monica is an attractive 40-year-old second generation Korean American woman with two young children married to a White American. We sit in the kitchen of her upscale Chicago home while she cuts up fresh fruit and vegetables for her children when they return home from school. Our conversation takes place during the morning and the early afternoon, the only time she can carve out before her children come back. Monica is a stay-at-home mom at the moment. Rather reserved at first, she quickly warms up to my questions and becomes progressively more reflective during the interview, especially about her childhood struggles with her ethnic and racial identity.[1]

Monica began with the story of her highly educated parents, who immigrated to the U.S. in the 1960s to pursue graduate degrees in the United States and the American dream. Her parents were a part of the 1950s and 1960s intellectual migration from Asia. During her growing-up years, Monica remembers that her parents primarily spoke English to her and her siblings and hewed to a rather assimilationist stance in the hopes that the children would be accepted by U.S. society. Although her parents retreated from this position a bit when the kids were in their pre-teens by sending the kids to Korean language schools, Monica reports that by then it was "too late."

Monica grew up in a predominantly White suburban Chicago neighborhood and describes her youth as characterized by a considerable amount of angst and confusion about her racial identity and social belonging.[2] Although considered pretty by her classmates and generally well liked, Monica emphasized that a painful sense of being split between two cultures and selves, American and Korean, dominated her youth. In fact, a powerful memory from that period of childhood is Monica's sense of the keen disjunction between how she felt American "inside" versus her external appearance—looking Asian (how others see her), which spawned an ongoing, inner struggle with a sense of internal "splitting." Monica describes her first racial epiphany this way:

> I went to a high school that was predominantly White. I think that I was one of three Asians. There were only two African Americans in the whole school . . . and there was a day when I was in elementary school and I remember looking in the mirror and seeing my face being Asian, and I burst into tears because I felt that I was exactly like everyone else, but I saw that I was different on the outside.

Although Monica did have some opportunities to interact with other Asian American kids through her parents' personal networks, she never developed enduring friendships with them. She came into contact with a significant number of Asian Americans for the first time in the large state university she attended but she said she was never one of "those" kids from the suburbs who became part of the university's Asian American community. In fact, she states that she found the Asian American students' insularity alienating and rejected that community; she instead joined a mostly White sorority. Despite the pain of realizing that she would always be set apart from her White peers by her non-White looks and a nagging sense of inferiority, she felt that she had even less in common with most Asian Americans she encountered. Instead of bonding with other Asian Americans, Monica developed racially transgressive desires regarding friendships and romance, particularly for White-ethnics.

How did the interracially married Asian-ethnics in my study become racial boundary-crossers in marriage, particularly in the face of general pressures toward endogamy in the larger U.S. society and in most ethnic communities? This chapter will explore these questions by examining the participants' narratives about the evolution of their romantic desires and identities, and situating them within the framework of contextual factors that shape these seemingly individual preferences for and choices of interracial partnering.

Although an individual's foundational desires in terms of romance or marriage, as noted in previous chapters, are molded by a combination of structural as well as cultural factors, I have argued that structural factors are inadequate to fully explain romantic or marital desires and choices of individuals. Structural factors provide what Matthijs Kalmijn refers to as the "supply contact," configured within local demographic settings, such as the size and racial/ethnic compositions of the community and neighborhoods.[3] Within this demographic framework, people develop the proclivity toward interacting with certain types of people and not others, constituting preferences. Some of this can be conditioned by the demographic dynamics themselves, but without consideration of cultural-ideological universes in which people operate, people's romantic preferences and choices cannot be fully understood.

In prior chapters, I highlighted the significance of race as one of these global-/ local-level cultural-ideological paradigms central to explaining interracial marriage choices. In examining the cross-racial romantic and marital choices of the Asian-ethnic participants in this chapter, I call attention in particular to the power of the globally circulating hegemony of whiteness that affects how the participants not only contend with the fractured development of their identities and self-image but also shape their romantic preferences for the White "other." Although my participants often talked about their romantic or marital choices in personal terms, the impact of whiteness as the marker of normativity/superiority on the formation of people's desires and subjectivities and the powerful pull of assimilation into White middle-class culture emerge clearly in their narratives. Despite the ascendant discourses of celebratory multiculturalism and racial diversity that appear to neutralize the hegemonic power of whiteness, the discursive universe in which whiteness stands as the standard bearer of beauty/normalcy and the core to the definition of being American is still the cultural framework within which racial minorities are embedded.

Notably, about 90% of the interracially married respondents in my study, like Monica, grew up in predominantly White neighborhoods. Given the demographic configurations in these cases during the growing-up years, that is, being part of a small-sized minority group in largely White areas, a demographically oriented explanation, as discussed in the last chapter, would predict a high likelihood of outmarriages for these Asian-ethnics. Such structural explanations however reveal little about the participants' experiences in subjective terms, how romantic desires and preferences develop internally, the meanings people attach to their romantic choices, or even how individuals might overcome endogamous pressures from the family or the ethnic community.[4] My findings suggest that the participants' development of racially transgressive romantic preferences/desires were not simply a "numbers game"— dating or marrying Whites because they became what was most familiar to the participants—but that these romantic preferences/desires were powerfully conditioned by the ideological power of racial hierarchy and of White superiority pervasive in the community around them, which produced a lasting desire for whiteness. This desire for whiteness and whitening, even if accompanied by painful identity struggles, was powerful enough that it was able to withstand the ethnically endogamous pressures of college life, a key turning point in terms of "ethnic discovery" for many middle-class racial minority youths in this chapter, and motivated the participants to continue conscious ethnic-distancing.

## Identity Struggles and Assimilative Yearnings

Like Monica, all Asian Americans in my study, interracially and interethnically married alike, talked about undergoing intense struggles with their racial and ethnic identity while growing up, particularly related to their desire to be accepted as "normal Americans." Due to the fact that they had to contend with being one of the few persons of color in predominantly White environments, all of the participants in the interracial group seem to have been subject to a particularly overwhelming sense of "othering" and subsequent experiences of internal "splitting" that left searing psychological scars.[5]

As kids, these participants wrestled with unabating feelings of self consciousness as persons of Asian-descent, especially in the face of frequent racist treatment, and all made concerted, if not desperate, efforts to fit in and be accepted in their schools and neighborhoods. As it was for Monica, the first epiphanic moments of racial awareness for many participants often occurred during the early elementary school years that would mark the beginning of such identity and cultural struggles. Vicky, a 39-year-old Chinese American, describes her experiences in terms that reverberate with Monica's words:

> We grew up in an all White neighborhood . . . and that impacted me. In the beginning, it was very negative because I was the only Chinese girl. . . . At the time, the idea of diversity wasn't as super promoted as it is now . . . and I grew up being actually embarrassed about being Chinese and, you know, eating Chinese food . . . like for instance I always remember this in kindergarten—kids do not like vegetables and I didn't understand why because I loved it . . . I would bring foods that my mom made from home, and people would make fun of my food. So I eventually told my mom I didn't want that kind of food at school. I wanted sandwiches and Wonder Bread. Looking back on it, I laugh about it, but at that time, it was about being embarrassed. I got beat up a lot. I don't think I had identity issues when I was little. I didn't realize it until I grew up more. It was so bad that when I would look in the mirror, I was shocked to see that I wasn't White. . . . because to me American meant White. . . . It bothered me when someone said "The Chinese girl." It still bothers me, you know, I don't know why. I'm not just the Chinese girl.

This description of reflecting on one's identity and "difference" while literally gazing in the mirror is a recurring trope in the narratives of Asian Americans.[6] Furthermore, both Monica and Vicky's epiphanic encounters with the mirror as the pivotal moment of racial self-recognition at similar ages are striking and appear to illustrate the ambivalent identificatory process of internal division as central to human identity formation discussed in the introduction. In this case, a bit of twist in the psychoanalytical model is that the original imaginary identification with "whiteness" is *shattered* in the encounter with the mirror as the two women consciously become aware for the first time of the Asian part of themselves that they had split off in that original identification process but now must face.

Like Monica and Vicky, Matt, a 41-year-old Chinese American, struggled with a disjunction between being perceived as racially Asian but internally feeling "White": "I felt that I was pretty much a White kid . . . I always wanted to be White and assimilate with everybody else." Despite this, Matt recalls routinely being "discriminated against" and rejected because, although he did not particularly identify as being Asian, he knew that the majority of students in the school did not perceive him as "one of them." Andrew, a 34-year-old Vietnamese American who grew up in a White environment, talked about his attempts at ethnic and racial self denial in his effort to blend in: "In general, I don't honestly think that I identified myself as Asian in any way until I got to college. You know, through high school, it was like yeah, I just happened to have yellow skin, you know. For the Rotary Honors Club picture that we had in our senior year, it was like me and seven White guys, and I looked at the picture and went, man, I look really yellow." Though written so many decades earlier, the narratives of these participants echo the searing words of Franz Fanon in *Black Skin, White Masks*, which describe a similar epiphanic realization of Fanon's own "raced body" through "mirroring" by way of the eyes of a White French child who, upon seeing Fanon, yells, "Mom, see the Negro! I'm frightened!" Fanon describes his instantaneous reaction: "My body was given back to me sprawled out, distorted, recolored, clad in mourning that White winter day."[7]

This inability to escape physical difference complicates the acculturation process of most of the participants who, throughout their youth, could not simply "assimilate" unproblematically by leaving cultural ethnic markers behind and physically blend in with the White majority; they had to come to terms with their ethnic/racial identity by negotiating how much or which aspects of whiteness and mainstream culture to identify with and how much of their ethnic culture to retain or discard. This was the case for Pauline, a 42-year-old Indian American who grew up in a highly assimilation-oriented family: "You know, I think I was . . . confused. I'm like, well, should I want to be more Indian or should I want to just be who I am? And it wasn't like I'm making a conscious effort to be . . . White. I think I was just trying to be just whoever I was." Unlike some of the others mentioned, Pauline does not objectify or problematize whiteness as something for which she was striving but nonetheless grapples with how much to incorporate and identify with her "Indianness." Pauline talked about being confused when her White friends treated her like an "honorary White," with ostensible "compliments" such as "We don't see you as Indian; we see you as White," while subtly reminding her that she is not White. One example of this was her friends' assumption that Pauline should date Indian men only: "So when it comes to important things . . . a lot of the White women I was friendly with—they never wanted to set me up with their brothers because they were like well . . . don't you think it would be better if you married an Indian guy? . . . Don't your parents want you to marry an Indian guy?"

With the participants, reports of experiences with racial microaggressions, both overt and covert, were uniform, affirming most historical and current findings regarding Asian American experiences.[8] Each of my participants talked about being targets of racist slurs and bullying when growing up, such as being called "chink" and told to go back to "where you came from" and other familiar racial taunts; "It was the stereotypical thing, a little of the 'ching-ching' and 'twing-twing' thing," said one participant. Marvin, a 41-year-old Korean American, offered this recollection:

> I grew up subconsciously, you know, as a minority. So I think I grew up insecure. I went through the name calling . . . by all kinds of people, by other minorities too. Yeah. So I got into lot[s] of fights when I was younger, third and fourth grade. And then I felt like I fit in and grew up as a normal American child until junior high. . . . I would feel insecure all over again because I felt like I had to do so much to find a friend. Playing sports helped, but still the teasing went on.

Another male participant, a Korean American named George who recalls being routinely beat up, feeling completely isolated in his predominantly White town and being called "every type of racial slur you can imagine," disclosed how things were made worse for him when the movie *Sixteen Candles* came out, and with it, the appearance of the now-infamous Asian male character Long Duk Dong, the clumsy and nerdy foreign exchange student played by the Japanese American actor Gedde Watanabe.

Some endured racist behaviors as a family unit; one participant related that in his predominantly White neighborhood, his house was vandalized after they moved in, and neighborhood kids, for months, would go by the house and call the whole family names like "chink." Another recalled when some kids from the neighborhood came to the house and broke the Christmas lights on purpose: "When my mother went to one of the kids' house[s] to complain, the mother of the kid said, 'Why don't you go back to your country?'" These behaviors served as reminders of the chilling and disheartening reality that racism and nativistic sentiments were still alive and well, behaviors designed to constantly remind Asian Americans of their "foreignness" and social exclusion.

I found that there were two major types of reactions to these racist behaviors; one was to confront and combat them, and the other, to minimize or deny their occurrence and impact. George stated that by the time he was in junior high school, he got so tired of being beaten up and being called names that he took up karate to fight back and talked about how important this became to him:

> Chink, gook, I got into fights. . . . I got beat up by older kids, like junior and senior years [of high school] because I actually fought back and they

insulted me in the locker room. It affects you and I definitely do have a chip on my shoulder. And even to this day, I feel like if I am getting animosity from somebody, right off the bat I immediately think do they not like me, or do they have something against Asians, and it could very well be that he is not a nice person and most of the times I find that is the case . . . but I very much internalize it as something against Asians. . . . One of the role models that I found comfort in was of course Bruce Lee like a lot of Asian males at that time. Because there was no sign of Asian masculinity or power and there was very much the attitude that like the Long Duk Dong character, Asians are weak and easily pushed around. But in him [Bruce Lee] there was this dynamic of somebody who could fight back that Caucasians would fear, not only by his physical presence but his attitude, this kind of fight to the death attitude, so later on I felt like I had to take martial arts also because that was a way of me developing my character.

Conversely, about half of the participants engaged in minimization of racism; when asked about instances of racism or discrimination when growing up, these participants would initially have trouble remembering, although most would end up recalling at least a few such instances. A small number of these participants admitted that while they recognized that racism against Asians existed, they did not experience it too much because they played sports or because they were not viewed as geeky as other Asians. This recalls observations made by some studies that many Asian-ethnics, buying into society's view of them as the "model minority" who might eventually come to be accepted, tend to write off or downplay repeated occurrence of discriminatory and racist treatment as acts of ignorant persons.[9] In doing so, these individuals also implicitly distance themselves from other minorities, especially Blacks, who are "looked down on by Whites for admitting their experiences with racism."[10]

Either way, the painful growing-up experiences of the participants in my study reflect the struggle with "double consciousness" discussed earlier, endured by subjugated minorities who have to contend with the two "warring selves" within—one denoting an "American" self idealized by society and the other, the disparaged self stemming from pejorative stereotypes heaped upon minorities of color that can lead to internalized oppression. I have found that one commonplace consequence of self-denigration is a strategy of disassociation from the denigrated part of one's identity, the "Asian" self, which includes an active effort at distancing from "Asian" stereotypes as well as from fellow Asian-ethnics.

## Practicing Ethnic-Distancing

During pre-college years, ethnic- and racial-distancing and dis-identification with Asian stereotypes and other Asian-ethnics was one of the main strategies by which some of the participants in this chapter weathered the challenges of racism, prejudice, and social "othering." The story of Sarah, a 41-year-old mother of two, is representative. Sarah relates that when she was growing up, none of the second generation Chinese kids she knew "wanted to be Chinese." Sarah professed that she grew up relatively unscathed as a Chinese American because she engaged in a variety of ethnic stereotype-distancing tactics. She made concerted efforts to become outgoing and participated in activities that challenged stereotypes of Asians, such as taking leadership positions in student organizations. Her tactics also included Westernizing her looks, such as by curling her hair and wearing makeup, and later, joining a mostly White sorority in college, though she did do some "stereotypical" things like play the violin and piano. Sarah said her goal was to ensure that she was "positioned where no one would ever tease me . . . I didn't want to be made fun of because I was Chinese, and I wasn't very much, but I would somehow get myself to a point where no one could make fun of me." Sarah also said that it helped that she did not possess the "typical Asian look" in the first place by, for instance, having large eyes. To drive home this point, Sarah contrasted herself with her sister who "had it harder" because she was "quiet" and more "overtly Chinese" in terms of her behavior; her sister, for example, played the violin seriously and hung out more with Chinese peers.[11]

This process of disassociating from other Asian-ethnics, coupled with the strategy of diverting attention from one's "Asianness," has been observed by a number of scholars.[12] Dislike of other Asian-ethnics, especially by framing recent arrivals/immigrants as "FOBS (fresh off the boat)," is a form of self-hatred or internalized racism that Osajima (1993) refers to as a "hidden injury" of race: "The desire to distance themselves from [a] stereotypical Asian image constitutes another hidden injury, a sense of discomfort around and disgust toward other Asians."[13] Karen Pyke and Tran Dang refer to this process as "intraethnic othering," especially where Asian Americans pit themselves against one another on the scale of assimilation by constructing sub-ethnic categories of the immigrant FOBs, blamed for perpetuating negative Asian stereotypes, juxtaposed against the "White Washed (or alternatively, "Banana" or "Twinkie")."[14]

Matt, discussed earlier, also dealt with his sense of non-belonging and marginalization by trying to distance himself from the male stereotype of the Asian male as much as possible. Even though he was rather quiet and shy as a youngster, Matt tried to overcome these personality traits as he grew up, trying to be viewed as a "normal" mainstream American kid by becoming as sociable as possible. Even though Matt was aware that he could never become one of the popular "jocks," he succeeded in getting out of the bottom of the high school pecking order by becoming a likable "band geek" type and distancing himself even further from the Asian American stereotypes in college. Describing himself in school, he said:

> I was a shy type, but I really didn't become that awkward, completely shy or anything like that. I wasn't a weird kid; I was pretty mainstream and I had a lot of friends and different groups I enjoyed in school. I was in the band, but I was a popular member of the band because I was pretty good at it and was involved in a lot of activities. . . . Then I came out of my shell in junior high school and became a very sociable person. . . . My friends were outgoing, but we were not crazy outgoing sporty types. We were just a couple of steps down from that. We were, you know, band geeks basically, but good band geeks, and moved outside of the circle of the band quite a lot. In college, I tried even harder to break out of the geek mold, to be even more outgoing than I was already. And I joined a fraternity, so I had a lot of role models.

Discussing the subtle and cumulative effects of racial marginalization, Mia Tuan reflects on ethnic-distancing strategy this way:

> With racial marginalization, the effect is incremental, slowly chipping away at one's self concept. Rationalizations are offered and incidents shrugged off in order to protect one's self-esteem. But all the while a running tab is kept on these "acts of ignorance," and increasingly the person spends more mental and emotional energy to short-circuit future incidents. Deflecting attention away from one's Asianness, avoiding associating with, and otherwise looking down upon other Asian Americans, all reflect a steep price paid to overcome alienation.[15]

It is worthwhile emphasizing that many of the individuals in the interracially married group did not grow up isolated from other Asian Americans and associated with some Asian-ethnics, even if they had resided in primarily White neighborhoods. In fact, at least half of those in this group interacted with and cultivated friendships with fellow Asian-ethnics through ethnically oriented networks the parents provided, such as the parents' social networks, ethnic churches, or language schools. For the Chinese Americans, in particular, Chinese language schools emerged as a central feature of this ethnic subculture—although these participants uniformly reported disliking these schools[16]—and for Korean Americans, the ethnic churches did. Carla, a 43-year-old mother of two, remarked:

> My parents had tons of Chinese friends. Their friends, like my parents, all moved here [to the U.S.] to go to graduate school, so their community of friends was primarily well-educated Chinese couples. So their children

were our friends, mine and my brother's and sister's, and we all went to Chinese school together though we didn't necessarily to go the same high school. In my regular schools, there were very few Chinese families. . . . But there were always Chinese people calling on the phone asking for our parents. They'd come over and play *mahjong* at night and you go to sleep with the sound of the *mahjong* tiles on the table. . . . And we got most of the Chinese culture from the Chinese schools. I did Chinese dancing for many years. We'd organize Chinese volleyball teams. We even had a student government at our Chinese school. . . . So my social life definitely had a lot of Chinese kids that were not in my regular high school. . . . I definitely had a separate and different social life with almost all Chinese kids.

As intimated by Carla's narrative, association with fellow Asian-ethnics, for my participants, often took the form of a double life in terms of social life and friendship groups, one American and one ethnic, where the two sub-groups intersected little. In fact, many of my participants explicitly discussed feeling like they led a kind of double social existence.

Previous studies of Asian Americans have identified a similar phenomenon among Asian-ethnics who grew up in White communities. While my participants saw their association with fellow Asian-ethnics as driven mainly by parental wishes, other scholars have observed that young Asian Americans seeking out other Asian Americans through ethnic organizations also serves as a strategy to fight a sense of marginalization, although both the participants and the Asian-ethnics they sought out were typically well-assimilated.[17] Either way, for those growing up in highly assimilationist and White-dominated environments, the impact on co-ethnic bonding and identification generated by sporadic ethnic interactions can be tenuous and fragile. In her research on U.S.-born Filipinos, for example, Yen Le Espiritu found that while many second generation Filipino Americans she studied tried to actively maintain social ties with other Filipinos through interactions with kin and ethnic institutions, sustaining such ties was an uphill battle in White-majority locations, as often these interactions amounted to "ethnic events" that were "periodic, brief, and disconnected from their otherwise White-dominated environment."[18] Thus, it is not surprising that for most interracially married Asian Americans in my study, this early exposure to fellow co-ethnics or Asian-ethnics did not translate into significant development of co-ethnic or panethnic consciousness and bonding, nor romantic interest in fellow Asian-ethnics, until, in a few cases, after college, which will be later discussed.

## Early Romantic Longings

The majority of my participants, both men and women, stated that dating during secondary school was not encouraged by their parents.[19] Most did, however, reflect on their budding romantic feelings during their teenage years, and all of my interracially married participants professed preferences and romantic orientations toward non-Asians from a young age, though some experimented with Asian-ethnic partners. One 39-year-old Chinese American named Kira said that very early in her life, her parents attempted to pressure their children to marry within their ethnic group. But these kinds of admonitions did not make much of a difference to her as she never developed much attraction for Asian American boys:

> My parents used to say that if I married somebody who wasn't Chinese that they would disown me. . . . They never really explained why. I think it was more that they just thought it would be easier because the backgrounds would be similar. They never said this, but I'm guessing that they probably thought it would be easier for them to get along with him as well. At the time, I think they were thinking it's more of a family thing . . . but all along junior high school until I met my one and only Chinese boyfriend, I had crushes on the nice, White, cute boy with blonde hair or lighter hair and blue eyes.

Besides this one Chinese boyfriend, who was so Americanized (second generation, spoke no Chinese) that he "didn't really count as being Chinese" to her parents, Kira did not date an Asian American again. In fact, she remembers being resentful in school because other kids, as with Pauline earlier, would automatically assume that she should be with an Asian-ethnic boy: "I remember there was one kid, one boy who was Chinese. Of course, all the other kids, they used to—I don't think they were trying to be mean or anything—but they would tease us and they used to leave Valentine's card[s] on my desk signed from him." She added: "But I was just not attracted to them [Asian boys] in general. I guess if I go all the way back, they were all just my parents' friends' kids and I just thought, I do have to go play with them. But I never really found anybody attractive. It could have been because they were Asian. It could have been because they were my parents' friends."

Monica, who said she never really wanted to be with a Korean guy, though she did date a few, put it this way:

> I don't really know why. I don't know if it's because I never met a Korean guy that I really like. . . . I was so Americanized. I was born here, I could speak perfect English, and a lot of my peers who were my age or older, they weren't in that position. They were still very, very 'Korean.' You know, so I found a little bit of disconnect . . . they were too Korean, for lack of a better phrase . . . I don't know. I feel like I was in that kind of first wave of immigrant children coming up and living in America and having really two cultures in the household, one that was really truly their parents' and one

that was mine, which was in the manner of meshing of the two. But if I had to identify myself at the core, in terms of the cultural description, it would probably be more American but with the indefinable Korean.

Monica's interpretation of her lack of attraction to Asian-ethnics, or fellow Koreans, seems to be that she was too "Americanized" and that she was unable to find her match in any Asian-ethnic boys she met, rather than finding Asian boys unattractive per se. She does not admit active efforts at dissociation with, nor a dislike of, Asian-ethnics, just a "disconnect." In either case, what we observe is her implicit conflation of "American" with complete assimilation into mainstream Anglo American culture; it is difficult to tell whether she could have ended up with an Asian-ethnic even if she had encountered one whom she felt was as assimilated or as "American" as she was.

A number of women more explicitly stated their lack of attraction to Asians in terms of the undesirability of the "nerdy" qualities of the Asian male. Sarah, who only dated one Asian American in her life, confessed:

> You know, Asian guys, they really don't work for me. Well, I think there are variations or whatever, and I don't want to stereotype . . . but I like more of an athletic kind of guy, more of an outgoing personality. I sort of found Asian guys not to be that way. . . . Our interests were also different too. And later in college, when I was in the sorority, there weren't many Asian guys in fraternities. So there was not a lot of opportunity to hang out with them.

Another simply said about Asian boys: "There was no attraction no matter how much I tried. There are a lot of good-looking Asian guys that have wonderful personalities, but I just don't feel attracted to any of them. I don't know why."

There were a few female participants who were "turned off" by men of Asian descent because of their dislike of "Asian patriarchy," which they believed inflicted terrible injuries on women. I found this attitude to be most pronounced among women of Korean descent, although studies of women of other ethnic/racial groups have uncovered similar patterns.[20] Many spoke from personal experiences in their natal families. Joy, a 33-year-old mother of one, for instance, came from a single-parent family after her mother divorced Joy's abusive father. She recalled an incident in college where a foreign student from Korea, who had been a platonic friend, suddenly proposed to her, taking Joy completely by surprise. Since Joy had never dated an Asian man and never thought of dating one, Joy rejected the proposal, but it also helped her clarify her feelings about marriage in general: "That was when I realized that maybe the reason why I'm not really seeking out other Asian men is that the interest just isn't there, and it might have been because I associated them with my dad. . . . I just figured every Asian guy is going to be like my father."

Janet, another Korean American woman who caused a "scandal" in her family by marrying a man who was Black mixed-race, explained that her early outright rejection of her Korean heritage came largely from the patriarchal ways of the men in her family, in addition to being ashamed of being Korean. She remarked: "I was embarrassed, I didn't want to be Korean, because I have to look different from everybody else. Also, I think it was because I saw early on the way my dad treated my mom, and the way the guys, the men, are in this culture. . . . I didn't like that from the start. So I think all that combined, yes, I was like, 'Okay, I don't want to be Korean. I'm going to dissociate myself and stay as far away from them as I can.'" Thus, while many female participants' narratives did show an awareness of the emasculating consequences of larger society's negative Asian male stereotypes, individuals such as Joy and Janet focused on the reality of Asian male privilege within Asian American community and families.[21] Similar aversion to the patriarchy of one's ethnic culture as a reason for outmarrying among women is found in recent literature on Latinos as well, for example, of Latinas citing Latino patriarchy and *machismo* culture as a reason for avoiding marrying men of Latino heritage.[22]

I found similar romantic patterns among interracially married Asian American men as well; that is, their non-Asian romantic orientation as youths appeared to be no less strong than the women's, despite the greater barriers to cross-racial dating they faced. None of the interracially married men I interviewed reported having much curiosity about Asian females or finding them attractive growing up but said they were attracted to non-Asian women, especially White women. Matt reported:

> In high school, the times I felt most different was when it came to girls. I really was attracted to White girls mainly because I guess that is mostly what there was around. And a couple of crushes I had—I couldn't help the feeling that if I weren't Asian, that I would have a better chance with these girls, and so I was rejected a lot. Again, I wasn't a total geek. I mean, I had lots of dates. I can go to things with girls, but it was never with the ones I wanted to go with.

Observing that there was hardly any interracial dating when he was growing up in the 1970s and 1980s, Lance, a 41-year-old Chinese American, said that he definitely did not feel that the White women he grew up with were interested in dating Asian men, even though he desired cross-racial dating. Being Asian, he felt, was an obstacle to dating: "In regards to dating when I was growing up, it just wasn't fun." Another participant, a Vietnamese American, echoed how the White girls he liked were always "out of his league," so he never had dates until later.[23] In the meantime, he did not feel any attraction to Asian girls.

## Discerning Racial Inequities in the Romance Market

Given the perceived barriers men faced regarding cross-racial romance, it was not surprising that all participants, male and female, articulated that women probably had an easier time getting dates than men of Asian-descent. Still, it is important to note that many women did not believe that attention from White men necessarily meant that they were on equal footing with White women in terms of desirability. Many of the women were surprisingly frank about the feelings of racial inferiority they felt growing up due to the prevalence of White beauty standards, wondering if they were being rejected by men because of their race or non-White status. Pauline, the Indian American who struggled with considerable identity conflict growing up, reflected on these nagging feelings of low self-worth:

> I struggled a lot with my identity growing up, especially in high school, and a lot of it was because of boys. . . . The [White boys] sometimes just didn't want to date me. I would like a boy and they would think yeah, I like her at school, or whatever, but they would never want to bring me home. . . . I knew it was because I wasn't White . . . mostly the boys liked me as being a great friend. In other words, I felt like I knew my limitations.[24]

Pauline mentioned, however, that by the time she was at the end of high school, the social climate had changed to an extent where there was a "growing curiosity among some of the boys to date me just to see what kissing an Indian girl would be like" and "it was more cool to be ethnic."[25] But still, she felt that even though there was a lot of flirting and "fascination" with Indian girls, she was not taken seriously as a girlfriend nor as a potential mate. In either case, Pauline's narrative reveals the objectification and dehumanization she experienced as an Asian-ethnic woman, first based on the "nerdy" and "foreign" stereotype, and later on the "exotic" stereotype resuscitated in a more palatable package within the current multicultural climate.

Even for those who had a great deal of success with cross-racial dating, the theme of not being taken seriously as potential marriage material surfaced; Carla, discussed earlier, explicitly addressed her long-held suspicion about some of her past White boyfriends may not have been enthusiastic about marrying her because they wanted to have "blond-haired and blue-eyed" children. Curiously distinguishing between "race" and "genetics," she tried to explain this away with a view that their preference had to do with "genetics" and not race, that is, not necessarily thinking that the Chinese were "racially inferior" but that they didn't have the right "genes" in terms of appearance. In other words, Chinese were not seen as racially inferior in terms of intelligence but that she was not going to be able to provide White children who had the desired physical attributes. She recalls:

> I was dating this guy who . . . was a football player in college, and that whole thing was very important to him. He never came out and said this, but I definitely got the feeling that he needed to have children who were going to be able to play football or be physically big. . . . And I definitely have had friends, guy [White male] friends who always said that they are looking to improve their gene pool. They wanted to marry women who were tall so they can put more height into their family. . . . But I never thought it was because they thought Asians are racially inferior or anything . . . they [previous White boyfriends and friends] always thought that Asians were incredibly smart as a race . . . but if there was any hesitancy about getting married, it was because of looks and genetics.

For the women, as I will discuss at length in Chapter 7, accompanying these insecure feelings, not altogether surprisingly, was the universal suspicion of the "Asian fetish," that the non-Asian men who *would* date them did so because the women became objects of heightened desire as "exotic" beings. In fact, sardonic discussions of "Asian fetish" or "yellow fever" emerged spontaneously in almost every conversation I had with the women. Most women were hyper-aware of this phenomenon and keenly alert to the possibility that non-Asian men may be attracted to them because they were Asian. Kira, for example, described some guys in her college dorm room who only pursued Asian women: "So it was at my university I had my first chance running into guys with Asian fetishes. It makes me cringe. . . . You know, do you even care about who I am or is it just how I look? . . . It just makes you feel so objectified." Vicky said that when she started dating, she was already very sensitive to the "yellow fever thing." Whenever a White man showed interest in her, she made a habit of testing them to see if they had preferences for Asian women, such as trying to find out if they had Asian girlfriends before, or outright asking them if they had a "yellow fever": "I was always trying to find out their motivations, why they wanted to date me."[26]

Although interracially married women may attain the objects of their desire (White husbands), these women, in their concerns and fears of the "Asian fetish," displayed at the same time an awareness of a potentially submerged and lurking dynamic of racial inequality in their relationship with their White husbands. More specifically, many could not quite shake the suspicion that, as possible objects of Orientalized fantasies, they did not occupy a fully human and equal status in the relationship.

## Repudiation of Ethnic Self-Discovery and Same-Race Partnering

A number of recent works on second generation Asian-ethnics address the phenomenon of ethnic "rediscovery" in college; these works highlight the importance of college as a life phase when ethnic identity-transformations can occur.[27] This is because college is when extensive ethnic interaction is experienced by many Asian-ethnic youths, especially in the context of socioeconomic homogamy. In a dedicated discussion of ethnic identity development of Asian-ethnics during college years, Nazli Kibria, in her book, *Becoming Asian American,* describes three different pathways of ethnic identity development in college; the first path is a turn toward ethnic rediscovery whereby being in college and joining pan-Asian organizations becomes a watershed event for embracing Asian American identity. Kibria describes two alternative processes however: one is developing Asian-ethnic friendships and identity without developing a pan-Asian identity, and two, "rejecting pan-Asianism" altogether which includes individuals who described themselves as "not ethnically oriented" in college, not developing connections with Asian-ethnics, and having mostly White friends.[28]

I have found that interracially married individuals in my study, all of whom came into contact with a critical mass of Asian Americans in college, by and large belonged to the last group described by Kibria, those who did not experience meaningful ethnic self-discovery in college.[29] About 10% of this group belonged to the category that maintained some Asian-ethnic friendships but without developing a strong pan-Asian identity. Only one participant shifted to having more Asian friends in college than in high school. With this one exception, however, the outmarried participants were similar in that they did not develop dense co-ethnic/co-racial associations in college nor a strong panethnic identity. In fact, just like some of the individuals discussed by Kibria, the majority of my interracially married participants comprised those who willfully turned away from close associations with co-ethnics/Asian-ethnics and avoided ethnic organizations, with a common complaint that they were turned off by the insularity of Asian American groups in college.[30]

Monica's narrative about her college experience is typical of this group: "In college I didn't hang out with many Koreans. There was a huge Korean population, and either you are in that group or you are not. And I remember being extremely turned off by the gossipiness of some of the groups, and just generally the Koreans. So I think from my sophomore year on, I really broke away and I didn't hang out with them at all." Almost all of the respondents complained of Asian-ethnic student groups as being too "cliquey" and insular. Kira, who got accused of being a "banana" because her friends in college mainly ended up being White, had this to say:

> I think almost all the friends I had in college were White, actually. Some kids who grow up in all-White neighborhoods go to the university and find these Asians, right, and then have various reactions to it. Some very negatively, like why are they so cliquish? They don't want to hang out with anybody else. Some discover their ethnicity by meeting these Asian kids. You know what I mean. So people go in these two different directions.

And I was definitely in the former group. . . . I was just amazed that, why would you automatically exclude, I mean—even people who join sororities have friends who are not in sororities—so why would you basically go, you cannot hang out with anybody else? Why does that make me a traitor? Why would I drop friends I've already got? And why could I not be friends with somebody because they're not the same ethnicity?

Sandra, a 36-year-old Korean American, described a college experience that echoed Monica's and Kira's. Sandra was one of the few who asserted that although she spent her high school years in a predominantly White suburb, she also had connections with Korean American friends through church. In college, however, she decided to limit her association with Korean Americans because they were "suffocating," and she set out to look for "other social outlets" which led her to join a sorority:

And I think I got to the point where, you know, this is college and it's supposed to be something new and different and exciting but it just felt like the same old thing. So I started seeking out other social outlets . . . then for some reason, I think I decided I wanted to rush [a sorority]. . . . It [my university] was a big-time Greek school. . . . And it seemed like fun and I thought I'd meet new groups of people.

Sandra initially kept some of her friendships within the Korean community; however, this led her to feel like she kept living a double life, "living in two separate worlds." Finally accepting the fact that she had a "personality that will not just follow the crowd," and one that did not suffer from a "lack of independent thinking" that she attributed to cliquey Asian-ethnics, she eventually disconnected further from the Asian American community. This narrative strikingly parallels those respondents by Kibria who objected to associating with fellow Asian-ethnics because of their "opposition to individuality," tendencies toward "clannishness," and "group conformity," as well as "gender traditionalism."[31] It also illustrates identifying these "Asian" ways as inferior and unenlightened, compared to the supposedly progressive ways and values of the White culture, such as "independent thinking" and "individualism."[32]

Reflecting a more overt case of ethnic-distancing, Sarah, the 41-year-old Chinese American who had little connection to the Asian American college community, recalls how she and her like-minded Asian American friends expressed their distaste of the perceived insularity of fellow Asian-ethnics by going as far as to make fun of fellow Chinese American students as being too "Chinesey." She mused, "We used to make fun—though we were Chinese ourselves—and we'd call them 'Chinesey'. And I think maybe that was it, that a lot of Chinese people that were *not* fresh off the boat, that were American-born, that were really cliquey. They were so cliquey and not really too friendly to me, and it wasn't like I was dying to hang out with them either." One man even talked about a "hatred" he shared with some other like-minded Asian Americans of "the whole Asianness type thing" as a "lack of individuality, lack of wanting to assimilate," which he found "offensive" and unrelatable. The narratives of the highly assimilated participants presented here seem to go beyond a mere disinterest in engaging in ethnicity and connecting with Asian-ethnics to representing an active desire to detach from them by stigmatizing the majority of Asian-ethnics with "fobbish" qualities noted earlier.

Resonant of remarks earlier in the chapter by women who expressed a dislike of Asian patriarchy, the following comments by Pauline, the Indian American participant, clarify her dislike of the "gender traditionalism" dimension of Asian-ethnics she encountered in college that played into her dissociation from Asian-ethnics:

> I tried to join the Indian Student Association when I was a . . . freshman, but all the girls were extremely cliquey . . . none of them in a sorority and they were all very prim and proper . . . the notion that I want to have a beer with a pizza at the pizza night . . . they all looked at me like I was some kind of a heathen . . . wearing a scarlet "A" on my chest. I just felt very unwelcomed by the women at that organization . . . that put a really bad taste in my mouth about Indian women, and I never became close friends with any Indian women in college or in grad school as a result. I always felt like they judged me too harshly.

The traditional gender expectations of women in these groups clearly do not appeal to Pauline, and she demonstrates disdain for the fellow Indian American women whom she sees as complicit in conforming to such expectations. Studies of other racial minority women report similar aversion to ethnic patriarchal elements as a primary motivator for many women deciding to enlarge their social and dating circles beyond the ethnic group in college, leading to interracial dating and marriage.[33]

## Avoidance of Same-Race Partnering

A small number of interracially married participants professed to having had friends who were racially diverse, which included Asian-ethnics. At least one woman, Carla, said she became active in an Asian American student association, though she had many non-Asian and White friends. However, for her, these involvements did not lead to interethnic dating. Although she was somewhat involved in the Asian American student organizations, she did not come to find Asian men appealing: "it seemed like they were all stereotypical engineering, kind of geeky-type Asian boys. That's not very nice, but that's kind of—that's how I felt about them. They were very nice, but I was just not interested." Indeed, for most of those who distanced themselves from the Asian American student community in college, this distancing also involved avoidance of Asian dating partners.

Most of my respondents not only refused to limit their socializing to Asian Americans by making efforts to attain social circles outside of the Asian American community by, for example, joining sororities or fraternities, but they also found no reason to change their dating patterns in college.[34] Most participants, claiming that they did so because it was "all they were familiar with," simply continued the pattern of dating Whites or other non-Asians, to the chagrin of many of the parents, although some did experiment with Asian American partners during college.[35] Some emphasized that college was when they came to the realization of how "American" they really were and that they had no desire to seek out co-ethnics or co-racials as dating or marriage partners. For others, being exposed to the "insular" Asian American groups did nothing to disabuse them of the unflattering images they held of Asians; college only reinforced such images.

In terms of dating, many of the women, like Carla, continued to hold on to their image of the nerdy qualities of Asian males as reasons for these men's undesirability or on to the dislike of Asian patriarchy. Outmarried Asian-ethnic men also subscribed to the undesirability of Asian-ethnic women in college, but of particular interest is that outmarried Asian American men in my study rarely mentioned nerdiness or physical unattractiveness as reasons for finding Asian-ethnic women unappealing. The Asian American men focused on different reasons; several men stated that they found Asian females "boring" and "uninteresting" (even if physically attractive), which is also often a code for the "unprogressive" and tradition-bound Asian female. Another reason that rendered Asian American women less desirable, mentioned most frequently by Chinese American men in the study, was that Asian-ethnic women reminded the men of their mothers or sisters in terms of their personalities. One Chinese American man spoke of how dating Chinese American women was unsuccessful because they reminded him of his mother by being "overbearing" and "possessive" He said:

> There were two things. One was the jealousy thing. . . . The second issue was that this aspect, and she [my ex-girlfriend], reminded me of my mother. Which isn't a bad thing—I love my mother and I am very close to my mother, but this is kind of awful to say, but my ex-girlfriend was—I felt very caged in. . . . I've met jealous people, but not like that. It didn't turn me off to Asian women forever, because it didn't, but it looks that way, doesn't it? Because I never paid attention to Asian women after that, not until after graduate school.

Assimilative desires and distancing from ethnic cultures, often reflected in the form of rejecting those in the same ethnic-racial group as romantic partners, is just as much a male as it is a female phenomenon. The interracially married Asian-ethnic men in my study expressed a similar level of assimilative and cross-racial romantic desires for non-Asian women throughout their young adult years. For the men, desiring non-Asian women, especially White women, typically went hand in hand with idealizing whiteness; for example, these men tended to elevate White females as paragons of ideal femininity, both in terms of physical appearance and personality or character.[36] Matt, for example, explicitly compared his White American wife in an opposite and favorable way to the few Chinese women he dated, describing his wife as "easy going" and "happy-go-lucky"; everything his ex-girlfriends were not. Even though he did not speak of Asian women in a negative way in any physical terms, his comparison implicitly placed Asian-ethnic women and White women in two contrasting and separate categories: Asian-ethnic women as accomplished and smart but possessive and emasculating, and White women as more free-spirited, progressive, and somehow more "evolved" in their dealings with men.[37]

While all the interracially married men in my study married out due to their desire to do so, it is important to register that the situation was slightly different and more complicated for the women. Although the majority of the interracially married women in my study confessed to their lifelong attraction to non-Asian men, there were a small number of women who asserted that they would have *preferred* to have dated or married Asian-ethnic men, attesting to the complexity of feelings toward intermarriage among some of the participants. This, however, proved difficult because these women did not fit the stereotype of a "typical" Asian woman. Vicky, a professional with an opinionated personality, related that because she did not fit this "ideal Asian femininity," many Asian men she was interested in did not reciprocate her interest in them. Describing a typical reaction by Asian men in conversation, she said, "They find you physically attractive, but once you open your mouth, they think, this one is too much work."[38] Vicky explained that after a number of such rejections during her college years, she actually felt freed from the Asian female stereotype and the pressure to "be" Asian and was able to give herself the permission to be herself and to be with whomever she wanted, especially those who would not be threatened by her personality.

Pauline, explaining what she perceived as a unique situation for Indian American women, stated that for many Indian Americans, women marrying non-Indian men is often not necessarily a result of assimilative desires or the wish for White privilege, but, to the contrary, a consequence of being "rejected" by Indian men:

> Yeah . . . We Indian women don't feel that way. Indian women never felt I want to date a White man so I can feel attractive. No, in fact, a lot of Indian women would say that dating a White guy is because you probably

don't think you are good enough to date an Indian guy. . . . It's very different from the East Asian case.

But she, too, did go on to qualify her remarks and echo Vicky's comment that it
was the "bold" ones who tended to get rejected by Indian men. She said, "They
might be like, oh, she doesn't want to date an Indian guy because she can't get
an Indian guy. . . . In the long run . . . I think it also has more to do with the
strength of personality. . . . I always found that the stronger Indian women, those
who [are] more bold, more Western . . . more worldly and outspoken, were
rejected predominantly by Indian men." My findings here parallel other studies
which show that antipathy for ethnic community gender traditionalism plays a
significant role in women's motivations behind outmarriage, but also introduce
the possibility that in some cases, out marriages for Asian-ethnic women may
not simply denote a rejection of same-race or -ethnic men but may be a consequence of being "unable to compete successfully for a marital partner within
their own ethnic group" in terms of the standards of the ethnic community, and
thus being "forced to settle for a less desirable choice outside the group."[39] Vicky
and Pauline's remarks indicate that for some Asian-ethnic women, the process
of "assimilation" or the decision to outmarry may not necessarily go hand in
hand with a rejection of their heritage, or a desire to "Whiten" through marriage
or avoid Asian-ethnic men, but reflect a complicated relationship to their ethnic
community's gender expectations.

## Ethnic-Racial Re-Identification After College

An intriguing theme that emerged was that for a number of interracially married participants, ethnic rediscovery came *after* college,[40] typically in professional
settings where they were able to meet other assimilated and successful fellow
Asian Americans like themselves. Matt describes vividly how he was awakened
to the positive qualities of fellow Asian Americans only after he had the occasion
to interact with them in professional settings, which gave him the chance, for
the first time, to work with and interact with a critical mass of successful, well-
assimilated, and attractive Asian Americans. Matt admitted that he decided to get
involved in his professional organization because he thought it would be a good
networking opportunity. When he attended the professional meeting for the first
time, he still thought the Asian Americans were going to be "cliquey" and insular
as they were in college. However, he quickly realized how different things were
and how differently he felt. He remarked on attending an all-Asian professional
meeting for the first time:

> I didn't know a single person, and I went to this convention that had
> about 300 to 400 people there. I've never done anything like that, gone

somewhere where I didn't know anybody. But I went and it was the most welcoming crowd. They embraced me right away. I went to a panel on Vincent Chin,[41] and I'm sitting there and listening to this, and I couldn't believe that there are these people that are so dedicated to the Asian American community and were such advocates. The whole weekend, every single person, every face I saw was Asian. And you know there was a banquet on the last night and everybody is wearing tuxedos, and there are some good-looking people. First, I was noticing—all these women there were like, wow, amazing. It was great . . . after spending my whole weekend enclosed and encapsulated with just Asian people who looked just like me, spoke perfect English, were professionals, successful, I felt very different than I had ever felt before, and I had that feeling with me ever since then.

He added: "And the weirdest thing that happened was that when I left that convention that Sunday to go [to] the airport and I walked into the airport, and it was a shock how different I felt walking around with all these other [non-Asian] people all of a sudden. And it was literally a marked moment that I felt so different from everybody else in the way I never felt before. . . . This convention didn't totally break the [Asian] stereotype, but it made me realize that I was thinking in stereotypes and made me realize that . . . it's okay to be different and that you can thrive on difference."

After this experience, Matt became actively involved in Asian American issues and advocacy at the community and professional level. For him, these experiences not only catalyzed his reassessment of fellow Asian-ethnics and involvement in the Asian American community but also provided a kind of ethnic rediscovery, a sense of ethnic/racial pride and then self-acceptance. The irony is that this ethnic rediscovery only transpired after involvement with a highly select group of professional and well-assimilated Asian Americans like himself, suggesting that rekindled desire for ethnic re-attachment did not signify freedom from White-identification for the "model minority" Asian Americans.

Similarly, Pauline said that it was only after she joined a network of Indian American professionals after graduate school that she was finally able to connect with other Indian Americans in a meaningful way. After describing her negative experiences with "cliquey" Indian Americans in college who made her feel bad, she said that after professional school:

I decided, you know, I was willing to join this group [the Indian American professional group] and re-identify with people my age or who are Indians who grew up in this country like me, and that was a great experience. These were people who felt the same way I did, a lot of people who grew up kind of isolated . . . with no other Indian friends. Two of my very best friends who are Indian today I met through that group. And I even dated some guys in that group.

Like Matt, Pauline said she felt a "renewed sense of pride" in being Indian American with this group and became inspired to serve the Indian American community, including projects to help underprivileged and immigrant Indians. However, like Matt, this connection was similarly forged with those who shared experiences of being a particular kind of Indian American: American-born, highly acculturated individuals, most of whom had practiced ethnic-distancing and struggled with identity conflicts well into their adult years.

## Assimilation and Ambivalence: The Role of Parents

The portrayals thus far of interracially married individuals show a general pattern of ethnic and racial distancing along with a high level of acculturation, but the participants' assimilationist desires include varying degrees of ambivalence. Even while they may have desired mainstream society acceptance throughout the growing-up years, many of my participants were not categorically dismissive of their ethnic heritage and identity but were, in at least in two-thirds of the cases, torn between a sense of cultural/ethnic pride or attachment and the wish to attain mainstream societal acceptance and White privilege.

This ethnic attachment and pride were often instilled by the parents, though a common trait of parents of interracially married participants in my study was that they fell on the assimilationist rather than the preservationist end of the spectrum. For parents who fall on the assimilationist end of the spectrum, attitudes regarding acculturation/assimilation can however be highly contradictory, and this often introduces confused feelings in their children regarding identity. For instance, most of the assimilationist-oriented parents were keen on promoting and ensuring their children's professional and educational success, and this typically signified fostering children's acculturation (or cultural assimilation), including speaking English fluently and becoming proficient in American culture and customs so that the children could be socially and professionally adept. These parents, many of whom were well-educated, wanted to ensure that their children acquired whatever cultural and educational capital necessary to succeed. For some families, this included parents insisting that only English be spoken at home or encouraging the children's Americanization.

Pauline, a Hindu, related that although her parents did attempt to teach her native language and about Indian culture, they were so committed to making sure that she and her sibling were going to be comfortable in American culture that they went so far as to make a conscious decision to let the kids eat meat: "Yes, so, we were raised very American. I don't know how to put it. . . . My mom felt like it would be a lot easier for my brother and I . . . in socializing with friends, if we can have sausage, pizza, pepperoni, hamburgers at McDonalds. . . . I think it was [a] smart move on my mom's part. . . . How do you go to a birthday party when you know that the family is White, cooking hamburgers and steaks on the grill?" This assimilationist stance however, which in many cases served to steer the children toward exogamy,[42] did not preclude many of these parents from being proud of their culture, and the parents often simultaneously transmitted messages that their kids should value their ethnic culture and made efforts, even if minimal, to try to pass down native language (for example, by speaking it at home or forcing kids to go to language schools) and certain cultural practices and values.[43]

The result of such mixed messages was that my participants often retained confused or mixed feelings toward their ethnicity and countries of origin, as well as toward assimilation and the desire for White privilege. On the one hand, the majority did engage in varying degrees of repudiation of their ethnic culture and identity as youths, but for some, such repudiation was not categorical; ethnic-distancing was also accompanied by a level of pride in and acknowledgment of their ethnic communities and cultures of origin, even if with ambivalent feelings.[44] This ambivalence often came in the form of regret expressed by a number of participants that they did not try harder to learn the language or culture of their parents. For all the participants, this ambivalence formed the basis for catalyzation of ethnic rediscovery upon marriage and having mixed-race children, which will be explored in the next chapter.

## Conclusion

Despite what appears to be a commonplace assumption that people generally want to "stick to their own kind," racially, ethnically, culturally, or religiously, the findings presented in this chapter suggest that desires for crossing or staying within racial or ethnic boundaries are context-bound. For my interracially married Asian-ethnic participants, their growing up experiences as racial minorities in White-dominated communities seem to have had a powerful impact on their assimilative and romantic desires.[45] Subject to an ongoing process of "othering," social marginalization, and racist treatment by peers and members of the dominant group, all of my participants responded by developing strong desires to assimilate and be accepted by the mainstream White middle-class culture, which was often accompanied by ethnic-racial distancing from their own groups. Another way of looking at this is that such desires to assimilate may lead to rapid acculturation, and for Asian–ethnics, high level of acculturation has indeed been found to be a strong predictor of interracial marriage.[46]

In contrast to what has been theorized within pluralistically oriented assimilation models, my findings therefore indicate the possibility that even in the present-day U.S., the drive for White privilege and "Anglo-conformity" may be alive and compelling, suggesting that we should not overestimate the diminishing impact of the hegemony of whiteness and its perceived role as a route to social incorporation and acceptance.[47] That said, a great deal of ambivalence can accompany this desire for whiteness, which highlights the inherent psychological complexities related to desire and identification within an unequal racial structure.

In tracing the evolution of ethnic-racial identity of the participants over time, this chapter has also begun to delineate the ways in which ethnic-racial identity is a shifting phenomenon in an individual's life. The next chapter will focus on the politics of identity development in the context of interracial marriage and explore further the evolution of participants' racial-ethnic identification and their navigation of these identity shifts within the context of marriage and multiracial/multicultural family-making.

## Notes

1. Parts of this chapter have appeared in Chong 2013.
2. Cf. Min and Kim 2000.
3. Kalmijn 2010, 282.
4. See DaCosta 2007, 186.
5. Tuan (1998, chap. 5) also finds that respondents who grew up in predominantly White communities struggled most with racial marginalization. See also Espiritu 2003, 190–91. Since ethnic-racial identity struggles are universal, I incorporate a few examples from my interethnically and intra-ethnically married respondents who also grew up in White neighborhoods in this part of the discussion.
6. Cf. Osajima1993; Dhingra 2007; Min and Kim 2000.
7. Fanon 1967, 112–13.
8. National indicators of crime and safety show that Asians or Asian American students are subject to more racial bullying than any other minority group. And when Asian-ethnics report them or protest against them, they are less likely to be taken seriously (Chang 2016, 29–50).
9. Cf. Dhingra 2007, 105; Lee 1996; O'Brien 2008, 75, 86, 124–62.
10. O'Brien 2008, 86. Kasinitz et al. (2004) note that although Asian-ethnics in their study were overall less likely to report experiences with discrimination than Latinos, Asian-ethnics who hailed from big cities like New York were more likely to report conflictual encounters with other *minority* groups, such as Latinos or Blacks, while Asian-ethnics from more White areas report discrimination by Whites (11).
11. Sarah also commented that all the Chinese American girls she knew growing up ended up marrying White-ethnic men.
12. Kibria 2002; Min and Kim 2000, 745, 747–48; Osajima1993; Tuan 1998, 88.
13. Osajima 1993, 86.
14. Pyke and Dang 2003.
15. Tuan 1998, 90.
16. Cf. Min and Kim 2000, 745.
17. Tuan 1998, 91–92, 102–3.
18. Tuan 1998, 188.
19. Cf. O'Brien 2008, 103.
20. Cf. Fong and Yung 2000; Espiritu 2003, 176; Kibria 2002, 126; Min and Kim 2000, 749; Pyke and Johnson 2003; Vasquez 2011b, 2017.
21. The misogynist behaviors of some men against women within the Asian American community may be a mechanism for coping with racist oppression from the larger society. See Kibria 1990; Collins 1990; Hongdagneu-Sotelo and Messner 1994.

22. Vasquez 2011b, 118, 2017.
23. Cf. Tuan 1998, 59.
24. Cf. Purkayastha 2005, 14.
25. See Purkayastha 2005, 50. In her book on South Asian Americans, some of Purkayastha's respondents similarly discuss how their dating options expanded in college and beyond because "rigid boundaries they encountered earlier in school had become somewhat permeable within the [college] dating scene." In the world of college and beyond, "multiple norms of desirability existed with White norms," even though lines between non-Whites and Whites did not entirely disappear.
26. Cf. Vasquez 2017.
27. Butterfield 2004, 300–1; Espiritu 1992; Kibria 2002; Min and Kim 2000, 745; Dhingra 2007, 73; Shinagawa and Pang 1996.
28. Kibria 2002, 125.
29. Pawan Dhingra similarly identifies a category of respondents in his book, *Managing Multicultural Lives* (2007, Chap. 3), that parallels my participants in this chapter. The other two categories he also identifies are those that discover/strengthen ethnic identity in college and those who always possessed a strong sense of ethnic identity/culture.
30. Nazli Kibria (2002) also discusses various types of engagement with Asian American identity itself in college. These include those who embrace politically focused "pan-Asianism," socially focused "ethnic pan-Asianism," and those who reject pan-Asianism altogether by either preferring fellowship with co-ethnics (e.g., Korean or Chinese) or with non-Asians.
31. Kibria 1999, 125.
32. Cf. Pyke and Johnson 2003.
33. See Vasquez 2017, 41.
34. At least half of my interracially married participants had joined sororities or fraternities.
35. Tuan (1998, 121) reports that most of her respondents with White spouses had almost exclusively dated Whites before marrying their partner. This was the case with most of my participants, though not all.
36. See, for example, Wielding 2003, 47–48. Similar to what appears in the next chapter for Asian Americans, the Latino participants in Wielding's study come to realize that such an attitude is expressive of being "racist" against their own people, and this becomes underscored with the appearance of children (Wielding 2003, 48–49).
37. Cf. Chow 2000.
38. Cf. Tuan 1998, 121.
39. Chen and Takeuchi 2011, 886.
40. Cf. Kibria 2002, 130.
41. Vincent Chin was a young Chinese American who was beaten and murdered by two White Chrysler plant auto workers in Highland Park, Michigan, a Detroit suburb, in June 1982, after being mistaken for a Japanese-ethnic. The lack of justice meted out in the case of Chin's murder galvanized a pan-Asian movement.
42. Studies have shown that the degree of parental stance toward assimilation and/or exogamy/endogamy varies by the gender of their children in most Asian-ethnic communities, with girls typically steered more toward "traditionalism" and endogamy. However, this can vary; in certain ethnic communities, the importance of boys marrying within the ethnic group is highly emphasized because of the importance of patrilineality. See for example Espiritu (2003) and DasGupta and DasGupta (1996).
43. Thus, for some parents, enabling of interracial marriages in their children can be seen as an unintended consequence of the parents' quest for the children's success and acculturation. See Alba and Nee 2003, 65.
44. Tuan (1998, 104) also notes the mixture of ethnic pride and an emphasis on being American on the part of some of her participants.

45. Cf. Chou and Feagin 2015.
46. See Hwang et al. 1997; Mok 1999. In her study, Mok finds that the "likelihood of dating White Americans might be influenced more by higher levels of acculturation than by lower ethnic identity. In other words, the degree to which the dominant White culture is seen as the reference group may be more important than lack of identification with one's own ethnic group" (115). She adds: "Finding that ethnic identity is less powerful a force than acculturation speaks to the most charged claims made against interracial daters: that they are 'sell-outs' to their race" (115).
47. The desire for White partners as reflective of a desire for White privilege and whiteness is not confined to Asian Americans. Studies of interracially partnered Latinos, for example, also revealed similar findings, where the Latino participants "idealized" Whites as preferred partners because of the privileging of whiteness. See Chang 2016; O'Brien 2008; Vasquez 2017.

# 4

# MULTIRACIAL FAMILY-MAKING AND THE REVITALIZATION OF ETHNIC IDENTITY AND CULTURE

I met Joy, a 33-year-old Korean American, at a busy coffee shop one sunny weekend afternoon in the uptown area of Chicago. Joy was born in a large East Coast city but raised mostly in a smallish Midwestern town with very few Asians or racial minorities and currently works in education. Her affable husband of European descent, Marshall, came along, pushing their toddler Brittany in a stroller. Marshall entertained Brittany while Joy and I talked first at a corner table. Joy began by telling me about her experiences growing up in a mostly White neighborhood where she was the only person of Asian descent in her high school and her struggles with ethnic-racial identity. Much like the participants in Chapter 3, Joy experienced racism while growing up, including being routinely made fun of and being subject to racially driven verbal and physical violence by peers. She said that because she was so "naïve" and desperately wanted to fit in, she did not even perceive these incidents as racist, preferring to think of herself as a White person.[1]

Even after encountering a large group of Asian-descent students in college for the first time, Joy did not strive to reclaim ethnic identity and association. She did make an effort to engage with Korean and "Asian" culture, making some Asian-ethnic friends and taking Korean-language classes, but she confessed that it was in college where she actually realized how much more comfortable she was with Whites than she was with Asian-ethnics.[2] Most importantly, it was in college that she realized she did not wish to marry a Korean: "There were a lot of good-looking Asian guys that had wonderful personalities, but I just wasn't attracted to any of them. I don't know why; it just didn't happen."

Joy ultimately married Marshall, but to my surprise began to talk passionately about how her entire perspective and feelings toward her ethnicity and race began to change when her daughter was born, something she did not expect: "Yeah, I wasn't one of those people who discovered their ethnicities in college. . . . but now that Brittney's here, I want to know more about it and I want to push it on her." Joy was "thrilled" with her daughter's daycare's "Diversity Night," an event for which she collected various Korean cultural items and displayed them for the group, surprising even herself. She further ruminated: "You know she [Brittany] just had her one-year birthday. And we did the whole, you know, *Doljabi*[3] and we got a *hanbok* (traditional Korean dress) for her. . . . Now we do all this Korean stuff, and I get all excited and I certainly wasn't like that when I was growing up. But now that she's here, it's different. It was like a renewed focus on it [Korean culture] that wasn't there before."

In the previous chapter, one of the prominent themes that appeared in the narratives of the participants was the extent to which the power of Anglo-conformity and the desire for mainstream social acceptance still forcefully shapes self-identities and romantic desires of the Asian American men and women in a society still structured by racial hierarchy. As discussed, individual romantic preferences cannot be understood apart from their embeddedness in societal discourses, attitudes, and images regarding race and/or gender. But once the participants marry and embark on family-making, what happens? Do interracial marriage and multiracial family-making represent a continued path of assimilation into the mainstream society, as traditional assimilation theories would predict, or do they represent something more complex and unexpected?

This chapter provides substantial evidence supporting that interracial marriage for Asian Americans may not serve as a smooth or uninterrupted path of transition to greater depths of assimilation and "Americanization"; on the contrary, it represents a critical turning point and marker for revitalization of ethnic/racial consciousness and identity that opens up possibilities for multicultural family-making. This surprising process occurs especially once the participants begin to raise mixed-race children, whose presence awakens in the participants a reassessment of the importance of their own ethnic-racial identities and those of their children. This chapter explores the ways in which this dynamic plays out for Asian Americans and the politics surrounding cultural-identity negotiations between the married couples in the process of family formation.

## Children and the Revitalized Desire for Ethnic Identification and Culture

Classic theories of assimilation not only popularized the view that an individual would follow a "straight-line" path of assimilation into the dominant White culture/society over their lifetime (or down the generations), ideally culminating in intermarriage with Whites, but also suggested that intermarriage itself would lead to greater assimilation for the minority partner. As scholars have pointed out, however, such views may be speculative, based on the assumption that a "wholesale cultural assimilation of minority spouse into the White mainstream"[4] is both inevitable and desirable. In what follows,

I show that most of my interracially married participants unexpectedly experienced an intensification of racial/ethnic consciousness and identity upon marriage and worked to incorporate this enhanced ethnic awareness into assembling their multicultural family lives. Efforts at multicultural family-making for most of the Asian-ethnic participants, while meeting with varying levels of success, are, however, a constant uphill battle in the face of pressures for conformity to the dominant culture, the participants' own cultural thinness, and ideologies of colorblindness that pervade their social and family lives. As I will argue, however, a large part of such efforts appear to be reflective of the participants' struggle to stave off the possible tide of ethnic cultural loss and also of a strategy against racism.

When asked, Joy continued that she could not articulate exactly where this fervent desire for ethnic engagement came from since she cared so little about knowing Korean culture while growing up, but she explained that it is simply important for her daughter to know Korean culture to "help her understand why people act the way they do." She added: "I didn't really care about that before, but now I do because I want *her* to know." She also explained that this realization has transformed her own sense of self:

> I really don't know where it came from. I don't know if it's because when you have a child, you feel like you have to pass something onto them, some sort of legacy or something. I don't know if that's what it is. And I don't really identify myself by my job or how much money I make. Most of the identification for me now is my ethnic background, and it wasn't that way before.

She also reflected that another pivotal motivation might have been the death of her maternal grandmother two years before her daughter was born, a grandmother who had helped raise Joy. Although Joy took her grandmother's presence in her life for granted when she was growing up, the significance of her deceased grandmother in her life was thrown into relief after her own daughter was born; Joy realized that her "grandmother's story had ended because she was no longer here to tell it," and so "we have to continue it on somehow, and it's only through your children." She admitted that now she has become very proud of her Korean culture and traditions.

The journey of Monica, the Korean American from the previous chapter, closely parallels Joy's story. Despite her intense identity struggles growing up, she also discussed how her life and self-perception changed upon having children. Although she always felt "shallow" culturally, Monica felt lucky in meeting a man who was open minded enough to allow her to begin engaging her ethnicity. She observed: "I think I'm so American that in our marriage, there aren't too many things that come up. You know, I don't go to Korean church; I can't speak Korean. But you know it's funny because at my kids' school, they do a lot of, you know, ethnic share days where you can volunteer to bring an ethnic dish or things like that. So I now actually find myself reaching deeper down to find my culture and heritage in the hopes of bringing it out to my children." However, adding that "it can't be forced, you know," Monica displayed a lot more ambivalence about this issue of cultural negotiation than Joy. In fact, when asked whether she would care as much about ethnic cultural maintenance had her kids been Euro-ethnic instead of half Asian-ethnic, she confessed that she would not care as much, and that the reason she feels the need to reconnect to her ethnic culture is because her kids have an "Asian appearance" which cannot be denied.

In fact, Monica recalled the following incident that was extremely disturbing to her. When it was pointed out to her six-year-old son explicitly for the first time that he was half-Korean, she recalled that he became angry retorting, "No I'm not!" and ran out of the room. She felt profoundly sad since this was reminiscent of the time when she was shocked by her own image when looking into a mirror, and she wondered if her son was feeling what she had felt then, though she thought his violent reaction curious in light of the fact that he was only *half* Korean. Such incidents, which made her feel as if her own son was rejecting her, precipitated conversations between Monica and her two sons about their ethnic heritage, skin color, and racial differences. They also motivated her to participate more in school and community diversity events because she realized it was important for her kids to understand that their "differences were valuable."

At the same time, Monica struggled mightily between a desire not to put too much emphasis on race/color and the need to attend to the reality of "difference," since she, to a large extent, desired a colorblind world:

> Now, I'm participating more at school . . . and the cultural differences are brought out to them more. I commend the school for that, too . . . and I realized that you do have to point out to the kids that there are differences, that different cultures exist in the world and also how they're different, because if you don't point it out, it's something they may not pay attention to. . . . But maybe later, once they do realize there are differences, I also want them to realize that the differences, you know, are superficial. . . . So in our household, I try very hard not to talk about somebody's skin color, or the way somebody looks, or whether they are thin or not, you know what I mean? . . . [T]here is a part of me that is glad that at this young age, my kids are not attaching very great value to these differences.

Monica's struggles with the issue of "difference" are clear in this narrative; she vacillates in a confused way between her needing to recognize "difference" and not wanting to, the desire to teach her kids about "difference" and not wanting them to put too much stock on "difference," a stance that reflects our present-day tension between ideologies of multiculturalism and colorblindness. Monica, however, did take comfort in the fact that there is now a pool of mixed-raced children where she lives, children with whom she believes her kids may be able to identify and share identity struggles as they grow up.

Unlike Monica, Kira seemed to have no qualms about the inherent necessity of transmitting Chinese culture to her biracial kids and fostering her children's appreciation of "difference," even though she herself is highly assimilated. For one thing, she said that she received strong messages of the importance of ethnic pride from her parents, something Monica did not mention. Although, when growing up, she "just wanted to be White," Kira said she gained an appreciation for having knowledge about her culture and for "cultural and ethnic difference" when her parents took the family to live in Taiwan for a couple of years when she was in high school. Although she resented having been "ripped out" of her comfort zone and taken to live in a place that she initially hated, she felt glad afterward because it made her realize that the world was made of different types of people and that the world was a bigger place than just the United States. She reflected:

> Maybe they [her kids] will have more of an appreciation for the crazy things that my parents do, and my grandparents too. I think it's always good for them to have exposure to different languages and to know where their family came from, so if they do get teased, they'll be able to appreciate some of the things that are unique about them. If they don't get teased, they can still appreciate some of the unique things about themselves and have this kind of appreciation of other people too, that even if someone looks white bread White, they could be Croatian, Italian, Swedish, whatever. There could be something that's interesting in people's backgrounds that's informative for you that might make you think differently.

It turns out, however, that Kira's children *did* get teased in school; one event she recalls was an "eye-pulling incident" where the kids in school made "Chinese eyes" (pulling eyes horizontally to make them look narrow) at her six-year-old son. Kira at first tried to downplay the incident by rationalizing that it may not have been malicious, but when she saw how much it bothered her son, she called the teacher to complain and asked the teacher to address this issue in her class. Incidents like these confirmed for Kira the absolute necessity of teaching her children about their cultural heritage.

Since the day they were born, Kira made sure to speak to her kids in Chinese, even though her husband does not speak any Chinese. Her kids can converse with her in Chinese, and she encourages them to do so whenever she can, even though she admits that it is becoming increasingly difficult now that her kids are in elementary school and out of the home environment more often. Like Monica, Kira feels fortunate in that she has a husband who is wholeheartedly on board with transmitting Chinese culture, but she is a bit bothered because she feels that she has to "take the lead." And as the kids grow up, she is afraid that the Chinese they learned will not be reinforced because her parents do not live nearby, whom she, as many others do, sees as key conduits of ethnic culture.[5] As I elaborate later in this chapter, her husband, as supportive as he is about passing down Chinese culture to the kids if his wife wants to, does not himself feel that this is that important.

## The Dilemma of Cultural Incompetence

In almost all of the cases, my participants, like Kira, faced a dilemma because, even though they wanted to teach their kids about their ethnic culture, it was difficult for them to do so since their cultural knowledge was so thin, starting with the language. Although Kira was unusual in that she was relatively proficient in Chinese, others were not so fortunate. Sarah, another assimilated 41-year-old Chinese American who felt strongly about helping her three kids retain their ethnic culture, experienced this dilemma keenly since she speaks little Chinese, though she understands it:

> It becomes hard because I really want my kids to learn Chinese. And so I had them watching some Chinese videos and reading some Chinese books early on, but then they had non-Chinese nannies a lot of the time. So they weren't hearing Chinese since I don't speak it. So it sort of fell by the wayside and it is unfortunate. . . . Besides, even if they learn it, who's going to talk to them so it gets reinforced? Unless they have Chinese babysitters or something, they are just not surrounded enough by it. . . . But I think it's a nice thing that more and more schools are teaching Mandarin, because I find that for work and stuff like that it's such an important thing nowadays, a good skill to have.

Whereas Sarah was not able to send her kids to Chinese language school, to her regret, like some other participants, she would like for her kids to take Mandarin in their regular school and eventually take them to China since it is really important for them to "know where they are from and who they are": "I want them to know that they are half-Chinese—they look like they are, too, so I think you would need to be in touch with it."

Aside from language, what the participants knew of their culture consisted mostly of major holiday rituals, food, and some family or national history, and "values." In our conversation about cultural transmission, Monica, who is now trying very hard to learn more about Korean culture for the sake of her children, even put it this way:

> Well, I'm laughing because there isn't much to pass down. I feel very shallow [culturally], and if you ask me what Korean traditions do you have in your home right now, I would say none, really. I've really just had to rely upon my

mom who is a pretty important part of our lives, in our family life, and just maybe through her random stories, and, you know, through her making *jap-chae* and *bulgogi* every time she comes over. You know, through something as subtle as that, Korean culture can get maintained. But I truly feel that other than that . . . maybe there are some morals and values that I do identify as being more Korean . . . such as a strong family value, a strong loyalty, respect for elders. I'm really trying to instill that. I'm trying very hard to instill respect and value for parents in the household . . . growing up, I saw that that's one thing that American families lacked. I saw a lot of rebellion and I saw a lot of kids that were doing just the worst things in the world and the parents had no control. So as a mom now with children who will eventually face that phase, my goal is to instill that of respecting parents whether or not you agree. . . . But other than that, I feel like I don't have that much to share.

Joy echoed some of Monica's comments regarding what customs and values she was attempting to pass down; to Joy, language transmission was situated somewhat high on the priority list, although she hoped her child would know other languages besides Korean. She also mentioned "respecting elders," even "playing piano or violin, no kidding," and "being well-educated," although she wasn't sure if the latter was necessarily a Korean thing.

When talking about "values," which I will elaborate more on in the next two chapters, "respecting elders" was consistently mentioned as one identifiable feature. Ted, a 38-year-old Vietnamese American and a father of three put it this way:

You understand that growing up in an Asian household there's this kind of hierarchy, right? Like your older brother is higher than you. You don't speak to your parents in a certain way. You have to speak to your parents with respect even if you're mad. That's how I grew up. Lately I've been having this issue with my ten-year-old who acts out. That's not acceptable. That's not how I was brought up. We're starting to go there, and I'm wondering if I'm being too strict.

As is evident in the above narrative however, Ted, echoing many of the others, found that passing down even the more identifiable aspects of his culture, such as elder respect or even basic customs, is challenging when raising kids in the mainstream U.S. culture, let alone in a biracial/bicultural household. Ted, therefore, imposed upon himself a more modest aim; he said that if he is not too successful in transmitting ethnic culture, he wants his biracial children at least to have a strong *awareness* of their ethnic identity:

My mom had a lot of customs and things that she tried to pass down that I have not managed to pass down to my kids. . . . I guess for me those cultural things aren't that important. I just want them to kind of have that ethnic identity to know that they're half Vietnamese and not get lost in the mix, just kind of going through life thinking, "Hey, you know, I'm just another White kid." I just want them to have that and then figure it out for themselves. Lot[s] of things I learned about my culture, I learned in college because my mom didn't teach me. . . . But I do want my kids to have the curiosity, and to know that they're half Vietnamese.

That some highly assimilated Asian American parents, such as Ted, settled for helping to instill ethnic consciousness or pride in their children rather than pursuing the more difficult task of sustaining cultural traditions parallels findings in other works on Asian Americans.[6]

It is apparent that participants like Monica, Sarah, and Ted, those who self-admittedly are culturally thin, tended to display more conflict about the issue of cultural transmission than those who deemed themselves more culturally competent like Kira. Sarah, for example, felt more conflicted not only because she felt less fluent in ethnic culture and less connected to it- for instance, she remembered hating Chinese school as a youngster- but also because she felt torn about what should be prioritized in her kids' education, between instilling "mainstream" skills and ethnic knowledge. For instance, though she would ideally like for her kids to learn Chinese, her "overscheduled" kids are involved in many other activities that she deemed just as important for learning life skills. This includes soccer, a sport she thought would teach team skills and which her husband coaches.

Referring to her husband, Sarah said, "It's hard because I've always liked someone who's active and my husband likes sports and he's very involved with the kids in terms of like coaching their teams and all that. And I like that but that is the conflict in terms of time. If we had to pick between soccer and going to Chinese school, all the kids are going to pick soccer." Clearly, in Sarah's case, this sense of conflict is due to a combination of her own inability to transmit Chinese culture adequately and her desire for her kids to acquire the educational tools and social skills to be part of the mainstream. Although a number of scholars have discussed the possibility and benefits of a relatively high level of ethnic retention among Asian Americans, even as they "assimilate,"[7] formidable barriers make the reality of this retention very challenging. Interestingly, Sarah also hinted that part of her conflict about ethnic cultural retention was also due to the fact that her husband, unlike Kira's husband who was "enthusiastic" about Chinese culture, was not exactly active in taking the initiative in Chinese activities, although he was not against them and even found them "interesting."

## Ethnic Revitalization as a Fear of Cultural Erasure and Strategy Against Racism

A number of scholars have addressed the issue of fear of cultural erasure or "loss." In her study of Chinese and Korean Americans, Nazli Kibria discusses the fears that her informants had of "ethnic loss" in intermarriage that lay not only in mixing of blood but also in the "production of culture gaps or dissonances in cultural orientations and practices" within their family and marital relations.[8] Aside from the possible tensions intermarriage would engender between the families of the spouses, Kibria's informants were concerned especially about the potential for conflict over passing of culture to children if they married spouses who did not value their ethnic culture. But while Kibria's interviewees were for the most part not yet married, Sarah and others, all of whom had already chosen the path of interracial marriage, were just as acutely concerned about the potential obliteration of their children's cultural heritage. A major reason for this concern, despite their own sense of inadequacy in relation to ethnic culture, was driven by the conviction that their kids should retain a sense of strong ethnic identity and cultural knowledge as a strategy against potential racism and exclusion.[9] As I will explore further later in the chapter, this was usually in contrast to the non-Asian spouses who did not seem to give this issue as much thought.

Reminiscent of Monica's story, Sarah related her young daughter's reaction when Sarah pointed out to her daughter about her racial mix in anticipation of our interview: "I was talking to her about how you were coming to interview us, and my little daughter asked me, 'Mom, you are a different race than daddy?' And I said, 'Yeah, you know I'm Asian.' And she knows that, but I don't think she ever really thought about it, like there are different people in the world. So I told her, you are half Asian/half White, and she was like, 'We thought we were White.'" Even though Sarah was aware that young children may not explicitly "see" race unless pointed out, what bothered Sarah was that when asked, her kids identified themselves only as White.

What bothered Sarah even more was an incident involving a school project that required her daughter to conduct research about China and make a presentation. Sarah was aghast to discover that all her daughter chose to present about China were a series of negative cultural features:

> Her presentation would center around things like how kids eat bugs in ancient China and how they had slavery. It was all about negative things. So I got mad at her and said, "Listen, you know you are half Asian. There is so much more to say than that. Why are you picking these? Look at all these things, like the inventions that originated in China." So I told her to talk to her teacher about what her teacher thinks of what she had so far, and the teacher said "Fine!" I was really irritated by that. I was like, "My gosh, you're going to stand up and you're talking about bugs and fleas. You could be talking about this invention or that; there are so many things". . . . I don't know what was going through her head there. I mean there weren't a lot of ethnic kids in her gifted program, but there was a Jewish girl there, and she did her presentation about ancient Judaism and stuff. I'm sure she wasn't talking about bugs. And what made me even more irritated was that she ended up getting a good grade. I was mad at my daughter, but I was also kind of mad at that teacher. This whole thing really bothered me.

Sarah clearly interpreted her daughter's actions, despite her young age, as the result of already having absorbed the subtle, negative stereotypes about China and as reflecting self-denigration in relation to her Chinese heritage. Another Chinese American mom, Carol, related a similarly disturbing incident: her young daughter, who looks more Asian than her sister, suddenly announced one day that she does not like Chinese people or anyone with black hair and dark skin. When asked to choose a book for a class project, this daughter explained that she chose her book because it had light-skinned people on the cover and she did not like dark-skinned people.[10]

In some cases, staving off cultural loss was not narrated necessarily as a strategy for defending against potential racism and exclusion, but as a simple fear that one's ethnic culture and identity would become "absorbed" by the mainstream culture. Indeed, numerous studies document the challenges that the minority partner in an intermarriage, or their children, may face in maintaining minority identity against the dominant and typically more highly valued majority identity.[11] Ted, who grew up in a diverse town in California but now lives in a smaller Midwestern town, related how he began to feel the keen need to reclaim his ethnic identity and culture when he got married to a White woman, began having children, and moved to a predominantly White area:

> So after I got married, we're living here [in the Midwestern town]. I realized that here, I am a minority. . . . At first, I was feeling like I'm just living here . . . but my home is in California . . . but the more I live here, the more I realize that this is home for me. But then I find myself wanting to reach back to my roots to where I grew up and identify. So I started identifying things that I think were Vietnamese. . . . My family is still there [California]. . . . So like when we take vacations and we go to Orange County, we'd take them [children] to Little Saigon and go have fun and do those things. And then we do the Lunar New Year here every year because I want to teach my kids that. But something that I do notice is that I see a little failure in myself that I didn't communicate to my kids in Vietnamese.

To Ted, the realization that he must make conscious efforts to maintain his ethnic roots for his children is strongly connected to the fact that he is now living in a mostly White environment. He very much regrets not "pushing" the Vietnamese language on his children more, and says, "I feel like the more I live here the more I lose my Vietnamese, too, because I'm not practicing it all the time until I talk to my parents, but that's about it. . . . So because I feel like I'm losing it . . . kind of like hair . . . I try to do little things to keep the Vietnamese identity." When asked what kinds of things he does, he replied:

> When my mom sends us gifts and asks every time "Hey, what shall I send the kids?" I only say, "Just send them a Vietnamese dress." Of course they [the kids] don't wear it. They only wear it when we take a photo. We always

celebrate Lunar New Year because to me that's a kind of a big ethnic thing. And then I cook for them, and I take pride in the fact that they like Vietnamese food. I cook for our friends and our neighbors and things like that. And I like to make Vietnamese coffee for them. So these are little things, but I try to do what I can to identify with my Vietnamese background.

Ted also added that, although he was very lucky to have a non-Asian wife who was highly supportive of his attempts to pass down Vietnamese culture to his kids—a wife who recognizes the need for the kids to have "some kind of a Vietnamese identity"—it was very difficult to accomplish this task because his spouse is not Vietnamese and does not speak Vietnamese.[12] Regarding teaching the Vietnamese language, he said, "I made some attempt to teach it to them, but it just didn't work. It doesn't work that I have this different language from my wife when we're trying to talk to them. And I wasn't always home with them."

This fear of cultural erasure that drives the renewed desire for ethnic identity and culture was brought home particularly forcefully by one Asian-White biracial man in my study, Kyle, who now identifies as Chinese American and is raising children who are one-quarter Chinese. He disclosed to me that while growing up in a small "monocultural" Midwestern town, he hardly identified as Chinese, although he knew he had another culture at home. His well-educated Chinese father did not impose the Chinese culture or language on the family, and the little he did learn about Chinese culture he learned by "osmosis" during occasional family events and interactions with Chinese relatives during holidays. He admitted to being called names a few times when young, but the smallness of his town where everyone knew each other, plus the relative high standing of his father in the community as a well-respected professional, protected him somewhat from racist behavior. Not surprisingly, he says his ethnic "awakening" started in college, a racially diverse, large state university. There, he came in close contact with international students, including those from Asia, and began identifying himself sometimes as Asian American.

His serious search for his ethnic identity, however, began when he got married and was about to have his first child, which coincided with his first trip to China with his Chinese part of the family and his non-Chinese wife. Once his first child was born, his search for his roots and efforts to learn more about his culture intensified. In the last few years, Kyle said he has been "learning more about different aspects of Chinese culture," such as "cultural events, festivals, and things like that." Part of it was because of his job, which involved business dealings with China, but he confessed that "I just wanted to know more about my Chinese heritage which, I felt, was completely off balance. I knew a lot about everyone else's culture but not mine." He also underscored that he felt the need to search out his Chinese cultural roots for his children's sake:

It's challenging because of the fact that she [his daughter] is even more mixed than I am, trying to figure out how we would work at getting the

Chinese culture into everyday life. But I am also very conscious and aware of this. . . . I know what it's like to grow up in a monoculture and so I really try to embrace diversity as much as I can. . . . It's definitely *not* okay for my kids to grow up without Chinese culture. It's a very conscious thing for me to want her to know about her heritage. If I don't teach her, her culture would become diluted . . . my niece [who is also biracial] goes to Chinese classes and speaks better Chinese than me now. And so, yes, I want to make sure it doesn't slip away for my kids.

Although Kyle referred at times to the concept of seeking "diversity" in referring to his ethnic quest, it was quite clear from his narrative that his quest was very much about retaining the Chinese part of his culture down the generations. For someone like Kyle, who, although biracial, looked quite Asian, and for whom the reminder of his Asian descent was constant in his life, the salience of ethnic identity could not easily be jettisoned, and he anticipated that would be the case for his kids. In particular, his fear that his culture and ethnic heritage would be "absorbed" by the mainstream culture through his marriage to a non-Asian woman intensified in his adult life.

The two Asian American participants in my sample who emphasized the benefits of "multicultural" or a "hybridized" upbringing more than a concern about "cultural loss" were 38-year-old Indian American Sonia, a mother of two, and Pauline, the Indian American from the last chapter. Sonia, despite her cognizance of racism, opined that no one has "much control" over how kids are going to turn out, and explained that in her case, she and her husband were not "overly doing" one culture over another but trying to raise the kids "multiculturally": "We do what's natural and what works and . . . just kind of go with the flow." Pauline, who was thus far childless, ruminated that she would be making sure her future kids will be educated in "both cultures" (American and Indian) and "have a sense of pride about being involved in both." She was not afraid that her ethnic culture would be "diluted" but saw racial/cultural mixing as a "building up," a kind of melting pot on equal terms where "everyone picks a little bit of everyone else's culture." She anticipated that her kids would be "American as apple pie and then a little Indian spice thrown in."

Sonia, on the other hand, did articulate some fear that her kids would experience identity conflicts when older, which could lead to cultural loss, whereas Pauline did not. Sonia reflected: "I feel like it probably is going to get harder as they get older and they will start having issues. I'm sure they're going to have that. How are they not going to have that? I had it, right? . . . at some point they will be embarrassed of one or the other and start rejecting one for the other. I would anticipate that will happen." Sonia was not sure how to deal with this potential problem, except to make sure to "give them the tools" like language and help them "make good decisions." Pauline, on the other hand, did not think language retention was of much value.

## Asian Cultural-Identity Capital and Its Benefits

Although the fear of cultural loss as a motivation for ethnic retention was a prominent theme in the narratives, what was interesting about certain aspects of Asian-ethnic culture was a recognition of their strategic value to many of the parents. This was particularly true of Chinese language acquisition. As illustrated by narratives like Sarah's, at least half of the Chinese American parents remarked that Chinese would be a useful language to learn in light of China's current economic ascendance. This perspective closely exemplifies what Kibria refers to as "globalism ethnicity," "a conception of ethnicity that draws attention to the globalization on the significance of ethnicity":

> Globalism ethnicity contributed to my informants' understanding that Chinese or Korean ethnic membership was strategically valuable, endowing them with a sort of ethnic identity capital that was of great value in the globalizing world economy. This value was increased when a Chinese or Korean identity was coupled with an American one, which connoted power and privilege.[13]

The recognition that some Asian-ethnic capital, especially the Chinese language, is becoming prevalent was highlighted by Carla's observation that so many non-Chinese children now attend Chinese language classes. Discussing one Indian American boy who was the best student in the Chinese language class, she commented: "Yes, he's amazing . . . and I think it's because he *wants* to be there. Obviously, there's no reason culturally, heritage-wise for his parents to make him go, because they don't speak Chinese. I think they're doing it because they think that Chinese is the wave of the future." This also attests to the fact that at least for the Chinese American parents, efforts to transmit the language may be easier in the current multicultural environment that stresses diversity and foreign language learning and in which China is ascending as a global cultural and economic force.

Most Chinese American spouses received support from, or at least did not face resistance from, their non-Asian spouses on Chinese language acquisition for this reason. Furthermore, as more regular schools teach Chinese, it makes it easy for parents to pass down the language. Nonetheless, my participants struggled with challenges in actually passing down such valued ethnic-cultural capital not only because they themselves were not well-versed culturally but also because their children faced pressures to accommodate to the dominant White culture. Korean American parents in this study, who were no less enthusiastic about their kids' ethnic language acquisition, seemed to face even greater difficulties in language transmission because they had to rely more on themselves and family members to teach children the language unless they were heavily involved in institutions such as ethnic churches, which was unusual for the interracially married.

Despite the possible growing significance of Asian ethnic-cultural cache, an interesting tension was that almost all of the participants felt that a multicultural environment with relatively less racism and more access to enjoying the benefits of Asian-ethnic identity-cultural capital could only be expected in metropolitan areas, where most of my participants already live. Many respondents, both Asian American and White, cited specific instances of overt and subtle racism they experienced as interracial couples and those that their children experienced in non-urban or more monoracial/monocultural areas, reiterating their calculated choice of neighborhoods. Even a White spouse, for example, said adamantly that she and her husband could not "imagine" considering a move to a predominantly White town deep in the Midwest or the South.

Despite what appears to be the participants' genuine optimism regarding the growing tolerance of U.S. society and the possibilities of "globalism ethnicity," this tension powerfully illustrates their awareness of the ongoing challenges of racism in the United States and the need to arm themselves and their kids with strategies to battle, or protect themselves from, such challenges. My findings echo other studies that show that places of residence were crucial for interracial couples and the ways in which racial issues come to the fore for the couples and their children. One study found that when interracial couples live in predominantly White areas, their racial differences become more visible to and emphasized for themselves, leading sometimes to relationship strife, whereas when they lived in more diverse/multicultural neighborhoods, racial issues and differences became less significant because community diversity kept them from dwelling on their own racial differences.[14] In terms of children, studies on mixed-race populations find that racial identifications and connections to racialized communities for mixed-race individuals would largely depend on where they live, not to mention with whom they live and what they look like.[15] The theme of residential location emerges in full force in the narrative of interethnic couples that will be discussed in the next two chapters, illuminating the crucial significance of ethnic communities/populations and interpersonal connections gained therein in the efforts to preserve ethnic cultures and identities.

## Cultural/Racial Dilution and Anxieties About Racial-Mixing

The participants' ever-present concern about cultural/ethnic erasure was also expressed poignantly in an unexpected manner by a few of them in terms of anxieties and ambivalence regarding the biraciality of children. Not surprisingly, most of my outmarried informants did not express negative sentiments regarding racial mixing per se. If anything, they tended to remark on racial-mixing, especially between Asians and Whites, in an optimistic, even celebratory manner, as demonstrated, for example, by their admiration of what they perceived as the greater beauty of their biracial children who possess some Caucasian features. Revealing their idealization of the White beauty standard, most of the Asian American respondents spoke of how biracial children were better looking than Asian children, since they would have, for example, bigger eyes and other Caucasian features like higher-bridged noses.

Nevertheless, a few of the parents simultaneously expressed conflicted feelings about biraciality, disclosing their trepidations about the potential "dilution" of Asian racial and cultural distinctiveness. Vicky, the out married Chinese American who does not yet have children, expresses her mixed feelings about biraciality in the following way:

> I have two feelings about biracial kids. First of all, they [biracial kids] are the best. . . . The body will naturally select the best genes of the parents. You will get a better child almost, unless something weird happened. So typically, biracial children are attractive or this or that. My only concern is that I really am proud of my heritage and what one thing I would be sad about is that my children won't look anything like me. They grow up and there are a lot of beautiful biracial children and they don't look Asian, maybe they do a little bit. . . . So while I don't think having biracial kids [is] a bad thing . . . I feel like I won't be able to pass on a legacy because I have children who won't physically look Asian, and other Asians won't identify with them as being Asian. . . . It will be kind of ironic for me because I worked so hard trying to champion API [Asian Pacific Islander] causes and then my own kids won't even look Asian and they won't need it. Does that make sense? Sometimes I feel guilty that I won't have Chinese kids. I want to look at my children and feel like they are little Chinese babies. I know it sounds crazy, but that's one of the reasons why I wanted to marry a Chinese guy. . . . So I love my husband, you love who you love, but I do feel a little sense of guilt about it.

Captured in this narrative about cultural/ethnic and racial erasure is the subtext of fear and concern about the "absorption" of the minority group, both culturally and racially, into the dominant Anglo one. This narrative also reflects conflicted feelings about "assimilation" and a recognition that assimilation in the American context is not a process of balanced ethnic-racial incorporation but one that can still imply Anglo-conformity. While this process may not be as problematic for White-ethnic groups whom most participants believed would eventually be embraced as a legitimate part of the Anglo-dominated culture—a number of participants mentioned recent Polish or the Russian immigrants as examples[16]— this process, for a group whose culture, values, and physiology are devalued, is experienced as an erasure of cultural/ethnic distinctiveness.

Explaining her strong commitment to passing down Chinese culture to her biracial children, Carla remarked on the difficulty she has experienced in coming to terms with the fact that her progeny may not be Chinese, especially racially:

> So I think for me, it [passing down Chinese culture] is sort of trying to preserve a little bit of my line of the family perhaps. . . . I guess I don't ever imagine myself having grandchildren that were different from my kids. I always think in my mind that they're going to look the same as my kids do. And it's kind of sweet, like my son has a 'girlfriend' in school right now who's half Korean. And so they look very similar. They're two mixed kids. . . . But yeah, I'm not so sure I'm prepared to have grandchildren that look 100% White or pretty close to it. I'm not sure I'm ready for that. I guess I always picture that they'd look like me. I guess we'll see.

This narrative is reminiscent of the discourses found in many existing studies on multiracial individuals, some of whom, even if they themselves were mixed-race, viewed their children as critical ethnic-racial symbols and even carriers of a family-ethnic tradition; thus, the race of their romantic/marital partners was seen to "portend the identification and commitment of their future children."[17] In a study by Kimberly DaCosta, a mixed-race individual married to a White spouse stated in no uncertain terms that she was unsure if she wished to "cast my whole genetic future" with Whites, "conveying the sense that the race of one's partner, inasmuch as it determines the race of one's children, marks a turning point that will determine the path she and future generations will take."[18] And similarly to Carla, most multiracial respondents in DaCosta's study found it difficult to think of their children as White, even if they had a White parent or if their imagined or real partner was White.

## Narratives of Non-Asian Spouses: Colorblind Discourses and Optional Ethnicity

While the discourses of most Asian American spouses illuminated a tense struggle between what they perceived as the continuing relevance of race in their and their kids' lives and a basic desire for a more race-less/colorblind world,[19] I found in my study that, with a few exceptions, the majority of White spouses hewed much more explicitly to a colorblind perspective that revealed a tendency to minimize the issue of race and racial differences of their spouses and of their mixed-race children. This is expressed in four major ways: first, by their desire to see their children as "race-less"; second, by their tendency to regard ethnic/racial identity as optional for their children; third, by their view of their children's Asian heritage, and any recognizable Asian racial features, as a source of harmless "difference" and "specialness"; and fourth, by downplaying of racial difference by conflating race with culture.

## Minimization of Race and Assumption of Optional Ethnicity

Colorblind discourses dominated the narratives of most of the White-ethnic spouses in my study. Colorblind ideology, the dominant racial ideology of the late twentieth and early twenty-first centuries, also referred to by Ruth Frankenberg as "color and power evasiveness,"[20] is the belief that color, or membership in a racial group, no longer matters and that "race is no longer viewed as a significant obstacle to social and economic participation and where racism is no longer a structural phenomenon."[21] Colorblind ideology has been roundly criticized because, by its call to ignore race and racial differences, it serves as a discursive strategy that occludes the reality of racism and racial inequalities. The ideology of colorblindness rests on the racial privilege conferred to Whites that allows them to subscribe guiltlessly to the idea that race has little impact on people of color. Indeed, although most of the White spouses in my study did recognize that their children had "mixed" features and were biracial, one theme that dominated these individuals' narratives was the extent to which they deemed their kids' "Asianness" as not having much significance or consequence for them, or that race mattered that much in general. For Calvin, for example, the husband of Carla, this meant not seeing his kids as having particular racial identification at all, that is, as being "raced"; "Well, my kids, I guess, I don't view them as Caucasian or Asian, I just view them as Susan and Tom. So to say you are one or the other doesn't make sense. To sort of force people into a box and pick, I always thought that was stupid."

The notable aspect about Calvin's view is, of course, that while he recognized the dilemmas involved in "racing," or racially categorizing people, he did not want to fully recognize the continuing reality of racialization in U.S. society and the very real consequences of this practice for minority groups, not to mention the potential daily salience of "race" for his biracial children. Furthermore, he sees racial identification as something people are forced to "pick" and which "boxes them in," but which is, and should be, voluntary and optional, at least in the case of his children. Not surprisingly, Calvin was most shocked when one of his children, when asked point blank by me during the interview about how he identified himself, definitively identified himself exclusively as "Chinese." Indeed, given the findings of some studies that Asian-White mixed-race individuals tend to identify more frequently as White as compared to Black-White mixed-race individuals, Calvin's reaction to his son's exclusive Asian-ethnic identification was not surprising.[22]

While Calvin objected to "racing" people in general, for some others, the colorblind perspective is reflected in the belief that the *Asian* racial characteristics of their children, even if acknowledged to exist, do not matter. In fact, Luke, the husband of Kira, admitted that although he does now identify his kids as biracial, he had always viewed biraciality as applying only to those who were half White/half Black. He recalled:

> There was a time years ago when a woman asked us, how do you guys feel about being in a biracial relationship? I didn't really understand what she was asking. Like, why was she asking me that because biracial to me always meant Black and White, not Asian and White, so I had to think about it. But I never thought that I was in a biracial relationship. I just thought I was White and Kira was Chinese. . . . So having kids with a Chinese, it's just that they'll grow up to be good looking kids. So it never really—it's not something I think about. I may think about it now since you brought it up, but it's not something that keeps me up at night. We just have too many other issues raising kids.

Luke's comments suggest that although he does recognize the racial "distinctiveness" of his kids, he does not seem to believe that the Asian racial dimension matters very much in that the kids' racial features do not make them "different" enough in any phenotypical nor practical sense to warrant major concern.

Aside from what Luke's comments indicate about the possibly divergent social perception of White/Black and White/Asian marriages,[23] my findings echo some other studies that have provided evidence that especially in cases where the husband is White, White privilege operates to enable the White spouse to choose to be colorblind about the marriage/relationship and their children. More specifically, the White male spouse has the freedom to exercise the privilege to view his relationship and his biracial children as White if he chooses. One example is provided by Maria Root in her book; in a focus study she conducted, she found that in some cases of White male/Asian female marriages, the White husbands, similar to my findings, will say that they do not see themselves as being in an interracial family, that they are just "human beings" in a family like anyone else, whereas Asian males married to White females will say they are in an "interracial family": "it's a different dynamic. One [the White male married to an Asian-ethnic woman] is very colorblind and the other one [Asian-ethnic male married to a White woman] cannot help but be color conscious."[24] Jessica Vasquez also notes in her study of interracially married Latino-White couples that the fact that twice as many White men than women in her study minimized race "begs the question as to whether male privilege makes racial inequalities less visible" to White men and that this observation is "in line with other findings that . . . White women [married to minority men] are likely to be [viewed as] 'race traitors' and to not endorse color-blind ideology."[25] Amy Steinbugler, in her study of White-Black interracial relationships, also notes that White heterosexual females, as opposed to men, feel more marked by interracial stereotypes: "The 'trashy' or 'slutty' White woman has no analogous male counterpart. When it is presumed to be heterosexual, White masculinity embodies extraordinary privilege, especially among middle-class or affluent men,"[26] subjecting men to less stigma in engaging in interracial relationships and also likely enabling them to hold onto a colorblind view of the world.

Consider Max, the 40 year-old White man married to the Indian American Sonia; Max said he did not even really consider his kids to be "biracial" because, since his wife is Indian and has more Caucasian features, his kids do not have as many "visual markers" of being Asian or being a minority. Therefore, Max believed that his kids had the freedom to "make up their own minds" about what they want to be and how they want to identify racially or ethnically. However, Max nonetheless thought that *culturally* it was an advantage to be "mixed-race" because the kids can get exposure to culture from both sides of the family. He said: "I think it's neat that the kids are getting everything. . . . You may lose some things [ethnic culture], especially down the generations, but I think it's an advantage to be a mixed-race because of that." In line with his view that his kids had the "best of both worlds," that is, not being stigmatized because of too much racial difference but getting the cultural benefits of being in a multiracial family, Max did not foresee any problems for their children in terms of racism or identity. This contrasted his wife's view; she definitely "anticipated" that their kids would have identity issues just as she had growing up. In fact, Max outrightly declared that: "I see interracial marriage as an instrument of assimilation."

This downplaying of the racial dimension also involved repeated assertions by many White spouses that they did not see their kids, or even their wives (except under certain circumstances), as "different" from themselves, and that it is not fruitful to dwell on the issue of race since it matters so little.[27] Regarding his wife, Luke said: "So, Asian-White is different from Black-White. I don't know why; it's just the way I've always felt. I'll use the poor example of my wife. . . . Most of the time, I don't even think that she's Chinese, and then I look at her and the light will hit her in a certain way, and I'm like, wow, I'm married to an American-Chinese."

To be sure, other works have shown that for many interracial couples, subjective awareness of racial differences subsides as they move more deeply into the relationship, where committed couples begin to see themselves more as individuals and human beings (despite how the wider society views them),[28] and that "deprioritizing racial difference" of mixed-race couples is often a strategy to deal with the society's negative stereotypes of interracial couples; couples often "cope with the negative attention and stereotypes associated with the discourse of homogamy by defining themselves as altogether unremarkable or unexceptional" and by claiming that race does not matter in their relationships and within the privacy of their homes, even if regarded as significant in public.[29] I suggest that for my participants, such deprioritizing of racial difference within interracial marriages also may occur, but that this may be more pronounced for the White partner.

When asked if he ever thought about the biraciality of his kids before they were born, Luke ruminated that before their kids were born, he and his wife Kira would speculate quite often about how their kids would look—wondering about what kinds of facial features the kids would have, including hair color, nose shape, and eyelids—suggesting the couple's obvious interest in and curiosity about the matter of racial blending. But when queried about whether he had anything to comment about challenges raising biracial kids, Luke did not think there was anything particularly worrisome; when I brought up the "pulling eye" incident suffered by his son in school that was mentioned to me by his wife Kira, he asserted that he did not think this was an insulting incident in the least since he thought "Asian eyes were cool."[30] Though cognizant of the racial difference of his kids to some degree, Luke is clearly uninvested in viewing that as an issue of great concern or even importance.[31]

Sam, Sarah's husband, similarly diverged from his wife's perspective, directly contradicting his wife's deep concerns about their children's identity and race issues and the school project incident that was fully disclosed to me earlier; he revealed no awareness of any difficulties that came from being biracial: "Yeah, I would say that they probably have as normal a childhood as you can have—I don't think anyone at school or anything has ever said anything to them. Although they look Asian—they look a lot more like Sarah than they look like me—I don't think people think of them as being Asian or different or anything." He also commented on the difference having an English-sounding last name may make for his kids: "I mean because their last names don't sound Asian . . . I don't think their friends or anyone at school has ever said anything to them. They're very active in sports and activities, and they are very busy with them."[32] In fact, Sam drew parallels between his kids' Asian heritage with his mixed-European heritage, which he did not have to "think about too much." When asked if he thought his kids identified with either race in particular, he said that he did not think they were much aware of their biraciality at all. He remarked: "I don't even know if they think about it to tell you the truth because sometimes, like we're waiting for dinner and all of a sudden, my daughter will say, 'Mommy, are you Chinese or something?'"[33]

While it may be true that kids at a young age may not be clearly aware of what biraciality entails—though some findings do indicate that race-learning actually begins for children at a very young age[34]—the point here is that Sam, in dramatic contrast to his wife, does not see such comments as a beginning of ethnic self-discovery or a potential challenge the kids will contend with when they are older. Furthermore, while he acknowledged that his wife "may have a different perspective from [his] own," he did not think that his kids would face much race-related adversity, implying his view of his kids' racial/ethnic identity as optional. In fact, he pointed out how his kids had mostly White friends and said that he envisioned them marrying Whites.[35]

## *Asianness as "Harmless" Difference and Discursive Displacement of Race with Culture*

Minimizing the significance of race and racial difference in the context of colorblind ideology also involves framing Asian racial and cultural difference as a source of harmless difference and/or uniqueness, unlike the difference posed for example by being Black, which is seen as having undesirable real-life consequences. First, this minimization involved downplaying the negative dimensions of Asian "difference" and highlighting instead the positive value of Asian-ethnic cultures as a kind of ethnic-cultural capital that may render the mixed-race children "special," "different," and "unique." When asked why she emphasizes Chinese culture in her family, Susan, Matt's White wife, commented: "Well, because there *is* something to emphasize. There is a cultural difference, there is different food, there's different clothing, and there are different stories, whereas I feel like with my own background, there is not a cultural difference. . . . It's really important to me that they [my kids] know their cultural background, to know the historical background. And you know, it's fun—it's fun to have something different." The sense that this cultural difference adds uniqueness and even "fun" to the kids' culture and identity is reverberated by one of the White husbands who commented: "I enjoy Chinese culture. I love my wife. I love her family. I think the customs are kind of cool. . . . Anything new for me is kind of cool. So I don't have any issue with the kids learning Chinese, and I am actually quite happy that they do it."

An interesting dimension was the extent to which some White spouses tended to contrast the "cool," "special," and "fun" difference of their children and their partners' culture/ethnicity by constructing their own backgrounds and their own families as "lacking" in culture and ethnic identity. Some specifically referred to their own families as being "cultureless," "white bread," and "boring," to which their non-White spouses can add exoticism and difference.[36] In fact, for Ellen, one of the reasons that she found the prospect of marrying her Chinese American husband exciting was because he was "different," a source of diversity for her in her life, and this was a major attraction for her. This characterization of Whites of their own families as being "cultureless" or "colorless" is quite commonplace, as attested by other studies:

> when Whites are prompted to discuss the matter [being White] . . . they often see whiteness as obscure, empty, or boring. . . . Many use racialized "others" . . . to construct White identity—in other words, they write of who they are by referring to who they are not. . . . White identities have three commonplace elements: they are constructed as empty, passive. . . . Mirrored against the cultures of people of color, whiteness often seems to lack content.[37]

The perception of whiteness's lack of content illustrates the "transparency" of whiteness, a situation in which because whiteness is such an unacknowledged norm that Whites are not aware of their own racial identity and privilege.[38] Calvin revealed this sentiment with his admission that his attraction to Chinese culture was due to the fact that he was "looking for something as different as possible" from the bland, undistinctive White culture that he grew up with, so he never saw marrying a Chinese-ethnic as a "big deal." This is in contrast to the considerable angst expressed by his wife about intermarriage. In Luke's words: "I like the difference. Being married to a Chinese woman is cool."

Second, for a number of White spouses, diffusing the "difference" of Asianness and formulating this difference in more innocuous terms involved varying forms of displacement of race with culture.[39] The first displacement of race with culture emerges in some of the White parents' construction of the race-related challenges their kids faced as arising from differences of their children's "culture" and "background" rather than of "race," disclosing their investment in, and desire for, a colorblind society that they felt could accept Asians. For example, relating an incident in which some peers made fun of her son about a Chinese custom, Susan explained: "And they [the White kids] were . . . doing it to my son because he was part Chinese, and it really upset him . . . But they weren't attacking him personally, but they were teasing him because of his background [culture]." I have found that this kind of displacement of race with culture is sometimes extended to the marital relationship. One White wife, when asked about any race-related marital challenges arising from being married to an Asian American, said there were challenges, but explained, "it has nothing to do with race. It's about our life experiences and how we grew up. . . . So it's more about that."

The second kind of such displacement of race with culture also took the form of downplaying racial difference, but this time by stressing the *similarity* of Asian "culture" with White middle-class culture. These similarities included such values as emphasis on education, expectations for delayed gratification and hard work, and high expectations regarding scholarly and other types of endeavors for children, values thought to be common to the "Asian" Confucian ethic and the Western Protestant ethic. Sam related that his parents were happy with his choice of wife despite the fact that she was not White, because, although he cannot say that his family did not care about religion or race, they did care that his mate be "smart, nice looking, and educated." In fact, his parents were unhappy with his brother's new White wife because she did not have a college education.

For most of the White husbands in my study, the generally high socioeconomic class status of their wives' families seemed to affirm their pre-conceptions of Asians as "smart," "educated," "good at math," "more intelligent than an average Caucasian," which they thought worked to the advantage of their children's upward mobility. Luke went as far as to state a belief that his son's high intelligence can be attributed partly to his being part Chinese: "So the other thing is that my first son is pretty smart. He is tested into the accelerated classes, so that's the Chinese part. Yeah, I associate Chinese with being really smart." Although emphasizing cross-racial similarities, rather than differences, is one feature of colorblindness,[40] what is suggested by these narratives is that with Asians Americans in particular, class can perhaps come to trump race in some instances, though this may not apply to other racial minority groups.

Not surprisingly, the White spouses are generally optimistic about their children's futures, in contrast to the guardedness shown by their Asian-ethnic spouses. This is particularly interesting because many White spouses were aware of the challenges their young children were already facing in school as mixed-raced children. Regarding her children's identity and personal development, Susan remarked:

> I think it will be smooth. I think that the environment that they're growing up in, they're not called out on their background. They're not teased consistently for being or looking a certain way or sounding a certain way. I actually think you know—I think their peers respect the fact that they're learning Chinese and that they were going to China. They think that's pretty cool. And like I said, the environment they are in at school, there are tons of biracial kids. And everybody is pretty much in the same socio-economic class.

Luke's statement, paralleling Susan's, presents a similar perspective. When asked if he ever worried about his kids facing any challenges in the future because they are biracial, he commented: "Not really . . . I myself didn't grow up with any of it [racism], so I didn't have to worry about it. I am White, I'm a guy. I'm okay . . . I grew up more noticing Black people than Asians, so if I had married maybe a Black woman, I might think about it more." Though admitting that there is always a possibility that his kids may face race-related challenges, he added, "But I think in today's society, there are so many differences and mixes that that's becoming fewer and fewer, so that you hope that by the time they get older, it won't be a problem. Plus, Kira and I gravitate towards the city more than lily-White towns . . . where the kids can feel comfortable." Again, as discussed earlier, surface optimism of both comments implies an important caveat, that their biracial children will be all right as long as they are in the right class and social environment, that is, in pockets of the urban, middle-/upper-middle class environment, revealing awareness of all the parents, White and Asian alike, of the ongoing pervasiveness of racism outside of these rarified spaces.

## Interracial Couples Negotiating Ethnic Cultures and Race: The Impact of Majority Spousal Support in Ethnic Retention

With mainstream, middle-class White culture operating as the "default," normative American culture, how do couples negotiate multicultural and multiracial family-making? More specifically, what difference does the Asian-ethnic spouses' revitalization of racial consciousness and ethnic culture/identity actually make in interracial marriage cultural negotiations, particularly against the colorblind worldviews embraced by the majority of the White spouses? As discerned thus far, interracial families are not spaces where racial and cultural differences will simply melt away as predicted by classic assimilation theories, but may be sites of ongoing contestation, controversy, and competing interests between the partners.[41] This is what the interracially married couples in this study experience, especially as the Asian-ethnic partners struggle to maintain and integrate elements of their cultures and identities in the face of possible cultural dilution. The quality and level of Asian-ethnic cultural integration, however, as well as the degree of contestation involved in this process, depends a great deal on the receptivity and cooperation of White spouses, as well as on the Asian-ethnic participants' own level of ethnic cultural competence and racial consciousness.

As discussed earlier, the colorblind ideologies of the White spouses in this study are tempered somewhat by the competing discourse of multiculturalism, with most of the White spouses viewing themselves as valuing Asian-ethnic/cultural difference as positive, special and unique, even if they also often trivialize it as something that adds color to the normative White experience. This stance at least renders most White spouses positively disposed toward including Asian-ethnic cultures in their family lives. This positive stance may explain my finding that the overall amount of *overt* conflict or tension involved in the couples' mutual cultural/ethnic negotiations was surprisingly low. I have found, however, that the level of support for Asian-ethnic cultural retention provided by the White spouse varied, falling into two general categories: 1) a laissez-faire approach to ethnic cultural retention in which the White spouses were on board in practice and by default as long as their spouses took the lead; 2) a more active support of and participation in Asian-ethnic cultural retention by spouses who were more aware of and attuned to the issues of race and ethnic/cultural identities in the lives of their spouse, children, and family. In both cases, however, Asian-ethnic cultural elements were selectively incorporated into the family lives only to the extent that the Asian-ethnic spouse was competent to do so and resulted in different levels of blending of Asian-ethnic and White mainstream cultural features, but in no case was the hybridized cultural outcome fully bi-cultural or configured on equal terms.

## Laissez-Faire Approach to Ethnic Cultural Retention

The power of the mainstream culture is reflected in the majority of White partners' narratives regarding ethnic cultural transmission of Asian-ethnic cultures, which were notably more "laissez-faire" than their Asian spouses' attitudes. As stated, most of the White spouses possessed a quite open-minded and positive attitude regarding Asian-ethnic cultural retention within their families; no one expressed problems with integrating Asian-ethnic cultures into their family lives, and most registered approval, even enthusiasm, of their kids learning aspects of their spouse's ethnic culture since it made kids different and special. Further, the White spouses' lack of resistance stemmed from their perception that ethnic cultural knowledge would be advantageous in the current global and multicultural environment. However, one caveat was that almost all White spouses in this group admitted that they were fine with it only if their spouses took the initiative. When asked how important it was for the kids to know about their Chinese culture and heritage, Luke, who is quite enthusiastic about his kids learning Chinese culture, put it this way: "Okay, so I think if there is anything I can do to open up their minds, that's good; difference is really good. So it's the Chinese part they get because Kira is Chinese, and I also find it really interesting. So I don't really have any issues with it. If Kira didn't push it though, I wouldn't be the one to push it." Indeed, this remark confirms Kira's earlier comment expressing frustration with her husband's passivity, as well as Sarah's disgruntlement with her husband's lack of initiative regarding ethnic cultural maintenance.

Saying that he just wanted his kids to learn foreign languages in general, Sam also had this to say: "We always wanted the kids to learn other languages. We had Polish nannies—we wanted them to learn that, also learn Spanish at school. But then obviously, Sarah and her parents had been able to teach them a little bit of Chinese. And I am perfectly fine with it if she wanted to go that route and teach them." In other words, what seems to be implied in these comments is that the kids' getting Chinese culture is almost an accidental benefit that comes from having a Chinese American spouse, but what is important is that the kids receive some kind of "global" education, which might include different languages and ethnic cultures, and if it is Chinese, the better. This affirms findings by other studies that parents of mixed-race children, especially those who tend to embrace colorblindness and elide race in favor of "culture," often want to see their children raised as "global citizens."[42]

In fact, as noted earlier, almost all mentioned the practical and strategic advantage of learning Chinese in this global environment. One White husband even confessed that if it were 20 years ago, he would probably not have been happy about his wife pushing Chinese language on the kids since he would have seen no use for it except as ethnic transmission. One clear effect of the positive valuation of "Asian" cultural features, at least among the middle-class, professional participants in our multicultural historical moment, is the general lack of conflict over efforts at minority cultural retention. On the other hand, these cases also clearly demonstrate the ongoing White majority privilege that allows the White partners the luxury of approaching ethnic retention within the families as an optional activity, or to view the mainstream culture as the "default," so that ethnic retention is unlikely unless the Asian-ethnic partner takes the initiative.

## Proactive Approach to Ethnic Cultural Retention

Although the majority of the White spouses in this study took a laissez-faire approach to Asian-ethnic/cultural retention, about one-fifth of White spouses took a more active approach to sustaining the Asian-ethnic culture and identity within the family. An interesting finding was that the White female spouses in my sample were generally less passive about Asian-ethnic cultural maintenance than their White male counterparts, and in some cases, they were more proactive about helping their children engage with their husbands' ethnic cultures. Furthermore, these wives were likely to be more concerned about their children's ethnic identity and were visibly more sensitive about enabling their children's awareness about their ethnic heritage.

The White wives in my study, for example, were keen on having their kids learn the language of their husbands and took an active interest in maintaining some of the major ethnic rituals of their husbands' families and instilling awareness in their children about their ethnic identity. Susan, for example, explained that the reason that her family tries hard to emphasize the "Chinese side of things" was precipitated by a disturbing incident that made her realize the need to transmit to her children the knowledge and value of Chinese culture:

> One day at a department store, when my daughter was about four, a big banner went up with different children's faces and she said, "Look mommy, that girl looks like me!" and I said, "She does. She's Chinese just like you," but then she said "I'm not Chinese!" So she visibly identified with an Asian child but that was it. That's when I realized, oh my gosh, we're doing something wrong! So then I said [to] my daughter, "Of course you are Chinese." And she said, "No, grandpa is Chinese, daddy is Chinese!"

Susan explained that after that, she and her husband made concerted efforts to transmit knowledge about their Chinese identity and culture to their kids and "really encouraged them to know that they're different and special and to be proud of who they are." In fact, she stated that she began taking the lead in this effort, as her husband was "highly assimilated" and up to then had been rather passive about keeping his ethnicity and culture alive. With her active support and encouragement, not only did she and her husband become a team in ethnic cultural retention, but her husband began to be more enthusiastic about embracing his ethnic culture. From then on, the couple made sure that they celebrated Chinese holidays, ate Chinese food, taught the kids about Chinese history, and made plans to teach the children the Chinese language.

Another such White spouse was Ellen, who very much saw herself as the "driving force" behind the family's efforts to include Chinese culture. She talked about her extremely "Americanized" husband, whom she said basically rejected his ethnic culture and identity and decided at an early age that he wanted "nothing to do with Asian women" and never dated one, and the extent to which she had to make most of the effort to keep the Chinese component alive. For example, she was the one who insisted that their kids attend Chinese language school; she complained that her husband did not even attempt to speak to their kids in Chinese or take them to Chinese school. She wondered if it was because the women in the family, of any race, tended to be the main force behind the passing on of ethnic culture: "I don't know if this is true, that it is the female that typically dominates the ethnic aspects of the family, but I feel like I have done my best in a lot of ways to do all the ethnic stuff, like stuff for Chinese New Year, reading books about China, and making sure we spend a lot of time in China-town, almost every weekend. . . . I was even ready to move to Chinatown. . . . My husband's mom thinks I'm basically Chinese." Ellen enviously observed that, whether true or not, families with Asian American moms tended to have much more "Asian" kids who seemed to be getting much more "exposure" to Asian cultures. Ellen also revealed some cognizance of the importance of race in saying that because her kids happened to *look* more Asian than White, it was important that they know that part of their heritage. Despite her husband's lack of involvement in Chinese culture, Ellen was also one of the few who explicitly believed that all her kids would likely identify as Chinese when they grew up, rather than biracial, because their dad was Chinese and they had Chinese last names.

## The Possible Significance of Gender

Although it is difficult to generalize about the particularities of the White wives' attitudes from the limited sample in this study, other studies have also provided similar evidence, suggesting what may be an intriguing pattern. Mia Tuan, for instance, describes one highly assimilated male respondent in her study whose White wife was also the "driving force" behind the couples' efforts to incorporate Chinese culture in their family life.[43] Jessica Vasquez, in her recent work on interracially married Latinos, also finds a similar pattern of White wives actively supporting or and even taking charge of maintaining the husband's Latino culture in the family, while conversely, even supportive White husbands took a more passive role in following their Hispanic wives' lead.[44] Why would this be the case? Why might White wives be more attuned to the issue of race regarding their mixed-race families?

Scholars have suggested that this may be because, in most cultures, women may be the "symbolic bearers of ethnicity."[45] In the case of interracially married women, they are similar to those described by Joane Nagel as "ethnic sojourners/ settlers," individuals who come to identify with their minority spouse's culture and work hard to pass it down, or what Tomas Jiménez refers to as those with "affiliative ethnic identity."[46] Another explanation may have to do with the fact that White women who are interracially married benefit a lot less from their own White privilege than White men who are married to women of color; White women who are married to men of color *lose* their White privilege by being viewed as less "White" than prior to being married and therefore become more cognizant of and attuned to the issues of race once they are married and have mixed-race children. Maria Root writes:

> In general, White women seemed to be most affected by how their biracial children changed them in the eyes of strangers. No longer quite White enough in the White world, and under suspicion in the non-White world, life gave these women a crash course in racial self-defense. For many of these mothers, awareness of White privilege was heightened by witnessing racial discrimination, however subtle, toward their children.[47]

This phenomenon of actively supportive White female spouses spotlights that White spouses can experience heightened racial consciousness through marriages with minority spouses and also challenges the classic assimilation theory that the minority cultures are likely to be "absorbed," or minimized, into the dominant majority culture through interracial marriage. This also parallels findings by Eileen O'Brien, who has argued that cross-racial/ethnic intimacies can sometimes foster a "racially progressive" stance in the majority partner as the majority partner comes to experience and empathize with the racialized experiences of the minority partner or the couple's mixed-race children.[48]

Only one female respondent in my study stated that her non-Asian husband was more enthusiastic about transmitting ethnic culture than she was, and that was Janet, the Korean American woman mentioned in Chapter 3, who is married to a Black mixed-race man. Janet's case was extremely interesting because Janet's trajectory involved a radical rejection of her family in her early adulthood due to her family's restrictive approach to women. But because her Black mixed-race husband had intimate knowledge about the issues and challenges faced by mixed-race kids, he led the charge regarding cultural retention, including "coaching" and coaxing Janet herself with regard to these issues and in making sure that the kids would know about their Korean heritage, in addition to their White and Black heritage, and take pride in them.

## Inter-Family Dynamics

While overt conflicts over Asian-ethnic cultural maintenance within these marriages appear minimal, what were the dynamics between the families of the couples? Studies of interracial marriages between Blacks and Whites in particular document hostile reactions of both White and Black families toward these interracial unions.[49] In the case of my participants, stories of overt resistance or opposition to the participants' marriages, or to their efforts at ethnic maintenance, from respective families were minimal. This is not to deny the existence of some initial tensions and of the racial/cultural dynamics between the families of which the participants were aware. Sonia, the 38-year-old Indian American, reported, for example, that while her immigrant parents did not object to her White spouse because they deemed him reliable, educated, and a "good husband" material, there were initially some tensions between the two families, which came to a head in some "cultural clashes" during wedding planning. Although Sonia claimed that these tensions have since mostly dissipated, she also vacillated in her discussion about this; while she said the interaction between the families has been pretty "positive" and that there was no racially inflected "power issue" between the two families, she belied this comment by registering an awareness of a subtle racial hierarchy.

Sonia suspected that her husband's family might be respectful toward hers because her parents are "successful" and highly educated. Then she demurred that there was no overt "power issue" between the families, at the same time admitting that there *was* the "issue of culture," especially in relation to the kids. She described this in the following way: "I don't sense a power issue, like you should do it our way because we are superior . . . but there is definitely that issue of culture. Like I could sense that they might feel like oh, our kids [are] going to turn out more Indian, you know what I mean? Or, my parents also feel like my kids are going to turn out to be [the] other way . . . and they actually verbalized it. . . . They were worried that they [the kids] would identify more strongly with his [the husband's] culture."

Others also stressed the relative decline of any family-related "conflicts" having to do with race- or culture-related tensions as time went on, but some participants registered the presence of subtle and backhanded racism against the Asian-ethnic side. According to Susan, this took the form of a not-altogether positive reaction her husband received from her grandparents when she first brought him to their home, wherein he received cringe-worthy race-related remarks such as being asked whether her husband's family owned a restaurant, and whether they use chopsticks for eating turkey for Thanksgiving, and so on. Sarah, the Chinese American participant, also related that when she and her husband first announced their marriage, her husband's parents repeatedly questioned him in a backhanded way about the sagacity of marrying Sarah owing to their "very different cultural backgrounds." According to both Sonia and Sarah, any initial tensions between the families have all but disappeared since the marriage and the birth of children, and Sarah in particular emphasized that the lack of or decline in "cultural issues" within their family-making was due to their similarity in the two families' "values"—echoing remarks presented earlier by White spouses Sam and Luke—such as agreements on the importance of education, a focus on academics, and hard work. Again, for interracially married participants in this study, the convergence between White professional middle-class American and Asian "model minority" virtues appears to serve as a common ground for White and Asian American couples that may help mitigate challenges arising from racial differences.

Indeed, it might bear reiterating that compared to White-Black couples, Asian-White couples, especially if they share similar class backgrounds, face less opposition from the families and society at large because of the dividends Asian-ethnics garner as the putative "model minority." Surprising views held by some White participants discussed earlier that the term interracial applied to White-Black couplings only, and not to White-Asian couplings, were paralleled in the narratives of other White spouses as well. Helen, a 42-year-old spouse of a Chinese American, noted similarly that her family held "prejudices," but it was "more for Blacks," an "African American kind of thing." When she and her husband decided to get married, it raised a few eyebrows—she heard a few of her parents' friends saying things such as "Well, at least he's [Helen's husband] not Black"—but no outright opposition because "He's not White but he's not Black either." As for her Asian in-laws, Helen described a satisfactory relationship with her mother-in-law, who "went out of her way" to make Helen feel accepted, and Helen registered a high degree of enthusiasm for the goal of Chinese cultural retention, expressing particular admiration for the "demanding" and discipline-focused nature of "Asian" cultures to which she, as a more "relaxed" non-Asian, felt could bring a "happy balance."[50]

## Conclusion

One of the central findings of this chapter is the Asian American parents' unexpected rekindling of interest in ethnic identity and culture as they begin having and raising children. This reawakened interest is activated by their realization of the need to pass down elements of ethnic culture and identity to their mixed-race children, which then leads to a serious reevaluation of their own relationship to their ethnic identity/culture and the issues of race. As discussed, most participants in my study who are interracially married belong in the category of those who sought an assimilative path into the mainstream U.S. culture as youths, so this rekindled passion about their ethnic identity/culture and racial issues upon marriage and children is arresting, especially in light of unilinear assimilation theories that suggest interracial marriage contributes to the gradual process of sloughing of one's ethnic identity and culture.

What this chapter has illustrated is that one of the major reasons for this recommitment to ethnic revitalization, in whatever form, is connected to fear of cultural erasure, and is an important strategy against racism and potential racism, even when the participants themselves may have wished to continue distancing themselves from their own ethnicity. Several participants explicitly stated that they would not be bothering with ethnic transmission were it not for their kids. However, given the ongoing prevalence of racism and social marginalization of minority persons of color in the United States, and the recognition that even some of the mixed-raced children may be undergoing racist treatment that may lead to "internalized racism," participants begin to recognize the acute need to teach their children about having pride in themselves and who they are.[51] Even if the majority of the participants may wish to accept a benign form of multi-culturalist discourse, this racial awareness becomes a necessity for the participants and their children.

This finding connects to many existing studies on mixed-raced children, which counterintuitively show that the strength of ethnic and/or racial identi-fication for biracial individuals may not necessarily decrease with "assimilation" but may actually increase with the higher generational status.[52] Another eye-opening finding of this chapter arises from the discourses of the White partners, especially the ways in which the White partners are able to cleave closer to a colorblind discourse when talking about their marital relationships and their children, indicating their access to the invisible but still powerful White privi-lege that offers them the ability to more realistically imagine a colorless world ideally devoid of racial inequalities. My findings here are also supported by existing studies; a study by Goar et al. for instance finds that although White parents of mixed-race children actually tend to embrace two main discursive frames, "colorblindness" and "race consciousness," White participants fell for the most part into the "colorblind" spectrum although there were some who operated within intertwined discursive frameworks of "colorblindness" *and* "race consciousness."[53] Indeed, as we saw in this chapter, some White spouses' comparative lack of awareness about race that accompany their preference for a colorblind worldview is underscored by some White spouses' admission that being married to an Asian-ethnic partner has helped them become much more aware of race over time.[54] Others, whether or not they were cognizant of racial issues, still viewed their children and their spouses as adding a kind of "flavor" to their lives; this dovetails with Kimberly DaCosta's observation about the wider society's perspective on multiracial families: "The legalization of intermarriage, along with popular representations of multiracial families as heterosexual and nuclear, leads to interpretations of multiracial families as an interesting 'flavor' of the normative family."[55]

The interracial couples in this study did not appear to engage in many overt conflicts over cultural transmission issues, in most cases indicating benign forms of agreement about what to do. With both partners broadly operating within an implicit worldview of benevolent multiculturalism, the couples seemed to deal with cultural or ethnic issues as they came up, mostly because none of them seemed quite prepared for the kinds of experiences that they and their children would undergo. This does not mean, however, that tensions between the couples did not exist. The ethnic-racial "awakening" of the Asian American partner in itself can be inherently politicizing even if in subtle ways, and I certainly detected subtle jockeying between the couples about what to privilege in the cultural transmission to their children.

Despite the shared discursive context of multiculturalism, the most common outcome of the cultural/ethnic negotiations for the couples appears to be a form of selective incorporation of the minority ethnic culture into the family life but rarely on equal terms with the majority culture. This departs from findings by some recent studies that portray possibilities for a more optimistic and egalitarian picture of bicultural blending between the majority and minority cultures within interracial families.[56] The level and kind of cultural blending achieved within the families in this study depend first on the competence and efforts of the Asian-ethnic spouse, and second, on the cooperation of the non-Asian spouse, but in either case, efforts to configure biculturalism on an equal basis are an uphill battle in the face of overwhelming pull of mainstream culture and rarely met with success. The next two chapters will explore these themes closely in the context of Asian interethnic couples and family-making.

## Notes

1. Parts of this chapter has appeared in Chong 2013.
2. Rediscovery of "Americanness" during efforts to reclaim ethnic heritage is a part of the "in-betweenness" that is a recurring theme in literature on second generation immigrants. For example, see Kasinitz et al. (2004, 12, Chaps. 6, 8).
3. *Doljabi* is a traditional Korean celebration of a child's first birthday.
4. Song 2009, 340.
5. The view that grandparents acted as critical conduits of ethnic culture, especially for the kids, arose repeatedly in the narratives. One respondent said that because she had little knowledge of ethnic culture, she relied almost entirely on her mother to provide this knowledge, from language and cooking to stories (Cf. Dhingra 2007, 177; Kibria 2002, 2002; Tuan 1998, 110–11).
6. See for example Tuan 1998, 114, 134. Such findings are present in works on White ethnicity. Alba 1999; Gans 1979; Waters 1990.
7. For example, Dhingra 2007; Gibson 1988; Rumbaut 1997; Zhou and Bankston 1998.
8. Kibria 2002, 182. See also Song 2003; Yu 1999; and Yancey and Lewis 2009, 92–93.
9. See also O'Brien's study comparing Asian Americans and Latinos (2008, 95–123); she finds that for both groups, "fear of cultural/language loss" is a major concern for first generation parents in regard to their offspring and the most important motivation for encouraging inmarriage, although the strength of this concern is greater for Asian immigrants. See also Dhingra 2007, 177–81.
10. Cf. Sharon H. Chang 2016, 107. For a similar in-depth study of mixed-raced individuals and multiracial identities, see also works by Kimberly McClain DaCosta (2007). All these works document the extent to which mixed-race individuals are not exempt from racist treatment, racial stereotyping, and internalized racism. Chang (2016) notes that every single Asian multiracial parent in her study was racially targeted in their lives, and half of the Asian multiracial children interviewed already had been (52, 84).
11. See Lieberson and Waters 1988; Murguia 1982; O'Brien 2008; Saenz et al. 1995; Spickard 1989; Waters 1990. Yancey and Lewis (2009, 92–93) observe that although the extent to which biracial and multiracial individuals lose their identity with their minority community is unknown, the likelihood of their "leakage" or assimilation into the majority group, culture, and identity is high, the group/culture that is more

highly valued by society and to which biracial or multiracials will likely be more accepted than monoracial minorities. This is the case especially if efforts are not made by the parents to help retain the minority culture/identity.

12. Cf. Kibria 2002, 105–6.
13. Kibria 2002, 166–68.
14. Bystydizienski 2011, 63–68. Studies of interracially married Latinos reveal a similar influence of children that leads parents to a more positive shift toward and valuing of their ethnic cultures, as well as a desire to live in parts of the country with a larger number of co-ethnics or co-racials. See Wielding 2003, 49–50.
15. DaCosta 2007, 180.
16. Cf. Feliciano 2001.
17. For example, see DaCosta 2007, 132.
18. DaCosta 2007, 312.
19. Cf. O'Brien 2008, 206.
20. Frankenberg 1993.
21. Doane 2003, 13. See also Bonilla-Silva 2014; Carr 1997.
22. Lee and Bean 2004; Strmic-Pawl 2016.
23. Although the views expressed by my participants and also held by many in contemporary U.S. society would seem to suggest that Whites see Asians as closer to Whites—thereby viewing White-Asian marriages as more acceptable than White-Black marriages—there is also evidence that White-Asian marriages are still considered the *least* desirable to Whites, along with Black-White marriages (less desirable than Latino-White marriages, for example). See Steinbugler 2012, 119; Root 2001, 53.
24. Paul Spickard's (1989) notes that during WWII, interned Japanese American/White interracial families (about 1400 families) with White husbands were allowed to return to civilian life and relocate anywhere (i.e., they were considered "White"), whereas families with Japanese American husbands could relocate only to certain places. White women in interracial marriages are viewed to be less able to exercise this type of White privilege, but Whites in general, both males and females, have more power to construct their families in a colorblind way, or as White, if they so desire.
25. Vasquez 2017, 95; Cf. Chang 2016, 131.
26. Steinbugler 2012, 109.
27. Chang observes, "although all parents of mixed-race Asian children resisted talking about race, White parents were notably less likely to do so. This is distressing given over two-thirds of their multiracial Asian children had already shown race recognition and at least half of those same children had already experienced racism. By contrast, of the parents who said they did talk about race, 79 percent were parents of color" (Chang 2016, 128).
28. Bystydzienski 2011, 112.
29. Killian 2003, 11; Killian refers to this as a kind of "duality" or "double consciousness" in that the couples may see themselves one way, and see society as perceiving them in another way (15). Karis 2003, 28; Rosenblatt et al. 1995.
30. Cf. O'Brien 2008, 174. Cf. Chang (2016, 168)'s discussion about the present re-conceptualization of biracial or mixed-racial children and the glamorization of "hybrid vigor," a romanticization of mixed-race people as somehow genetically superior and better looking.
31. Other studies have also noted that the racial minority partners may be more acutely aware of racism and prejudices toward their interracial partnering and families in general but that they may be reluctant to talk about it to their partners (e.g., Killian 2003, 11). Another author states, "The limitations of current racial discourse make it difficult for members of multiracial families to communicate about the complicated racial realities of their lives. The assertion that race does not matter within the privacy

of interracial couples' homes might mean that race does not matter in the stereotypical ways that society assumes" (Karis 2003, 29). See also Dalmage 2000.

32. The results are mixed on this issue, with some studies showing that mothers in general have stronger influence in ethnic transmission (therefore children with non-White mothers tend to have stronger ethnic/racial identity) and other studies showing that children tend to more strongly identify with the ethnicity of the father. This appears to hold true whether the father is White or non-White. See, for example, Saenz et al. 1995, 186; Xie and Goyette 1997, 565; Waters 1989.

33. In her book on Asian mixed-race children, Chang (2016) notes the extent to which parents of such children tend to think that their mixed-race children are not that cognizant of race when young.

34. Chang 2016, Chap. 3.

35. See Root (2001, 152–53) for similar findings about how unprepared most parents of biracial or multiracial children are about challenging racial experiences of the children. Chang's (2016) study about White spouses' colorblind stance strongly echoes my findings (See Chapter 6 in particular).

36. Hughey 2012.

37. McKinney and Feagin 2003, 235, 248. See also Hughey 2012; Twine and Gallagher 2008.

38. Doane 2003; Frankenberg 1993.

39. Cf. Goar et al. 2017. Similar displacement of race with culture has also been found in other studies. See Vasquez 2017, 92.

40. Frankenberg 1993.

41. See DaCosta 2007, 186; Steinbugler 2012.

42. For example, see Goar et al. 2017, 349.

43. Tuan 1998, 114.

44. Vasquez 2017.

45. For examples, see DasGupta and DasGupta 1996; Vasquez 2017, 125–26. See also Yuval-Davis 1997, 46.

46. Jiménez 2010a; Nagel 2003.

47. Root 2001, 140. See also Reddy 1994.

48. O'Brien 2008. See also Steinbugler (2012), who points out that racial-awakening or a shift toward racial-progressiveness does not happen in all cases.

49. For example, see Childs 2005.

50. Like Ellen earlier, Helen also registered pride in her children identifying as Chinese and predicting they will identify as Chinese.

51. Cf. Song 2003; King-O'Riain 2014.

52. For example, see Xie and Goyette 1997. See also Ellman (1987) and Salgado de Snyder et al. (1982) which show that contrary to assimilationist perspectives, children of intermarriage do not always necessarily gravitate toward the majority parent identity or group.

53. Goar et al. 2017.

54. Cf. Vasquez 2017.

55. DaCosta 2007, 175.

56. For example, see Vasquez 2017. In her research on Latino interracial marriages, Vasquez outlines four typologies of "biculturalisms" (a two-way blending of cultures) that ranges from "Leaning White" to "Leaning Latino," with two middle categories "Everyday Biculturalism" and "Selective Blending." The two middle categories represent a balanced blending of Latino and mainstream American cultures.

# 5

# MARRYING WITHIN THE RACIAL FOLD

## Romantic Appeal of Co-Racials

Interethnic marriages are on the rise among Asian Americans.[1] In the last decade or so, mass media outlets began to take notice. A 2012 *New York Times* article by Rachel Swarns, "For Asian American Couples, A Tie That Binds," is one example.[2] The story spotlights the declining trend in interracial marriages among Asian Americans, especially to Whites, and the increase in pan-Asian interethnic marriages. Although the story includes examples of inmarried couples as well, it highlights the visibility and importance of growing intra-Asian attraction and unions. The story proffers two major reasons for this trend: mutual cultural comfort and understanding as well as the ability to maintain certain aspects of ethnic cultural traditions with greater ease. A 2012 *Wall Street Journal* article by Jeff Yang, "The Reason Why Asian Americans Are Outmarrying Less," is another in-depth attempt to tackle this mystery and also serves as a response to Swarns's article.[3] Yang has a slightly different take on the reasons; although Yang agrees with the "mutual cultural comfort" thesis that "allows aspects of life other than race and ethnicity" to come to the fore for interethnic couples, he disagrees that a burning desire to "preserve" ethnic culture serves as a main reason why Asian-ethnics marry other Asian-ethnics. In other words, while Asian Americans may achieve a life more insulated from the daily grind of race-related struggles by coupling with fellow Asian-ethnics, they are more "American" than we would think. Yang also speculates that improved societal and media images of Asian Americans may contribute to the growing interethnic attraction.

This chapter explores the important phenomenon of Asian American interethnic marriage, focusing on some of the reasons why U.S.-born/-raised Asian Americans may increasingly opt for co-racials as mates. As discussed in the introductory chapters, of all Asian Americans who intermarry, more Asian Americans still interracially marry than interethnically marry.[4] Between 2006 to 2010, however, the frequency of Asian interethnic marriage has increased by greater than 8% among all Asian Americans and over 15% for U.S.-raised and/or –born Asian Americans.[5] We do not know what the future holds for intra-Asian marriage, but the issue and dynamics of intra-Asian marriages beg a closer investigation because these marriages open up the question of the ongoing and changing salience of race and ethnic identification in the lives of Asian-ethnics in the United States and what "assimilation" might look like for this group.

In this chapter, I first tease out some key factors, informed from the stories of the interethnically married participants, which shape romantic preferences and marital choices of U.S.-raised and/or –born Asians. Moreover, this and the next chapter will investigate the nature of hybrid panethnic cultures and identities constructed within these marriages and families and discuss their implications for the incorporative process of Asian Americans.

## Development of Interethnic Romantic and Marital Preferences

Dennis is a 39-year-old second-generation Vietnamese American living in a West Coast city, married to a Korean American. He grew up in a West Coast town with diverse race and ethnic populations that included a large number of Asian Americans and Whites, as well as Latinos. The way Dennis describes it, he went through "distinct phases" growing up in terms of his attraction to the opposite sex. He grew up initially having crushes on White girls, like a lot of other Asian boys he knew, and then toward his high school years, became more attracted to a "wider range of" women, including Asian American women. According to Dennis, this is partly a result of his becoming involved primarily with the "smart," if not a bit "nerdy," Asian American cliques. In college, Dennis's friendship group widened to include diverse ethnic/racial individuals, but the core was Asian Americans. During this period and after college, Dennis dated women from different racial/ethnic backgrounds but found himself being attracted mainly to Asian American women. Dennis admits that during his post-college years, he consistently had in the back of his mind that marrying someone from an Asian background would be ideal because it would be easier "culturally," especially in relation to his parents. His parents never drummed into him to inmarry, although some of his relatives tried. He had come to a conclusion that he might want to marry someone who would understand his family dynamics and could get along with his aging parents.

In Chapter 3, we examined the ways in which desires for whiteness and White privilege played a substantial role in the identity development of interracially married Asian Americans. Whereas the majority of my participants in the interracially married group grew up in predominantly White neighborhoods,

which, in combination with parental stance on the desirability of acculturation and upward mobility, appears to have contributed to assimilative desires,
a notable aspect of the interethnically married individuals of my sample is that
their backgrounds in terms of neighborhoods and friendship associations were
far more varied. Like Dennis, the majority of interethnically married participants, about 75%, grew up in mixed-race/-ethnicity neighborhoods, with a
large concentration of Asian-ethnics. The rest grew up in predominantly White
neighborhoods. Again, while this study does not aim to generalize about the
effects of ethnic group size/composition, nor would it be possible to do so from
the limited qualitative sample of this study, the majority of interethnically married participants in this study report an early exposure to a critical mass of Asian
Americans within the context of racially diverse or predominantly Asian-ethnic
neighborhoods.

This situation suggests a couple of things. First, on a general level, such neigh-
borhoods/communities provide the demographic opportunity for same-race
contact. However, this does not constitute a sufficient explanation for interethnic
marriage since it does not explain why the participants chose to marry across
*ethnic* lines rather than within their own national/ethnic groups. For this, we
must look to the ways in which this environmental context comprises the cultural
backdrop for the development of panethnic identity/consciousness which can lay
the foundation for interethnic associations.[6]

Panethnicity, however, is an evolving process, and we will see that college—
often the place where the participants come into more extensive contact or engage
in more magnified interaction with other Asian-ethnics—serves as a pivotal period
for intensification or reinforcement of panethnicity. College was a particularly significant turning point for the small number in the sample who spent their early
years in primarily White neighborhoods because it provided opportunities to
experience ethnic rediscovery. Panethnic identification is only the starting point
for understanding interethnic marital choices, however. I argue that for my participants, parental attitudes about intermarriage interacts closely with panethnicity
as two major factors that can motivate cross-ethnic marriage. After a discussion of
intertwined influences of parental preferences and panethnic identity for fostering interethnic preferences, I highlight two reasons that are offered by my participants for considering other Asian-ethnics as desirable partners: one, a sense
of pan-Asian cultural affinity/compatibility that overrode desires for non-Asian
romantic partners, and two, preference for co-racials over co-ethnics (lack of desire
for inmarriage).

## The Role of Parental Influence

One surprisingly consistent factor in the narratives of my participants that contributed to their openness toward cross-ethnic marriage was parental position

regarding marriage.[7] The issue of parental influence was briefly discussed in Chapter 3, where for interracially married participants, the generally assimilative stance of many of the participants' parents toward their children—especially in regard to acculturation and the quest for academic and professional success coupled with being situated in a White-dominated environment—appeared to have influenced the participants' outlook regarding the viability of interracial marriages. Most parents of interethnically married participants demonstrated a similarly easygoing attitude toward marital choices, particularly in not pushing inmarriage, but about two-thirds of them seem to have differed from the parents of interracially married participants in communicating a stronger distaste for crossing "racial" boundaries in marriage.

As stated above, my interethnically married participants varied in terms of the kinds of neighborhoods in which they grew up, with a minority of my participants growing up in predominantly White areas and the majority, about 75%, growing up in ethnically/racially diverse neighborhoods with a strong presence of Asians. The mixture of friendship associations growing up varied also, depending on the neighborhood context. Those who grew up in areas with a critical mass of Asian Americans tended to form friendships that leaned heavily toward Asian Americans or co-ethnics, though this did not exclude friends of other race/ethnicities. Those who grew up mostly in White areas tended to have many White friends, though this did not necessarily exclude Asian American friendships. Regardless of the areas in which the participants grew up, or their friendship associations, one common theme that emerged in the narratives was related to parental attitudes toward and expectations regarding intermarriage, and the participants' desire to meet parental expectations.[8]

The majority of literature on Asian Americans highlights the existence of parental pressures on their children toward inmarriage; in this literature, the parents are often viewed as *obstacles* to outmarriage,[9] though the degree of success of these pressures remains unclear.[10] In contrast to these findings, what is pronounced in the narratives of my interethnically married participants is that the parents were relatively laissez-faire regarding the dating and marital choices of their children, though a few did express preference for co-ethnics when their children were young.[11] A Chinese American man married to a Japanese American stated that his parents did not care at all whom he married, while another Chinese American man married to a Japanese American, a 43-year-old named Cooper, explained that his family had "expectations" that he would marry a woman of Chinese ancestry but never pushed it on him:

> I think we had a family expectation to marry Chinese . . . not that my parents put down other races but they just kind held up, you know, Chinese as this is what we are so we continued to be kind of . . . yeah . . . but

they never really pushed it, you know, "you will marry Chinese" kind of thing. . . . I think that might have driven me away.

Aaron, a 37-year-old Korean American married to a Filipina American recalled:

My parents were just really laid back [about marriage issues]. . . . They weren't really involved in like who we were dating . . . who we were hanging out with. They didn't have any criteria and we never really sat down and talked about dating and things like that. . . . But, after meeting Gloria, whom they actually liked very much because she is a very genuine person and very, very considerate and respectful of elders . . . they did say one time "have you ever thought about marrying a Korean?"

Another Korean American married to an Asian Indian American, 38-year-old Daniel, had this to say about his parents regarding marital issues:

We were allowed to chart our own course . . . they never came out with guns blazing like . . . you have to marry that and you can't marry that. I just don't think it was a big issue . . . when we were young, they might have had a little bit more preference for Koreans, but they never came out and said that, not directly. And they were never trying to introduce me to their friends' daughters that were Korean, you know what I mean?

Lucy, a 35-year-old Filipina American married to a Korean American, similarly said of her parents: "My dad wasn't into me dating period. But they didn't really emphasize or encourage one way or another. If anything, when I first started dating, I did date some Filipinos because there were so many. And then after a while, I went on a stretch of dating non-Asian guys, mostly Caucasian." Pamela, a 36-year-old Korean American who initially sought out co-ethnics to date because she assumed it would please her parents, said her parents "never said Korean, Korean, Korean." In sum, unlike many immigrant parents who insist that their children select a co-ethnic/-national marital partner, parents of interethnically married participants in my study seemed relatively laid back in their approach to marriage issues, though they may have hinted at preferences for a co-ethnic.[12]

One interesting theme that emerged in my study, however, is that a large subset of my participants, about two-thirds, had parents who were generally laissez-faire, but not as much about their children marrying "non-Asians," including Whites. Most of these parents were flexible as long as the spouses were of Asian origin but drew a firm line for marrying across racial lines. Many expressed explicit displeasure. Daniel was surprised when his parents, despite their laid-back stance on marriage, objected when his sister wanted to marry a White man. Rachel, a 39-year-old Japanese American, commented of her parents, "I never felt any pressure [to marry a Japanese American guy]. . . . I think there was probably more of a pressure to marry an Asian person. . . . I think my parents . . . would have had a more difficult time I guess if we were to marry a non-Asian person." Justin, a 39-year-old Korean American married to a Cambodian American, commented: "Well, growing up, they would not mention. . . . I mean it wasn't something that we talked about often. I think it was more important to them that I did not marry a Caucasian person. Their impression of Caucasian people is that they divorce, they are not faithful, and they're all interested in money. My parents had those sorts of impressions." On the other hand, Justin also added that his parents did not mind that he did not choose a Korean American, as long as he remained within Asian racial boundaries: "As we got older, many of my parents' friends' children were in intermarriages, so they cared even less that I married a Korean. . . . Another sort of view my parents had was that Korean women were actually very materialistic, so they understood if I didn't want to marry a Korean. But it was still important that I didn't marry a Caucasian. . . . And at a subconscious level, year after year, 'Don't marry a White person, don't marry a White person, don't do that' rubbed off on me."

One participant, 49-year-old Jane, who spent some early years in Hawaii where Asian-ethnics enjoy high social status, said that her parents never explicitly stated their preference for the race or ethnicity of their children's mates but gave her sister a "really hard time" when she started dating a White man, making Jane aware for the first time that her parents had low preference for Whites as partners. Jane added that her parents subsequently cautioned the children about the possible dangers of marrying Whites, who were described as "not to be trusted" and "smooth talking." She speculated that this distrust of Whites came from the parents' perception of Whites as colonizers of the island. Rachel, also raised partly in Hawaii, similarly talked about the generally lower regard in Hawaii of Whites as romantic partners: "if you are Asian and you dated a Caucasian guy . . . people kind of . . . it wasn't as desirable as dating an Asian." James, a 38-year-old Taiwanese American whose parents made plain their preference for an Asian-ethnic partner, discussed how his preference for Asian-ethnics was shaped by his desire to please his parents: "I think it was more cultural and kind of being able to share, just growing-up issues, maybe you struggled with your parents. I don't think I am not *not* attracted to Caucasians, but just by the virtue of that I think." Shane, a 34-year-old Chinese American, remarked that although his parents "relaxed" over the years about their preferences to the point that he felt like he "can choose whomever and say that out loud," he still felt like he "definitely should marry an Asian. . . . I think my dad at one time said, 'Yeah, it's preferably Taiwanese American, but any Asian would be fine.'"[13]

For the rest, parents expressed a strong preference for Asian-ethnics as part-ners but did not explicitly forbid cross-racial coupling if it were with Whites, and there was one case where the parents were adamant into the participants' teenage years that the children inmarry but relaxed this demand as the children became adults, extending their blessings to Asian-ethnic partners. Thus, with parental consent to cross ethnic, if not racial, boundaries at least, most of my interethnically coupled participants reflected that they never thought that mar-rying outside their own national or ethnic group was a problem.[14] Even those participants whose parents appeared to assent to cross-racial marriages, almost all seemed to also have absorbed subtle or overt messages regarding the parents' preference for same-race marriages. As discussed next, the participants' choice of dating or marrying fellow Asian-ethnics was propelled by their movement toward pan-Asian identification, in tandem with the desire to meet familial and parental expectations.

## Pan-Asian Identification and Early Romantic Preferences

Parental influence did not mean that all of the respondents automatically became oriented toward fellow Asian-ethnics as romantic and marital partners from child-hood years, though liberal parental attitudes seemed to have at least removed the barriers to looking beyond co-ethnics. According to my research, another key foundational factor for those who ended up being interethnically coupled was the development of pan-Asian consciousness or identification during their growing-up years or in college,[15] the groundwork for which was often laid by parental/family attitudes or pressures.

The issue of Asian American panethnicity has been amply discussed.[16] Asian American panethnic identity first emerged in the 1960s primarily as a basis for political mobilization for Asian Americans. "Asian American" was a socially ascribed term, but it nevertheless reflected "heightened racial consciousness . . . and the institutionalization of race as a basis of access to government resources and of political mobilization for racial minority groups" following the 1960s civil rights struggles.[17] In recent decades, pan-Asian ethnicity has expanded into a cultural phenomenon as well, which fosters a stronger sense of identification as a racial group. Mia Tuan observes that increasing levels of inter-Asian couplings, over co-ethnic/national or interracial couplings, can be viewed as an example of a "new and thriving racial salience" of panethnicity: "this embracement of a panethnic identity and consciousness represents the latest development in the evolution of their emergent identities and cultures. Ethnicity's influence in their lives has shifted and changed, and for many, racial considerations have replaced it."[18] Diverging from the interracially married group of the previous chapters, almost all interethnically married participants in my study displayed high levels of such pan-Asian identification and identity, which they explained had developed throughout their growing-up years and/or in college.

All of those who were raised in areas with large concentrations of Asian-ethnics, areas which were also frequently racially/ethnically diverse, grew up associating along panethnic lines from early on. These individuals started developing identification as Asian Americans as children. For example, Carter, a 44-year-old Asian mixed-ethnicity individual identifying primarily as Chinese American was raised in heavily Asian parts of Los Angeles, where he felt that he grew up "surrounded" by Asians: "Everyone was Asian. . . . My friends were mainly [a] mixture of Asians—Chinese, Japanese, Korean. That's pretty much it." As Carter moved into dating, he remarked: "I kind of just pretty much stayed with just Asian people. Some people were mixed along the way—some were like half Mexican and half Japanese—but they were mainly a lot of Japanese girls, Chinese girls pretty much." Carter said he never thought about venturing outside of the Asian group, both in terms of friendships or dating.

Lucy, a 35-year-old Filipina American who grew up in a racially diverse, "well integrated" neighborhood with a critical mass of Asian Americans and Filipinos, remarked bluntly: "For me personally, I have natural gravitation towards other Asian people. I have found them the most—well let me back up. At times socially, when I meet someone, if they don't show as much an interest in getting to know me, I don't bother either. And I've noticed Asian people tend to be more, pulling me in, and making an effort. I haven't found that a whole lot with non-Asian people." Finally, Rachel, the Japanese American who grew up in Hawaii, describes how growing up in such an Asian-majority environment fostered a strong sense of panethnicity: "Well, growing up in Hawaii, most of my friends were Japanese Americans. I guess guys I was physically attracted to would be predominantly Asian American, but it wasn't always Japanese Americans, but also like Filipino . . . but always I guess an Asian." Rachel's preference always remained mostly with Asian American men, and she was one of the few participants who never dated a White person.

The effect of early friendship associations and co-ethnic networks, partly dependent on the neighborhoods in which the participants grew up and their exposure to Asian subgroups, has been found by a number of studies as having possible relevance to the development of proclivity toward co-racials and marrying within racial boundaries.[19] My study also suggests that co-ethnic/racial friendship associations are highly relevant, particularly via their effect on the development of panethnic identity. Aaron, the Korean American married to a Filipina American, grew up in a Chicago neighborhood which was highly diverse, an area which he estimates was something like "49% Caucasian, 22% Asian, and 29% Latino." Most of Aaron's friends were a mixture of different Asian Americans, and this did not change in college. Stella, a 34-year-old Cambodian American married to a Korean American, talked about a "transition" she underwent when she moved to an Asian-dominated area in a California high school—almost 90% Asian—from a far more White neighborhood; she reported that she always thought she would marry a White guy until she moved to this new town: "Yeah, so it was in high school that was kind of when the transition happened where I befriended more Asians . . . and the majority of my boyfriends after were Asians." Stella added that despite her changing preference for Asian-ethnic men, the earlier link in her mind about the "geekiness" of Asian guys persisted, so she almost always chose to date highly Americanized Asian men.

A 34-year-old Filipino American, Ed, also married to a Korean American, was a bit more unusual in that he had two distinct sets of friends growing up in a large East Coast city, a mostly White group of friends from school and a "Filipino crowd" who hung out together on the basis of their nationality, reminiscent of the "double life" led by some interracially married participants described in Chapter 3. But unlike some of the interracially married participants mentioned earlier who reported loose ties to Asian-ethnic youth subculture, Ed developed equally strong friendships and identification with his Filipino friends as he did with his White friends in school, and this strong ethnic identity he developed as a youth expanded into a broader Asian American identity when he later entered an ethnically diverse college located in the Chicago area.[20]

In terms of racial experiences growing up, participants who grew up in more diverse areas generally reported fewer struggles with identity conflict and racist treatment than those who grew up in predominantly White neighborhoods, though they were by no means immune.[21] These discriminatory experiences seem universal regardless of neighborhood, although, as I discuss in the next section, those from diverse areas appeared more able to defend themselves from psychological injuries. Justin, the 39-year-old Korean American from a large, racially diverse area in Los Angeles, related the typical narrative about how "kids at school would make Asian jokes or Chinese jokes." He also described micro-aggressions against Asian-ethnics even in the racially mixed area in which he grew up, including instances of indignities suffered by his parents, such as when they would not be offered the same treatment or service that was offered to Whites in stores or restaurants.

As expected, the few who spent their growing-up years in predominantly White areas struggled with "injuries of race" similar to those related by interracially married participants.[22] Growing up as minorities in White areas, these participants struggled with their minority status, feelings of inferiority as Asians, and desires for White privilege and acceptance. One participant remarked: "whiteness was the sea we swam in . . . it had a profound effect on my racial identity. I think we struggled a lot with inferiority and never wanting to be different and always just trying to conform and fit in." Reflecting on his attraction to White girls but his lack of early dating success, Jared, a 40-year-old Vietnamese American man who grew up moving mostly between predominantly White neighborhoods said, "When I was growing up, I absolutely had a general lack of self-confidence . . . it was a general kind of lack of self-esteem. At the time, I didn't think of it in racial terms, but now that I think about it, I realize that being Asian was definitely a deficit." Echoing many of the narratives of interracially married participants,

Becky, a 34-year-old Taiwanese American, related: "I wasn't a popular girl. And I think for me the definition of the popular was always like, White. I remember being like, I wish I had blonde hair . . . hazel eyes. . . . That's what was considered beautiful. . . . Those were the popular girls. If there were any popular Asians, they were always considered Whitewashed."

Not surprisingly, these individuals professed that they were not as strongly oriented toward Asian American or ethnic identity when young, nor particularly desired Asian Americans as dating partners, although this changed later. Jared, a 40-year-old Vietnamese American, spoke about his evolution of dating preferences in elementary and secondary school years:

> I think overwhelmingly the girls I liked were Caucasians probably simply because there were no other Asian people around. And then, when I started liking Asian girls later on in high school, it really was a revelation to find Asian girls . . . because of the media and standard portrayals of beauty and attractiveness . . . it really leads in one direction. I think it's a little bit different now, but at that time it was you know . . . the exemplar for attractiveness was . . . still very overwhelmingly White girls. . . . It's not that I didn't think Asian girls were attractive; it just never registered to me that I would be interested in Asian girls, you know what I'm saying . . . because of the culturally dominant view that the person you should date should be Caucasian.

Shane remarked that in secondary school, "all the girls he was interested in were White." His views toward Asian-ethnic women changed with his encounter with some Asian-ethnic girls in high school, after which he "started getting more into Asians" and realized that he had more "in common with other Asians instead of Caucasian people." This realization progressed further in college.

Nora, a 39-year-old Korean American, also spoke about how her White environment may have affected her dominant attraction to White boys when a young child. Nora, however, started to develop an awareness of her attraction to Asian-ethnic boys relatively early in her teenage years, a development she, in retrospect, attributes in part to her involvement in a religious camp for Asians that provided her with exposure to Asian American boys and dating opportunities. At this point, though, Nora also notes how distant she felt "culturally" from the more Asian-identified kids. Speaking of her experiences with one boy, she recalled, "So then at the camp I was like, wow, all these Asian boys are attracted to me. I am used to like that random White guy here and there being attracted to me, but like it was just nice. . . . I did have a boyfriend. He was my first kiss . . . but he was very Asian, Asian identified, hung out with Asians. . . . And I remember just feeling so different from him culturally, because I was so Whitewashed." Although Nora dated across racial lines as she grew up, this early subcultural involvement served as an important part of her eventual evolution toward pan-Asian identity and attraction toward Asian-ethnic partners. Pamela, the Korean American from earlier, also notes the important role of Korean ethnic church in her life; because of this involvement, she realized that she was always just "more comfortable with other Koreans and other Asians," and was able to better deal with the "discomfort" with White friends and dating non-White boys.

## Normalizing Effects of Asian-Ethnic Communities on Intraracial Dating

While Asian-ethnics growing up in largely White areas wrestled with feelings of inferiority and marginalization, a theme that emerged is that those who grew up in areas with large numbers of fellow Asian-ethnics tended to have developed a stronger sense of identity and confidence in being Asian American.[23] This parallels observations made by other scholars about the "protective effects" of growing up in areas with high concentrations of co-ethnic population, especially the ways in which this can shield individuals from racial self-consciousness, inferiority complexes, and other negative influences of the larger American culture.[24]

Male participants brought up these points more explicitly and often than female participants. Cooper, mentioned earlier, was born in San Francisco's Chinatown before moving to San Diego during his pre-teen years. What he recalls from his days in San Francisco is that most his friends were Chinese, and according to him "growing up in these neighborhoods really cemented my Chinese ethnic identity and was foundational for me." Thus, when he moved to a more White-dominated neighborhood in San Diego as a pre-teen he said that his early ethnic foundation "helped him feel confident, know who he is, and see that how he was and did things were 'normal.'" In effect, this confidence served as a defense against feeling marginalized, different, or inferior in relation to Whites.

Carter also grew up in a town with a large number of Asians. He said because he was surrounded by Asians, it made him confident about being Asian, mainly in that he did not even have to question who he was; that is, being in a largely Asian environment helped "normalize" his Asianness. To drive home his point, he added that when he moved to an "all-White" area in his teen years, he became more aware of racial differences and began to feel more "inferior"; nonetheless, coming from an Asian-dominated area made him retain more confidence even in this new setting.[25] Growing up among co-ethnics or Asian-ethnics, these individuals also seemed to have been largely insulated against media or societal assaults of negative stereotyping against Asians, which frequently produced desires for White privilege and acceptance socially or romantically. In short, for many of these individuals, associating with and dating Asian-ethnics was something far more normalized than it was for those from predominantly White environments.[26]

## Pan-Asian Identification in College and Beyond

All the interethnically married individuals in my study developed or cemented a strong pan-Asian identification in college. For those who had little pan-Asian identification before college, it was in college—many of which had large populations of Asian-ethnics—that identification along pan-Asian lines was often initiated through encounters and friendships with other Asian-ethnics. Some mentioned taking Asian American studies courses as a consciousness awakening experience. Indeed, particularly for middle-class Asian-ethnics, existing studies suggest that that the strength of panethnicity may be significantly related to college experiences, where interaction with large numbers of fellow Asian Americans increases the likelihood of developing pan-Asian identity.[27] My findings bear this out.

While participants from predominantly White areas generally underwent a more disruptive and consciously reflective process about their dating choices, often involving a process of ethnic "discovery" and exploration in college after coming into contact with large numbers of Asian Americans, many participants from more racially diverse neighborhoods who already had strong romantic and friendship associations with Asian Americans more seamlessly continued their pan-Asian identification and associations. Justin, the Korean American who grew up associating mostly with Asian Americans in secondary school, said that in college his friendships remained mostly with Asian Americans, which consisted not just of Korean Americans but "Chinese, Filipino, Indonesian, Japanese." Carter, who earlier noted that he maintained primarily pan-Asian friendships before college, also disclosed that he continued this panethnic association at a university where there was a large number of Asian American students: "In my university, there was a giant Asian community you could just hang out with. And some of these were all my friends to start with [from high school]. I just hung out with that group and pretty much ended up with these people."

Many in this group drew from their primary associational pool of Asian-ethnics for dating. Justin said that he dated only Asian-ethnics during his college years (with the exception of one person), mainly Chinese and Korean Americans, in keeping with his primary friendship links. Carter also put it this way: "As you are growing up, you look at everybody. . . . I see White people, I see Black people, I see Mexican people and everybody, but for me, my attractions just stayed with the Asian women. It's just the way it was." Jeff also echoed this view: "In college, it just happened to be again just that the group of friends I ended up being with dictated how I ended up meeting my wife. . . . She was across the dorm from me, and that's how we met and then we ended up being friends, and we ended up starting to go out, and then the rest is history from that point." Though making sure to point out that he was *not* attracted to the "fresh off the boat" types, he stated that shared Asian American "culture" and "values" were central to this attraction.

For those from White areas, the narratives were different. Vietnamese American Andrew, a self-described "Whitewashed" person and a "Twinkie" who grew up in a White Midwestern town and had never associated with or dated Asians much until college, described, in contrast, an ethnic discovery process that led him eventually to his preference for Asian American women. According to Andrew, he first formed friendships with fellow Asian-ethnics in college, a large university in an East Coast city, which activated his awareness as an Asian American. This was followed by a growing attraction to women of Asian descent. He describes how his path toward pan-Asian identification first began with the friendships he formed with Asian-ethnic male students in the dorm:

> When I went to college . . . I think that was when I started grasping more of a sense of my Asian identity . . . we had a game room at the bottom of our floor. And there was Street Fighter 2 down there, and that's when I think was the beginning of my transformation of being more Asian. So I remember going down to the game room with my roommate [a White student] . . . a few times to play Street Fighter 2, and there was this cadre of, like, six Asian dudes always there. It was kind of intimidating. And I come down, and the funny thing is like, I would become friends with all those guys, like really close friends. I'm still really close friends with them. . . . After hanging out with them, the next semester . . . I did some Asian student union stuff.

For Shane as well, college was an "eye-opening" experience where he realized that he had never been that "totally comfortable" with "Caucasian people." In college he started to feel more "proud" as an Asian American and forged a connection with Asian-ethnics: "I mean, I did have Caucasian friends . . . but it's just I don't feel totally at ease with Caucasians versus with Asians. . . . So maybe in college is where I started hanging out with other Asians . . . so with that, I realized that these people are cool and we have a lot in common." In college, Shane also began finding Asian women more attractive. This was particularly instigated by a brief but painful relationship with a White woman whose father expressed a highly racist attitude toward him with remarks like, "Oh, Shane is nice—too bad he's a chink." Such experiences made him realize that "race is . . . something that definitely mattered." He added, "I just feel that there is this really big gap in the culture between Asians and Caucasians and . . . I was one of those . . . I just can't cross. I can't bridge that gap. . . . I'm attracted to some [Caucasians], but in terms of settling down and having a family, I don't think that I could. I think that's just not for me."

Nora also discussed how her ethnic identification was further galvanized in college and beyond through her increased exposure to other Asian Americans and awareness of Asian American and race/ethnicity issues. This led to a conscious decision to marry a fellow Asian-ethnic, which followed several years of cross-racial dating. Speaking of her college years, she said:

> It [college] really politicized me in a lot of ways. . . . I had already kind of been slowly politicizing . . . in high school, and the fact that I was a minority, and the fact that what the White guys and the White people would say would piss me off so much. So I was already kind of there, and then of course I went to college, and college is such a politicizing institution.

Lewis, a 48-year-old Chinese American, explained that his journey of ethnic discovery began in college where his world became more "cosmopolitan" and diverse, but it was in graduate school that he was fully politicized as an Asian American: "It was the broader environment [of graduate school]. Most of my friends became people of color, Asian Americans, and being exposed to issues of race and ethnicity . . . so that was like a big transformative experience for me, going off to [graduate school] . . . being involved in left-wing politics." Polly, a 32-year-old Korean American who grew up mostly with Whites, relates how she transcended a narrower ethnic identity to a wider pan-Asian identity in college, even evolving from an earlier "social" pan-Asian involvement to a more political one later in college:

> I definitely would say college is where I found myself in terms of my ethnic identity. Before college . . . I definitely considered myself Korean American and was aware of discrimination and all that . . . but I didn't start an Asian Club at my school or anything . . . but I was intellectually aware and curious about those [Asian American] issues. So when I got to college . . . I honestly went crazy. My first boyfriend in college was Taiwanese . . . my freshman year was a party year where I hung around with all Asians; it was the first time there was like a large group of Asians and, oh, my God, there are a lot of people like me; I belonged, so I partied a lot. But then after that I got disillusioned. I thought oh, my God, what am I doing with my life? I need to do something about this. And I recognized that I'm not that social Asian party type. I identified as being Asian American, but I'm more civic-minded. Other people just hung around with other Asians because it was comfortable and easy. I didn't want to do that; I had a lot of different types of friends . . . so I joined . . . the umbrella organization for Asian groups. I did a lot of work through them, and I think I really grew my love for the Asian American community and started to think of myself as Asian American [as] compared to Korean American.[28]

## Romantic and Marital Appeal of Asian-Ethnics

This link to a strong Asian American identity, mediated through parental expectations, appears to be one of the starting points for my participants who chose interethnic marriage. However, as studies have shown, possessing a strong pan-Asian identity does not *in itself* lead to pan-Asian marriage.[29] This section will delineate some of the specific factors many interethnically married participants identified as underlying their attraction for Asian Americans. For these participants, these factors decidedly figured into their consideration of Asian Americans as ideal partners. The participants mentioned two main components underlying their attraction to and choice of Asian-ethnics as romantic/marital partners: 1) cultural affinity and compatibility; 2) preference for co-racials over co-ethnics.

## *Cultural Compatibility: It's Just Easier*

In my research, there was a small subgroup of interethnically married participants who were always primarily physically attracted to Asian Americans and did not seriously consider dating other races. Justin is one such case; he said that although his parents' admonition to him not to marry across racial lines affected him, "another factor" for him was physical attraction: "I find that I am not as physically attracted to Caucasians. I'm just more physically attracted to Asians in general." Charlie, a 52-year-old Chinese American, also admitted that although he did not think he cared about whom he ended up with, he simply "wasn't as attracted to" non-Asian women. Jeremy, a 39-year-old Korean American, commented, "Yeah, I think I'd say I am more physically attracted to someone of an Asian background, but I did recognize beauty in women of different backgrounds. . . . But, yes, I think maybe it's because I grew up with a Korean mom. I just found that particular body shape or whatever you want to call it more attractive."

As discussed in the last section, the rest of the individuals in the interethnically married group were not exclusively attracted to Asian–ethnics earlier in their lives but came to be so as they were growing up, especially through high school and college. In fact, it is worth pointing out that this group of respondents more often than not admitted that they were in reality attracted to many kinds of partners—Whites, Latinos, Blacks—but simply said that they came to prefer Asian Americans, especially as marriage partners. Aaron, the Korean American who ended up marrying a Filipina, admitted: "I found Whites attractive, and, you know, Latinos, Blacks, everyone. But in terms of settling down . . . I would have figured that it would have probably been within the Asian race, but not necessarily Korean, but I think, Asians in general." What ultimately drew him to his Filipina wife were shared values which turned out to be central to their marriage. Nora divulged that after a great deal of dating experimentation across racial lines, "I just got to the point where I just felt like I should just be with someone like me."

Indeed, one prominent reason given was the sense of greater cultural affinity provided by feelings of a shared "Asian" cultural connection, though almost no one in my study explicitly declared that the purpose of marrying a fellow Asian was to get back in touch with their ethnic roots or because of a particular desire to preserve the Asian race. One woman simply said, "Although growing up, there were no attractive Asian guys to admire on TV and stuff, when I started dating, I was attracted more to Asian guys. I just felt more comfortable with them." Aaron, who said that he "always thought he'd marry within the 'Asian race'" though not necessarily Korean, remarked, "It was because I felt more comfortable." With his Filipina wife, the final "clincher" was that she was instinctively "respectful of elders and considerate toward my parents," which made her the "next best thing" to a Korean American daughter-in-law. Indeed, although his parents had initial hesitation about the fact that she was not a Korean American, they quickly warmed up to her because she would do things like phone his dad all the time while they were only dating, coming over to his parents' house often and helping out in ways they felt that a Korean daughter-in-law would. Carter put it this way: "I think there are beautiful White people, everybody is beautiful, but when it comes to it, I think on the connection level, it's the values you share and the culture, like foods and customs. Those are very similar. So you kind of end up . . . that's where I felt more comfortable."

Cultural comfort and ease as a key source of attraction among Asian Americans had been brought up by other scholars.[30] Pamela, the Korean American from earlier, was an interesting case in that she grew up in a predominantly White area but with a strong friendship orientation toward Koreans as well as Whites, primarily because of the strong Korean ethnic church culture in which she was embedded growing up. Although Pamela herself did not see herself as a "typical" Korean American female—having a "tomboyish," "loud and boisterous" personality and not in the least "domesticated"—she was distinctive in that she thought she had a preference for a co-ethnic—a Korean American—as a potential mate. In late high school, however, her horizons expanded and she experienced an "awakening" where dating across racial and ethnic lines became an acceptable option for her. For Pamela, dating across racial lines never materialized as a reality, but she discovered her preference for fellow Asian-ethnics:

> I was first opened up to it [intermarriage] I think when I was in high school. I went out to visit my girlfriend in California . . . so on the campus, just sitting there and walking, you see all these interracial couples, Mexicans with Whites, Mexicans with Asian, and I'm like wow, this is . . . you hear of it on the news and all and you hear that change is starting to come and obviously the biggest thing was the whole Black and White thing. But to see like, these not-Black, not-White, but different Asians dating each other, and I was like wow, this is so novel and it's great and it made me happy! We can all get along! . . . I was attracted to a lot of people [of all races] . . . but for whatever reason it didn't work out. . . . And probably for Asian guys [in terms of dating], maybe it became more of a reality when I moved here. . . . And then for whatever reason I heard somewhere . . . you know, Chinese guy and the Korean woman are supposed to be a very good match. Um, so it probably became more of a reality when my sister married him [Chinese American man]. And realizing that his family is like almost identical to ours in the way that we grew up and stuff. So I thought that was really cool.

Regarding the special affinity among "Asians," she added about Asian-ethnics that: "they tend to take care of their families . . . honestly, I want to be treated equally, but I want to be taken care of as well . . . so we talk about that a lot that, us being both Asian and coming from Asian culture, we have the affinity and understanding of . . . taking care of each other, or taking care of parents or even our siblings."

Echoing this line of thinking, Carter said that what he found most attractive about his Asian American wife was what he perceived as her "traditional" values:

being responsible, hardworking, and family-oriented. Like Carter, another man said that, for him, it was a "conscious" decision to marry an Asian American because with Caucasians, one has a "vastly different cultural system." He said, "I'm talking about things like ambition, focus on education, certain common childhood experiences." Although many ethnic groups value education, he explained that the Asian focus was distinctive; in his case, it meant a willingness, for example, to put the kids through the best kind of schools, no matter how expensive." Another woman explained it this way: "even if I were attracted to them, to non-Asians, it's just too complicated. You have to explain too much." Indeed, the narrative that "it's just easier that she/he was Asian" arose again and again.

Filipina American Lucy elaborated further on this point; referring to her temporary "stretch" of dating White men, she recounted: "after a while I just really got tired of dating guys for whom I was the first non-White person they would date. As the very first Asian person, I would have to teach them about culture and introduce them to things and, you know, and some of them had [a] very rough transition to being respectful of my culture. I wasn't crazy about that, so I started to miss having someone whom I had more things in common with." She also added that facing a series of racist treatments from her past boyfriends' families did not help matters.[31] Stella, a 34-year-old Cambodian American, similarly discussed how her preferences for Asian-ethnic men intensified after the realization of the importance of her cultural differences with non-Asian men, such as with her former White boyfriends who could not understand certain traditional values she grew up with, like having curfews, pressure to do well in school, and "all that good stuff"; indeed, with her Korean American husband, she said, "I think for us, we focus on our values, our values about life and about family and career and all that stuff."

One interesting observation was that while a number of participants in this group declared that their choice to interethnically marry was a result of a "conscious" decision related to cultural affinity, a minority of participants, many of whom were raised in predominantly Asian-ethnic areas, distinctly downplayed the "conscious" or purposeful aspect of choosing an Asian-ethnic partner, instead explaining their choice matter-of-factly as growing organically out of existing "cultural compatibility," one that some of them did not even view as necessarily uniquely "Asian." Corinne, a 40-year-old Chinese American married to a Vietnamese American, remembered:

> My mom had earlier wanted me to marry a nice Chinese boy, if possible, so that was in the back of my mind, but marrying an Asian was not a conscious decision or anything. I was not unattracted to non-Asians, but I never thought about it much . . . we just met and fell in love, and for me, it wasn't even the Asian thing . . . but I do remember thinking it was easier that he was Asian.

Rachel, the Japanese American married to a Taiwanese American, expressed a similar sentiment: "My husband just happened to be Asian. I didn't have anything against anyone who was not Asian. . . . I met [my husband]; we had the same interests, we just clicked and we just got along really well. I think he is just a really nice guy and that was cool. And we didn't just have the same type of interests, but same types of tastes in things like travel—well, there were a lot of things in common." Samantha, a 41-year-old of Asian mixed-ethnicity ancestry who was the only one to make a point to say that she never planned to marry an Asian person just for the reasons of cultural ease, remarked:

> I could have married anybody . . . as long as we were compatible . . . but we [my husband and I] had similar backgrounds. And by background, I mean our upbringing, our values, and how we would choose to raise our children. Family values are particularly important. Family values for me is having that closeness. I don't know. You just see so much in families where families don't get along and it's sad. Growing up, though we had our differences and fights, we have always been close. We always knew we would be there for each other. . . . But I don't see these values as being particularly Asian values.

Another participant Jeff, a 35-year-old Korean American, used the word "gravitated" liberally, but qualified that these romantic and friendship gravitations toward Asian-ethnics were not particularly purposeful:

> At high school, I just naturally gravitated toward my core group of friends who were all Asian Americans. It just happened that way. I don't think . . . I was looking for that type of friendship, but I don't know if it was similar core values or it just . . . whatever it may be. It just happened that way. . . . In terms of dating . . . they were all Asian Americans. And again, it wasn't necessarily a specific requirement on my part . . . it's just how my friendships ended up becoming . . . and who I interacted with during high school and in middle school. I tended to just gravitate more toward Asian Americans.

Jeff, like Samantha, also believed that his attraction to his Chinese American wife that was based on strong shared "values" that were not particularly Asian (which contradicted his earlier statement that his shared "Asian American values" with fellow Asian-ethnics were important): "What kind of holds us together is the fact that we have similar values, and I feel that when our values are combined, it's good. I think that makes, for me, a successful marriage and that's what I'm looking for . . . you know, doing the right thing, treating people with respect, and trying to do good to others and things like that. I don't think it's anything more than that in my opinion . . . but it's not attributable to the Asian culture." Especially for those who grew up in Asian-dominated areas, such matter-of-factness about their marital decision seems to stem from the fact that dating and marrying a fellow Asian-ethnic was so normalized as to require no particular explanation.[32]

## I Want an Asian of a Different Flavor

Although it might appear that for many who interethnically marry, dating and marrying Asian-ethnics seemed to be the path of least resistance; especially in the face of parental disapproval of interracial marriage, there is an important and subtle dimension to their choices that bears scrutiny; desiring a fellow Asian-ethnic over a co-ethnic. The vast majority of the participants in the interethnically married group declared that they never particularly desired to marry co-ethnics/ nationals, or inmarry. In fact, as we have seen, the majority professed explicit preference for marrying someone within the Asian race, and not co-ethnics necessarily. Korean American Nora said that an important reason why she married a Vietnamese American was because although she was sure she wanted to marry an Asian-ethnic, "I wanted to be with someone that was *different* from me." She added, "I am actually excited to have non-Korean dynamics in my family at the same time that I find them bothersome and annoying, but I am like, oh, this is great. . . . Like [my daughter] will understand that . . . Asians are different. Asians have different experiences and different histories and different conflicts with even each other." For Nora, pan-Asian identification for herself and for her children overrides narrow ethnic identification.

Another Korean American, Polly, married to a Taiwanese American, offered up a number of reasons for wanting a non-Korean partner; first, she offered up "patriarchy" of the Korean family/gender structure as one reason for avoiding marriage with another Korean American—similar to narratives in Chapter 3—and said that although her younger years were more oriented toward co-ethnics, she made a conscious decision not to date Korean men by the time she got to college:

> The reasons why I decided not to date Korean guys was for all the stereotypical reasons. . . . Korean men are raised and socialized to believe that Korean men are better than Korean women. . . . Even with nice Korean guys, not that they are bad people, but I'm way too independent for that. I needed to be with someone that wasn't going to tie me down.

Second, as described earlier, Polly's decision to not date or marry Korean men was also driven by her strong, budding pan-Asian political consciousness and identity in college, and her desire to transcend the narrowness of co-ethnic identification as a Korean American. Echoing the narratives of some of the interracially married participants, Polly recalled that she developed a disliking for the cliquishness of the Korean American crowd in college and determined that she did not want to be just "immersed" in the Korean American world. As she developed a strong pan-Asian identification and involvement, Polly dated a number of men of color, but stayed within racial boundaries by primarily dating Asian-ethnic men. In terms of marriage, Polly stated that "Korean was definitely not on the top of my list" and said she knew she wanted to marry an "Asian," especially someone who "gets being a minority in America." Indeed, the importance of the potential partner's comprehension of race relations and racism appeared as a theme with other participants; Jeremy, a Korean American, described how turned off he became when a White date described her thoughts about racial differences with an old adage about how all skin colors were the same in God's eyes: "So yeah, I figured I can't be in a long-term relationship with someone that basically is at this point in their understanding of race relations."

Adding to her growing pan-Asian consciousness, Polly also became less attached to the idea of partnering within ethnic boundaries when she became critical of certain aspects of her Korean family's culture. The first was her eventual distaste for what she saw as strong ethnocentric tendencies of her family. She moved even further away from her Korean American identification when she discovered her parents' hypocritical stance regarding intermarriage; despite their oft-repeated preference for Koreans, Polly's parents ended up liking far less their tall, handsome, rich, and well-educated Korean son-in-law than a son-in-law who was only half-Korean, short, and dark skinned because the former turned out to be a terrible husband to Polly's sister: "So there I began to see 'aha,' there's hypocrisy in how my parents look at marriage and relationships. From that point on, honestly both parents' standards for what they want for me—there is no right or wrong reason to it. So I knew I needed to find someone for myself."

Participants such as Polly and Pamela stated that another deterrent to pursuing a co-ethnic/-national mate was a level of discomfort they had from not being fluent in Korean culture and the realization that they "weren't Koreans from Korea." Polly, for example, said that on her way to solidifying her pan-Asian identity, she went through a period where she tried to change herself by becoming more "Korean" but became "disillusioned": "I kind of went to the extreme. I only hung around with Korean FOBs and tried to speak Korean as much as I could, taking Korean classes. I was going to become a Korean historian; I took a short time exploring that route and realized I'm not a Korean from Korea." Pamela went through a similar phase, but in her case, it involved wanting for a while to marry a Korean because she "wanted to marry someone that's Korean who knows how to speak Korean, who knows the Korean culture" and then ending up dating Korean Americans who she described were even "Whiter" than she was. Like Polly, Pamela eventually came to the realization that rather than pigeonholing herself into a co-ethnic dating market, crossing ethnic boundaries in dating and marriage was going to be a far more sensible and comfortable choice for her.

In terms of meeting parental expectations, many, like Pamela and Polly, subconsciously absorbed and accepted parental wishes that they date and marry within the Asian racial boundary. Others, to meet the expectations of their parents, looked for Asian-ethnic partners, even though they claim that they themselves could have married "anybody." James, the 38-year-old Taiwanese American, for example, explicitly stated that he would have dated or married a non-Asian were it not for his parents. One individual, however, struggled mightily with the parental expectation that she marry within the ethnic/national fold. Sadie, 31-year-old Korean American, was one of the few participants whose parents were insistent on inmarriage into her adulthood. Sadie, however, had little attraction to, nor desire to marry, a Korean American. A self-described "banana," Sadie battled her parents about this demand from her teenage years, rebelling and dating across racial lines. Unwilling to completely disobey her parents' wishes, Sadie's "solution" was to meet their wishes "halfway" by marrying an Asian co-ethnic, a Chinese American.

## "Trade-offs" of Interethnic Marriage

Are all the participants comfortable with their choices to interethnically marry? How do they feel about it? Although many did not much question their choice to marry interethnically and felt at peace with it, others displayed more complex and conflicted feelings about interethnic marriage that spoke to the prevailing power of White hegemony. Although all of my participants did not explicitly question the wisdom of interethnic marriage, and emphasized the benefits of it, it was also surprising that some of the participants felt that there was a level of "trade-off" within the context of a society where race matters and that still equates being American with being "White": the trade-off was the loss of White privilege. Even the participants who did not fret over the decision to marry fellow Asian-ethnics believed to a certain extent that interracial marriages to Whites would have the benefit of elevating their status within the mainstream society, and that by marrying a fellow Asian-ethnic, they paid the "price" of relinquishing this potential access to White privilege.

Sophie, a 45-year-old Japanese American, made a surprising remark, "I might have made it more in the world, would have made it higher in the world, had I married a White guy, but I would not have been as comfortable." She also added that she has always felt that being with an Asian American partner did make her feel more "dismissed" than if she were with a White guy. Furthermore, because being Asian American is still not fully regarded as being "American," she feels that even as a couple, they are not regarded as fully American by society: "When people say American, they still mean White, and my parents even do that. And it's like, 'Okay guys. We're Asian American, just as American.' Still, when you say someone's American, you think that means White. . . . So there's that contradiction, and, yeah, as an Asian American couple, it seems like the two of you have to prove yourself."

Pamela's narrative below parallels Sophie's sentiments and thoughts. Remarking that she may have been "more accepted and fit in better if I were married to a White guy," Pamela commented:

> I feel like if I'm married to another Asian, the rest of this White society will just see us as like this, another Asian family that has done well. It's almost like people who are interracially married fit in with White society better. . . . I'm still trying to figure this out . . . but if I'm married to a White guy, that in some way that might make me look more White. But the weird

thing is that it's not like I want to look White. I know I'm not being clear, but it's hard to articulate. Unfortunately, I think what it is, is that I feel like people might give me more credence or more respect almost because they think, okay, look at this Asian woman who's married to a White guy. . . . I kind of feel like that the White society will give me more chances? But it sounds weird because they're not seeing me, but they'd be looking at my [White] husband. And it's not even that I'm thinking about my kids, that oh, my kids will look more White, whatever.

Scholars have discussed the ways in which some Asian American outmarriages to Whites can be considered a case of hypergamy; more specifically, as a case of racial hypergamy since one is "trading" whatever one has to offer (beauty or youth typically in the case of women, and economic ability in the case of men) for racial privileges associated with a White spouse.[33] Recent studies of inter-racially married Latinas similarly find that "Latina women position themselves for romance with White men as a way to consolidate class and racial privilege."[34] For Latinas, light-skinned women are positioned to be particularly successful at this. Though he did not articulate it in terms of a "trade-off," Jeff, a 35-year-old Korean American, made an interesting remark about how the "forever-foreigner" stereotype will continue to mark those who interethnically marry, implying a certain disadvantage: "In my own personal opinion, I think there is going to be always that element that you're foreign, especially if you are married intra-Asian. The folks that are Asian and marry White, their kids will be a little bit more non-traditional Asian-looking, and so I think it has a lot to do with just how you look, and there can be a natural tendency to discriminate based off that."[35]

Whether or not they are interethnically or interracially married, what the narratives of this section show is that most Asian-ethnics are keenly aware of the power and existence of White privilege. In particular, they are aware that for Asian Americans, social subordination means subordination along the lines of depriving them of the full social/cultural citizenship granted to Whites, that is, by racializing Asian Americans as "not Americans," as "forever foreigners," or as "inauthentic" Americans. This is the case no matter how many generations they have been in the United States, how much economic upward mobility they have achieved, or how high they are considered to be situated in a color hierar-chy.[36] At the same time, narratives such as Pamela's also reveal that while Asian Americans may acutely recognize the intensity and specificity of their oppression and inequality, not all Asian Americans necessarily *desire* to become free of this situation by becoming White, contradicting the traditional assimilation thesis.[37] Nonetheless, it is clear that pressure for assimilation into the dominant White mainstream culture remains strong, and some interethnically married participants struggle with the recognition that despite the comfortableness of, and pride in, their personal choice to marry interethnically, there are still possible costs in terms of continued social marginalization for themselves and their children.

## Conclusion

This chapter examined some of the factors that inform interethnic marital choices of my participants. One of the consistent themes among the interethnically married participants of this study is how their romantic desires and marital choices for co-racials are shaped by a close dialectic between parental/family expectations for same-race partnering and U.S. society's racialization of Asian Americans, which leads them to develop a strong sense of pan-Asian identity. This study confirms findings by earlier research that pan-Asian identification is a strengthening and expanding phenomenon among the younger generation of Asian Americans, who increasingly seek out and prefer to date Asian-ethnics for a variety of reasons: "the matter-of-fact attitude . . . toward interethnic dating is both the producer and product of an intense boundary shift currently taking place. More and more Asian-ethnics, particularly younger ones, are defining themselves panethnically as Asian Americans and identifying along racial lines. They subsequently can have a casual attitude because they believe it is still 'within the family,' the family of Asian Americans, that is."[38] An interesting finding of this study was how racially open minded many of the participants actually were about dating and even marriage, but ultimately felt that for the purposes of marriage, a fellow Asian-ethnic represented the best choice for them because of the ease with which they can mutually understand their racialized experiences and share cultural affinity.[39]

One issue that this chapter underscored is how race is still of central importance to the participants and in the development of a pan-Asian identity. Still considered "foreigners," and not fully granted the social/cultural citizenship as an authentic "American" regardless of their generational status, most participants in this study have come to accept and appropriate the externally imposed panethnic term "Asian American" as a meaningful category around which to identify themselves as a racially and culturally cohesive group. I suggest that this racial and panethnic category has become meaningful to the extent that it is able to even override proclivities toward cross-racial attraction and coupling, something that many participants had admitted they had desired as a possibility. For a few, interethnic coupling was sought purposefully and willfully, sometimes as a political statement, but for most it was sought in a more matter-of-fact manner, either as a normative path to take given their ongoing connections to Asian-ethnics or out of a desire to be with those who shared common understanding and life experiences.

It is also worth stressing that a strong sense of panethnic identity as a factor in the development of same-race romantic preferences is intertwined closely with parental attitudes—with parents in turn being the most powerful conduits to the children of ethnic community attitudes and values—and the children's desire to meet parental expectations.[40] After all, it is the parents who transmit the norms of the ethnic community by determining where the children grow up, go to school, and for instilling ethnic/racial consciousness/culture, thereby helping to lay the foundation for the development of panethnicity.[41] This observation also underscores the fact that social networks provided by proximate ethnic communities, kin, and family are key factors in helping to maintain ethnic identity/practices and communal participation, In the next chapter, I explore how participants from different Asian-ethnic groups negotiate respective identities and cultures within the context of family-making and marital relations.

## Notes

1. Parts of this chapter has appeared in Chong 2017.
2. Swarns 2012. See also Gowen 2009; Onishi 1996; Yip 1997.
3. Yang 2012.
4. Pew Research Center 2010.
5. Le 2013; Yang 2012.
6. Cf. Mok 1999.
7. Cf. Dhingra 2007; Kibria 2002; Kikumura and Kitano 1973; Kitano et al. 1984; Maira 2002; Min and Kim 2010; Mok 1999; Saenz et al. 1995; Spickard 1989; Sung 1990; Tuan 1998, 76.
8. Tuan (1998) also notes the importance of the respondents' desires to meet the expectations of their parents in regard to their marital and dating choices: "Quite clearly, some respondents have made a conscious decision to date other Asians and do so for many reasons. Explanations ranged from wanting to please their parents to wishing to maintain a pure bloodline" (119).
9. Kibria 2002; Kikumura and Kitano 1973; Kitana et al. 1984; Maira 2002; O'Brien 2008; Spickard 1989; Sung 1990.
10. One scholar (Mok 1999) found that parental influence was mostly non-significant in the dating partner choices of her respondents, while other studies suggest that parental influence does have some effect, including a recent study on Latino intermarriage that shows the strength of parental teachings in shaping children's outlooks on marriage/dating, including preference for outmarriage (Vasquez 2017, 8). Also see Dhingra 2007; Tuan 1998.
11. Cf. Tuan 1998, 58; Vasquez 2017.
12. Tuan 1998, 58–60.
13. For almost all the participants, African Americans were at the bottom of the parents' racial preference hierarchy.
14. Cf. Mok 1999; Tuan 1998.
15. Cf. Espiritu 1992; Mok 1999; Shinagawa and Pang 1996.
16. For example, Espiritu 1992; Kibria 2002, 1997; Tuan 1998.
17. Kibria 1997, 526.
18. Tuan 1998, 120.
19. See Kikumura and Kitano 1973; Mok 1999; Saenz et al. 1995; Spickard 1989; Sung 1990.
20. Cf. Tuan 1998, 103.
21. Cf. Tuan 1998; 97–98.
22. Osajima 1993.
23. Tuan's (1998, 96) respondents who grew up in Asian-dominated areas claimed that ethnic identity matters were a "non-issue" since everyone around them was of similar ancestry. Dhingra (2007, Chap. 2) also makes a similar observation about a group of his respondents.
24. For example, see Zhou and Bankston 1998. Such theories even maintain that such individuals may even be more academically and professionally successful owing to lesser dilution of important core ethnic values focused on success and achievement.

25. Tuan (1998, 82–83) gives a description, on the other hand, of participants who moved to White communities from predominantly Asian or racially mixed neighborhoods as children or teenagers who mostly reveal negative experiences of trauma, alienation, and lowered self-esteem. But she does qualify: "I am not suggesting here that all respondents who moved into White neighborhoods suffered from the same difficulties as Jerry. . . . What I am suggesting is that these respondents could articulate their feelings of hurt more clearly because they had a point of reference to compare their current experiences with. They experienced a sense of loss in addition to a general sense of marginalization" (86).

26. Racial privilege enjoyed here by these participants in their Asian-dominated environment is equivalent to White racial privilege: the liberty to not have to think about one's race, for one's race to be considered "normal" or "invisible" (Blauner 1972; Frankenberg 1993).

27. See for example Espiritu 1992; Shinagawa and Pang 1996.

28. Some psychological theories of identity development have found that many youths who start their lives ashamed of their racial differences and ethnic identity/culture can eventually reconcile these conflicting parts of their cultures and identities and become comfortable with both. The participants from the White areas described here appear to fit this model of identity development. See, for example, Phinney 1990; Tse 1999.

29. Mok 1999.

30. See Chow 2000; Fong and Yung 2000; Kibria 2002; Tuan 1998.

31. See Brenda Gambol (2016)'s contrasting of interethnic attraction of Filipinos/as for other Asian-ethnics, especially East Asians, based on a sense of cultural similarity versus Filipinos/as' interracial attraction for non-White partners that leads to distancing from Asian American identification.

32. Tuan (1998, 118), on the other hand, notes that one of the surprising findings of her study was not only the large presence of interethnically dating/marrying respondents but also the "purposefulness" with which they sought out other Asian-ethnics to date/marry.

33. Tuan 1998, 61. See Chou and Feagin 2015; Nemoto 2009.

34. Vasquez 2017, 47. See Chang 2016; Vallejo 2012.

35. Dhingra 2007, 197, 172. Dhingra finds similarly that some Asian Americans feel that associating or being partnered with co-racials or co-ethnics perpetuates and reinforces their image as "perpetual foreigners" and that dating or partnering with a White person signifies attaining a higher racial status as "normal" Americans.

36. Glenn 2002, 2011; Tuan 1998; Kim 1999, 2007; Ong 1996.

37. See Ong and Azores 1994; Rudrappa 2004; Song 2009.

38. Tuan 1998, 118.

39. It is interesting to speculate, however, whether the narratives of open-mindedness signify the participants' true desires for cross-racial dating, or whether they are simply the participants' way of signaling Americanness while they attempt to live up to ethnic norms and expectations. Cf. Dhingra 2007, 174.

40. See Hwang et al. 1997. In this article, the authors echo my findings that the impact of the norms regarding out or inmarriages stemming from the "institution of the family" within migrant sub-societies is an important overlooked variable in studies of Asian American intermarriages.

41. See Tuan 1998, 76; Rumbaut 1994: 790.

# 6

# CONSTRUCTING HYBRIDITY

## Cultural and Ethnic Negotiations in Interethnic Marriage and Family-Making

Once united, how do interethnic couples negotiate their ethnic cultures within the context of marriage and family?[1] If this is a kind of pan-Asian ethnogenesis, the formation of a race-based group and group identity, what is the nature of ethnic cultures being blended, retained, discarded, reconstructed, and in what ways? Are there any implications arising from tensions or hierarchies *within* the Asian American community? The widespread perception that people with Asian national origins share a common cultural core, often of Confucian derivation, is not only false but also fails to recognize that even "Confucian cultures" differ across nations and take on different forms and valences across national and ethnic boundaries within Asia. Expressing her incredulity, one respondent related how one White colleague, after watching an Asian American couple argue in a restaurant, made a statement, "What do they have to fight about? They're all the same!"

No matter the nationality or ethnic combination of my respondent couples, my findings suggest that a considerable amount of ethnic cultural and identity negotiations occur between partners, and that these negotiations constitute a process of identity and cultural reconstruction in response to and within the context of the larger, socially imposed definitions of the "Asian American." One of the most ironic aspects of the ethnic/cultural negotiations that can be observed among the couples occurs along two dimensions characterized by divergent motivations but similar outcomes: 1) couples who, once married, consciously or proactively make an effort to maintain respective ethnic cultures/identities within their marriages and pass them on to their children but end up with a diluted, "re-invented" form of amalgamated/hybrid "Asian American" culture due to cultural incompetence; 2) couples who do not view themselves as actively trying to preserve anything cultural, even in some cases emphasizing their "Americanness" for themselves and their families, but are nonetheless passively participating in a similar, diluted form of cultural retention by virtue of having chosen an Asian American mate and through primary association with Asian American family members, friends, and other networks.

The first category is made up of individuals who are relatively politicized about their Asian American identity and are purposive about maintaining "Asianness," together with individuals who did not necessarily see their ethnic assertions as a political statement but still believed in the importance of maintaining an Asian American identity and ethnic cultures. The second category is made up of individuals and couples, about three-fourths of the interethnically married group, who are de facto passing down what they refer to as "Asianness" but do not see themselves as making a particular effort to do so by virtue of the fact that they are in a marriage with a fellow Asian-ethnic. Nonetheless, regardless of the category to which the participants belonged, that is, whether the participants saw themselves as actively maintaining or transmitting ethnic cultures/ identities or not, what was being passed down and negotiated, frequently referred to by the participants as "Asianness," was mostly nebulous and ill-defined, with "Asianness" being a hybrid but a relatively amorphous concept. Indeed, "Asianness" as a concept and as a content were subject to ongoing construction and often crafted through a cultural blending in unreflexive and unpremeditated ways, and always in complex dialogue with the White-centered hegemonic conception of "Americanness" and "American culture." That is, "Asianness," though clearly a contested and emergent concept among the individuals in this study, is a concerted effort to delineate an ethnic boundary and group culture by way of defining some kind of an "ethnic core" that would also be acceptable to the wider society.[2]

## "Asianness" Under Construction

A quarter of my interethnic participants were articulate about their desire to maintain Asian American identity for themselves and their children. Having chosen an Asian American mate, often consciously, these individuals expressed that retaining Asian American identity and culture, especially in terms of passing it down to their children, was a necessity and a priority, whether in the form of a what they perceived as a hybrid form of pan-Asian culture/identity or in the combined form of multiple ethnic identities and cultures. This included participants who became strongly politicized about Asian American issues as young adults and those who had developed a pan-Asian identity as youths and came to feel strongly about ethnic cultural maintenance. As Sophie, the Japanese American married to a Chinese American, asserted, "I'm raising my kids as Asian American. I want them to retain a strong Asian American identity. I want them to see themselves as Americans of Asian descent." Nora, the Korean American, explicitly expressed a desire to instill in her young child both a strong panethnic "Asian American" identity and hyphenated, ethnic/national identities: "I want her to identify as Korean American, Vietnamese American *and* Asian American. I want her to know her ethnicity, but I would want her to know Asian Americanness."

Individuals who were politicized and self-aware about race and ethnicity issues were, not surprisingly, most articulate about the importance of ethnic cultural retention and identity. One such individual was Lewis, the 48-year-old Chinese American. Involved in Asian American activism since his college days, he was one of the participants who strongly emphasized the need for ethnic cultural maintenance for minority groups of color because of the challenges arising from racism and social marginalization. Asked why cultural maintenance was important for his kids, he explained, "My value system—I think of myself as not a part of the mainstream. I don't identify with the mainstream. I don't identify with it in terms of values, so that's where I come from. . . . It's like when W.E.B. Du Bois was talking about 'double consciousness.' That's what I feel like—double consciousness." Anticipating the likelihood that his children will experience similar forms of alienation and "double consciousness," the contradiction that comes from being both an Asian-ethnic and an "American," Lewis plans to help his kids learn how to psychologically arm themselves against this possibility through efforts at ethnic cultural and identity retention.

Those possessing stronger pan-Asian consciousness parallel the sentiments of Lewis and almost always point to the central significance of physiology; that is, their kids need to be aware of and carry an Asian American identity because their Asian appearance sets them apart. Charlie, the 52-year-old Chinese American married to a Japanese American, expressed this sentiment emphatically, "We are different because we *look* different. People treat us differently because we look different." Sophie asserted, "It has more to do with looks, because the kids only speak English anyway." According to Pamela, the Korean American introduced in the last chapter, "We want them to know the language, where they came from, culture, and be proud of their race. We don't want them to be ashamed." The participants repeatedly expressed that continuing racism against Asian Americans makes it necessary that the children be taught to be "proud" of themselves and not ashamed.

Pamela also agreed that, in her opinion, ethnic identity consisted first and foremost of "appearance," or the "look," although there is "more": "When I think of the word ethnicity, it's first appearance, and then secondly I would think culture. But it's even hard to say culture now, being Korean American growing up here in America. . . . But I guess secondly, I would have to say culture. But with culture, it's so vague because it could be mindset, it could be practice, it could be things you do, things that your family does and all that." While astutely observing the vagueness of ethnic "culture," Pamela nonetheless expresses a strong desire to pass it down, though in the context of a more benign pluralist view of American society:

> I see America as a mosaic; you see the different parts and different colors, but it makes one big picture. We all melt but we also retain our individual cultures. I don't want us to become homogeneous and of the same kind.

Certainly there's the American culture simply because there's a nation . . .
but I don't want us to lose our individual ethnic cultures. And certainly, as
we marry and have kids, these cultures will change, and [the] definition of
culture will change, obviously for the kids. My kids will be Vietnamese and
Korean, and that's a new culture. So I think that's why it's important for me
to be 100% Korean and my husband to be 100% Vietnamese so we can pass
it down, and spread, spread, spread.

The rest of my interethnic couples, those in the majority passive group, were
not nearly as explicit and articulate about their intentions to maintain ethnic
identity and culture and to fend off ethnic/racial erasure. What was intriguing
though is that the uncertainty of what ethnic culture constitutes, as articulated
by Pamela, was common to both groups in my study.[3] This was reflected by the
fact that almost all individuals in both groups admitted that they never explicitly discussed cultural transmission in a systematic or planned manner with their
partners, one reason being that what should be transmitted, or how, was initially
unclear. Jeremy, the Korean American married to a Chinese American, who does
not yet have kids, commented: "Yeah, I haven't discussed it with my wife, like
explicitly. . . . Do we have a plan on how to do it? . . . My wife is a great plan-
ner . . . but we've never had that kind of an explicit conversation. . . . I guess
there is some sort of cultural difference [between us], but I don't know how this
will play out when my wife and I have kids. How does she want to transmit her
Chinese culture to the kids? How would I want to transmit Korean culture? I'm
not sure how." Indeed, regardless of whether one was intentional or assertive
about cultural transmission, one theme that emerged repeatedly for both groups
was that the transmission of culture and ethnicity was often an uncoordinated,
unpremeditated affair, accompanied by the oft-repeated statement that "we make
it up as we go along," or "we just sort of do it."

### Making Stuff Up as We Go Along

One major irony was that due to the lack of ethnic and cultural competency on
the part of most parents, the content of what was being passed down was not
only being constructed on an ongoing basis but was not very different between
the two groups, one ethnically proactive and the other passive. That is, whether
the participants were consciously making it a goal to pass down ethnic culture
or doing it more passively, the de facto content of cultural elements being transmitted were similar and basically could be boiled down to four key elements:
language, food, holiday celebrations, and values. However, in my finding, food
and holiday rituals were the only cultural elements that were being passed down
in any concrete and consistent way.[4]

Almost all the respondents said that they ate foods belonging to the ethnicities of both parents at home. Although the parents routinely cooked mainstream

"American" food as well, such as spaghetti or hamburgers, and often described their foods as "multiethnic," Asian-ethnic foods were something that the parents themselves spent their lives eating, and thus was simply a practice that they had no reason to discontinue. Sophie, the Japanese American married to a Chinese American, commented: "Well, I cook the majority of the time . . . but it's multi-ethnic. . . . Cooper is actually a better cook than me because, when he grew up, he was expected to cook, whereas in my family, the boy wasn't expected to do anything because he was a prince, whereas I'm the servant. But yeah, our food preference runs the gamut. I mean, I'm comfortable cooking, like, teriyaki . . . but I don't cook only Japanese food. Like tonight, we'd have pasta."

Even if the participants perceived food as the biggest "tie" to ethnic culture because it was passed down concretely from their parents, ethnic foods that were transmitted were also almost never in their "pure," original form, demonstrating the makeshift, improvised nature of ethnic foods down the generations. Samantha, for example, stated, "Yeah, my husband is a good cook, and I think a lot of his influence is from his grandmother who is Chinese. But he's one of those cooks—he just improvises. He just kind of whips things up and throws things together, and I would have to say that most of his dishes are more Americanized than Chinese or Japanese." Such descriptions illustrate not only the hybridized construction of ethnic elements such as food by the non-immigrant generations but also the evolution of pan-Asian culture.

Other scholars have described similar findings that food tends to become the most important residual ethnic-cultural element that gets practiced: "when immigration fades, ethnic cuisine takes on a distinctly American flavor that begins to lose its resemblance to cuisine from the ethnic homeland. What is more, when immigration wanes, food becomes a primary means through which individuals experience a purely symbolic form of ethnicity centered on sporadically involved symbols."[5] However, among my participants, holiday celebrations like the Chinese New Year or the Korean 100th-day birth celebration, and certain customs of gift-giving tied to these holidays, were also marked as worthy of cultural transmission and something that did not require a lot of investment or effort. Nora, the Korean American, qualified that although there was no question she would make an effort to transmit such ethnic traditions to her children, she would do it as long as it did not take too much effort: "I don't think I'm going to follow everything related to tradition or break my back to make sure I make all the proper foods for *Seol-Nal* [Lunar New Year holiday] or whatever. . . . We'll celebrate like the *Chuseok* [Harvest Festival], we'll do things like that and they'll probably do, like, *Sebae* [formal ritual bow]. I just want them to know that they have other options than just the White American register."

Like Nora, who also added that she would definitely want her kids to visit her and her spouse's countries and would try to teach the kids the two ethnic languages, numerous other participants also mentioned wanting to take the children to visit the family's countries of origin as another way of connecting the children to their ethnic cultures. The desire to acquaint the children to the "homeland" is a wish that may be abetted by contemporary forms of globalization and increasing transnational flows, though it is not certain how successfully those desires are ultimately fulfilled or how strongly these transnational ties can be maintained down the generations.[6] Many also mentioned making efforts to attend pan-Asian or ethnic events in the communities in which they lived, such as cultural festivals, as something they tried to do for their kids. Like the interracially married Asian-ethnics in the previous chapters, encouraging children to read books that are "Asian," books about Asia or with Asian characters, as well as viewing videos of ethnic dramas or movies, was offered up as another strategy of cultural retention by a number of participants.

Surprisingly, language transmission was one cultural element with which the participants struggled the most and was not being passed down in a consistent manner. All but three of the participants expressed a strong desire for the kids to learn the languages of both spouses. However, they simultaneously lamented that this was difficult to do as they did not know the language well themselves. Like many of the interracially married Asian-ethnics, many interethnic couples often grew up in households where English was primarily spoken, although some grew up in bilingual households. In either case, by the time of my interviews, none of the interviewees claimed to be even proficient in the languages. Sophie, who was concerned about passing down certain aspects of both Japanese and Chinese cultures, described their paltry efforts at language transmission: "We speak to them only in English, except when he [the husband] is trying to tell them to hurry up or do stuff." Jane, another Japanese American, said also of her children: "It [language transmission] would have been nice. They could have learned Chinese or Japanese. But then it would have been hard because neither of us speak it, and then we don't have grandparents or generations before us who spoke that well, so it is just too difficult." Jeff, a Korean American married to a Chinese American, described it this way:

> I mean, like I said, I would love to expose both my kids to the Korean language. But I think to expect them to know the language is pretty ludicrous in my mind given the fact that I don't speak Korean and no one in the family would speak Korean to them, and that my parents aren't too involved in their daily life so I don't expect them to learn . . . like I said, I just want them to be exposed [to the language]. We'll try Korean schools, we'll try Chinese schools, see what they like, then go from there. But I'm not going to push Korean school by any means. . . . I don't necessarily need to have my kids fully engrossed in the Korean culture for me to feel like they've been exposed to Korean culture.

As briefly mentioned in Chapter 4 on interracial couples, many interethnic couples like Jane and Jeff also perceived the presence of family members, especially grandparents, as central to the efforts to pass down language; in a small number of cases, this was moderately successful, but in most cases, it was not because either the grandparents were not around as much as they expected, or the grandparents often chose to speak English to the grandchildren in order to remove barriers to communication. As Gloria, the Filipina American married to a Korean American, put it, "I think they [grandparents] want the favor of the children, and if they're making them [the children] work too hard or whatever, they don't want the kids to just give up and not want to communicate with them. . . . I think that's where they're coming from." The grandparents' preference for speaking English was also often motivated by the fact that the grandchildren were multicultural, and the grandparents were reluctant to seem like they were emphasizing one cultural side over the other; thus, they often "defaulted" to English. Commenting on her mother's reluctance to speak Korean to her kid, Nora said, "there is no one else around [to speak Korean] and then like I ask my mom and everybody else to do it but they don't . . . my mom is not around very much . . . I have had conversations with her about how disappointing it's been."

Three respondents surprisingly did not even consider language to be an important cultural capital to pass down and did not attempt to push it on their kids, apart from teaching "little phrases." Sending kids to weekend language schools was often expressed as an option, and something some parents themselves had done as kids, but the parents were skeptical as to the effectiveness of these schools. Sophie remarked that she did not think that the kids would go to these schools, "just because we're so busy with other stuff . . . if anything, we'd send them to, like you know . . . Boy Scouts or Cub Scouts and Chess Club or something." The precarious and uncertain status of language as part of "ethnic culture" is summed up well by Pamela: "I like to think it [language] is more important than the way it actually is. Let me put it this way: I want my kids to know the language, but apparently it must not be that important to me if I'm not learning it on my own. You know what I mean? I want them to learn it, so I'm going to send them to someone like my parents to teach it to them?"

As for "values," the answers resembled some mentioned by the interracially married participants and were surprisingly similar across the board. The "Asian" values the interethnic couples agreed upon as being common to Asian heritage were things like "respect of parents and elders," "importance of family," "hard work," "being stoic," "education," "not talking back to grownups all the time," or mundane practices like "taking off shoes inside the house." Speaking of how important values like respecting elders were to her, Pamela had this to say: "Absolutely [it's important] and I think that comes from the Asian culture. I can't just say Korean culture because it's Asian culture. I am thankful that we both [she and her husband] have that. And that's not to say American culture doesn't have that because they do have that. It's just to a different degree." Jeff agreed that "honoring" one's family and elders was an important "Asian" value to "instill" in his kids, but he was not so sure of anything else: "but in terms of other values from a Korean perspective, I don't really have any particular point that I try to emphasize with my kids. To be honest, I don't know that many values from the Korean perspective myself."

### "It's Just Who We Are": Minimizing Intentionality and Normalizing "Asian" Difference

One feature that distinguished the more culturally passive group and the assertive group was the extent to which the culturally passive group tended to downplay or minimize the intentionality of their ethnic cultural engagement and transmission. For example, many in the passively inclined group did not think of "values" or ethnic culture in general as something they were *consciously* trying to pass down to their children, but only upon reflection realized that these were central to their own upbringing and something that they were trying to instill in their children in unintentional ways. Corinne, the Chinese American married to a Vietnamese American, explained, "We pass down things because that's who we are. It's not intentional . . . even with food. You need to know how to eat rice because we are Asians, and it's more like we're eating rice tonight because we like it, so you [children] are going to eat it too." She added:

> So obviously, I am Chinese American, so in any of the values or the culture or things that we pass down, it's just who we are. So I guess I am kind of—I don't think I am making a conscious effort to say, okay, we take our shoes off when we come into the house, and that's a Chinese thing, or this is an Asian thing, so kids, take off your shoes. . . . like I don't think there is anything like that going on.

For participants such as Corinne, "Asian" culture constituted a part of their "normal" cultural habitus, which, by virtue of being part of an Asian family and of being "who they are" that their "American" children came to embrace; these participants did not see themselves making any concerted effort to perform "Asianness." This stance also suggests the degree to which the participants were living the tensions of being, and wanting to be, seen as "normal" Americans despite their ethnic/cultural/physical distinctiveness. *Feeling* American and asserting normality ("it's just who we are"), even while they enacted certain features of their ethnic culture that they still knew to be marginalizing, can then be viewed as making a claim to American cultural citizenship and asserting a sense of connection to the mainstream.

Indeed, a number of individuals who did not perceive themselves as actively passing down much Asian culture also often talked about how "Americanized," even "White," they and their kids were.[7] Gloria and Aaron, a Filipina and Korean American couple, related that when all of their Asian American couple friends get together, it "tends to be Americanized," including the way they celebrate holidays, such as Christmas. Gloria admitted that, "only food is sort of ethnic," but even there, it is a mixture of "Korean, Japanese, Mexican, pizza, pasta." Jane, the Japanese American married to a Chinese American, said something similar; when asked what she thinks made her kids "Asian," she first said, "I don't know. . . . They're so . . . I think they're White!" She then quickly deflected, "No, I don't know. I think the food. So we like a lot of Asian food. But we eat a lot of American [food] too. I think that we are very Americanized." Though humorously referring to his kids as "Japachinos," Charlie gave the same answer to the question: "Probably what we eat. Our parents, of course. Other than that, yeah, hmmm, what makes us Asian besides our food? Other than that, they are Americans." Many of these participants reported they speak only English at home. Samantha confessed that in regard to her kids, her child-raising was rather devoid of ethnic culture: "There is not a lot of [ethnic] culture. . . . We just raised them as, I guess, so Americanized. That's the only way I can put it . . . that's kind of sad when you think about it. I was raised that way and I'm so clueless when it comes to culture, and my kids are basically being raised that way."

In short, most of the passively oriented couples recognize that despite their awareness of the importance of ethnic retention to some degree, the "default" culture for the families and children sometimes ends up being what they refer to as "American" rather than ethnic; that is, the kids are just as culturally immersed in the mainstream even though they are connected to certain elements of ethnic culture, and the families feel that they are as "American" as anyone else.[8] Indeed Jeremy, saying that even his best efforts to transmit ethnic culture would "only go so far" because of his lack of cultural competence, even speculated whether he would, in the end, be raising "White kids with really Asian faces." The interesting point here however is that these couples *do* pass down ethnic cultures, even if passively, but they don't *see* themselves as doing so, or being able to do so, and whatever they pass down, they see themselves as doing it by virtue of just "being who they are"—Americans with mixed Asian heritage. As Corinne reflected, "it's hard to talk about what I'm passing down to my children because I myself struggle with what is Chinese, what is Chinese American, what is Vietnamese. It's really hard to distinguish because it's just who I am."[9]

### Living Among Asian Americans: "My Kids Are Asians by Association!"

For all the parents, whether ethnically proactive or passive, another important way in which they believed they could ensure the transmission of "Asianness" was the following: living among other Asian-ethnics. A number of individuals expressed how important it was for their kids to live in places with other Asians around so that they could maintain their ethnic identities and cultures and also feel normal about who they are. Sophie, who lives in an area of Los Angeles with large numbers of Asian-ethnics, reflected, "That all plays into where we choose to live because . . . I don't want the kids to live where they are tokens. . . . There are a lot of Asian Americans here, and they can be themselves." Corinne expressed a similar sentiment: "One thing I want to say is that even though we may not be intentional about these things [ethnic culture], it's important that they be around Asians." Samantha, who admitted that she never sat down and had any extended conversations with her kids about their backgrounds, said that "just by virtue of the fact that they're living amongst Asians in California, I know they're getting Asian culture. It's kind of sad, but my kids are Asian by association!" She further clarified: "So it's not that I'm ignoring Asian culture, but I just don't have to work very hard at it because we have the Asian environment."

Other works have reported findings similar to what I have just described: the focus Asian-ethnic parents put on co-ethnic and/or pan-Asian association and community for ethnic identity/cultural retention. Mia Tuan, for instance, shows that in the face of their ineffective efforts at cultural transmission, even for food or holiday rituals, Asian-ethnic parents tended to believe that "culture ultimately resides within a sense of community and association rather than the ability to speak Chinese or Japanese, practice rituals, or prepare ethnic foods."[10] She also adds that this form of cultural transmission signified not necessarily the hope that the children remain highly ethnic but that they were being encouraged to "live an American lifestyle but to do so with other Asian Americans."[11] My findings certainly show that the main interest of Asian-ethnic parents, especially in the face of their own ethnic cultural incompetence, was to assure that the children at least retain a connection to their ethnic identities, or "who they are," through interaction with other Asian-ethnics.

By the same token, couples in my study who lived in predominantly White suburban neighborhoods who were not well versed in their ethnic cultures lamented that there was little they could do to promote ethnic culture in kids if there were no Asians with whom to associate. Just as interracial couples in previous chapters noted the importance of living in an urban and racially diverse environment in which their multicultural children would not be subjected to excessive racial prejudice or marked as "different," interethnic couples pointed out the great significance of living among, or at least in close proximity to, an Asian American community or a critical mass of Asian-ethnics that can serve as cultural resources for the children.

Expounding on this, Lewis, who lived in a place without a significant Asian community, had this to say:

> I feel that the best way to have the kids learn their ethnic heritage is not to browbeat them into doing it; it has to be organic. It has to be something you do every day in your household, the language you speak, what type of food you eat . . . having a support of Asian peer group . . . for my kids—that is a very important thing and I don't see that here.

Lewis said he would eventually like to move to a place like California that could provide such a community for his kids. Claire, the Chinese American wife of Jeremy, echoed Lewis's observation; living in a predominantly White town means "It's just us. So, there is nothing you can really do to promote [ethnic] culture. Neither of us is very well-versed. I'm more well-versed than he [her husband] is, but there is nobody to negotiate with. I mean, there is no Korean school, there's no Chinese school. . . . We don't even have a lot of international students here."

Jared, the Vietnamese American married to Corinne and living in a mostly White town, also expressed a similar sentiment about his kids, whom he thinks consider themselves White: "I would consider leaving here just because I want my kids to be around Asian people . . . when we go back to California, they . . . really connect with their cousins in a way unlike how they connect with any kids here, and I don't know why that is, but I find that to be a really interesting dynamic. But it's a general sense that we mourn them not being around Asian people." Narratives like these illustrate the pivotal importance of the Asian-ethnic community presence and associational networks in helping to maintain ethnic culture, and the challenges for those without these resources.

In sum, one of my findings regarding interethnically married Asian-ethnics is that while some of them made extra efforts to transmit their ethnic cultures to their multicultural children because they feared ethnic cultural erasure at some level, others, counterintuitively, took a certain amount of cultural transmission for granted because they were in an Asian-ethnic family unit, obviating the need to try hard to actively pass down ethnic culture. This questions the possible thesis that all pan-Asian couples are highly bent on consciously preserving their ethnic cultures or that they are more successful in their efforts to pass down their cultures than, for example, interracial couples. Indeed, when asked to imagine what they would do if they were married to a White spouse, several individuals definitively stated that they would probably make *more* of an effort to pass down their ethnic culture to make sure the kids "got their side of the story." Carter, for instance, asserted that if he had been married to a White spouse, he would "make sure my half gets represented. . . . I think I would be pushing a lot more stuff."

## Couples Negotiating Ethnic Cultures

The spouses negotiate respective cultures and ethnic identities within the context of their partnership and family-making. To what extent do interethnic couples struggle over negotiation of their respective cultures? What kinds of conflicts arise? As noted earlier, the interethnic couples in my study seldom talked explicitly about cultural negotiations. Most were also reluctant to admit that explicit tensions and negotiations over culture existed, and some indeed did not report much. What I have found, however, is that when probed, there was a considerable degree of negotiation, and even conflicts, occurring, and like the interracial couples, these seemed to emerge almost always when children entered the picture. In all cases, the couples stated that they wanted their respective cultures to be passed down equally to their children, but the reality was that the contribution of each parent to the passing down of his or her ethnic culture, or the emphasis of it, was often uneven. This was sometimes openly admitted to me and did not appear to generate a great deal of overt conflict between the spouses, but in other cases, overt conflicts emerged, with one spouse complaining that the other emphasized his or her culture too much or not enough.

## Imbalances in Cultural Transmission and Negotiation Conflicts

About half of the couples did not report any conflicts or divergent expectations. With the other half, reports of efforts at active negotiation, of imbalances in cultural transmission and even of conflicts over negotiations, emerged. Corinne, the Chinese American married to Vietnamese American Jared, explained that there was definitely an imbalance in which side gets passed down; because of her greater ethnic cultural fluency and time with the kids, she ended up teaching them more "Chinese things," including language: "because I feel like I know more Chinese, and because I am with them more, I teach them the things that I know." Pamela makes a similar observation about her interethnically married sister: "Yeah . . . it's interesting because with my sister and her Taiwanese husband; they are both Americanized . . . and I think my sister wants to teach them [the kids] both cultures . . . but it's funny because they learn more Korean words than they do Taiwanese just because my sister is with them all the time . . . But the interesting thing is, her husband speaks the language pretty well, and my sister doesn't know Korean very well . . . but he doesn't really care." Jeff, a Korean American whose Chinese American wife Becky is a stay-at-home mom, observed the following: "Yes, I mean absolutely. I think they're getting more exposure to the Chinese culture, ethnicity, much more so than Korean. But I'm okay with that. I think it has more to do with the fact that my in-laws are interactive with my kids versus the fact that my wife is force-feeding Chinese culture on them."

A number of couples described similar concerns about and efforts at negotiating the two cultures. Similar to Jeremy's worries about how he would negotiate cultural transmission with his wife, Nora fretted about how she would handle the issue of cultural transmission equitably with her husband. Talking about language transmission in particular, she remarked: "Yeah, so I just feel like hopefully, we can find a way in which we can balance language schools for instance, and I'm not exactly sure how we're going to do this. . . . So it would be that maybe like one season, we'll put her [the child] in my husband's language school, and then we'll just kind of go back and forth . . . or . . . we could just start attending a church or temple or whatever where they teach the language as part of the service . . . so we'd sit in service and then she'd go learn the language. And maybe that way it [the two language classes] won't both be on Saturdays." Nora's narrative indicates how much thought and effort can go into trying to effect bicultural transmission for those who want to pass down both sides equitably.

Chinese American Becky spoke similarly about the increasing need to engage in complex cultural negotiations with her Korean American husband as their kids grow up, though cultural differences were never a problem when they were dating. She explained:

> They're not huge issues at this point, but we have had discussions about things like, how are we going to raise our kids, have them be aware of who they are, because they're half Chinese and half Korean. One simple example is, do we send kids to Chinese [language] school or Korean school? Is it beneficial to send them to both or to one . . . I'm Chinese and I want to teach my kids about their Chinese background, so I think we are going to have to address that as they get older. . . . But I don't know if either of us are willing to compromise. . . . So as they get older, we are going to have to face more decisions about how we expose them to their backgrounds. Another example is, my son is getting older and we want to enroll him in classes. So I was talking to another mom, a Korean woman, and she signed her kids up for Taekwondo before, and she realized that it was not that practical and signed them up for Jujitsu and . . . the kids find it very fun. . . . So I said to my husband, why don't we just sign our son up for Jujitsu, and he was like nope, our son *has* to take Taekwondo. He said, "That's the one thing that I want him to keep. He doesn't have to continue it, but as a Korean man, it's one thing I want him to try and do". . . . So now as we are raising our kids, our opinions about kids come up.

What is clearly conveyed in Becky's comments is that she not only foresaw a substantial need for cultural negotiation with her husband, but even possibly conflicts, because both she and her husband felt equally strongly about transmitting their respective cultures and Becky wanted to make sure that her side did not get subordinated.

Becky's husband Jeff, in contrast, presents himself as more laid-back about the possible imbalance, though he definitely seemed concerned about it:

> Yeah . . . as long as I give them the opportunity to get exposure to it [Korean culture] that's all I ask. If it was something where Becky was adamant that it's only going to be, let's say, just Chinese school and nothing else . . . I would be a little offended by that. It would feel to me that she is rejecting half of who our kids are and rejecting my culture, and I guess in a sense, rejecting me as a result of that. But Becky has never once been opposed from that perspective so that's never been a problem.

But he adds:

> Just for my own . . . I don't know if ego is the right word, but I would like
> to be able to stoke the national pride of Korea in my kids. I want them to
> be proud to be Korean, just like I'm proud to be Korean. But at the same
> time, I make it a point to tell my kids they're also part Chinese as well. . . .
> But I think because I'm not too attached to Korean culture, it's easier for
> me to have my wife and my in-laws kind of having them [kids] gravitate
> toward the Chinese culture just because they [in-laws] are around more.
> And that's fine. I mean, for the most part, my expectation is that they're
> going to be very American.

Justin, another highly Americanized Korean American, observed that his
Cambodian American wife wants to draw on her cultural side in the upbringing
of their children and worried that there might be a conflict between his wife and
himself about this:

> I would like my children to know who they are and know what being
> Korean is about. So one of the things I'm worried about is that there might
> be a sort of a clash, where more would be based on my wife's side and my
> wife's culture and the influence of her family. It's a very narrow time frame
> when it comes to grabbing hold of the kids, and I know that my wife's
> culture is going to be probably more because of the importance she has
> placed on that.

Some participants outrightly complained about what they perceived as inequities in cultural transmission. Japanese American Sophie thought that her husband Cooper's Chinese side definitely overshadowed her Japanese side, because
her husband's family was into maintaining its cultural traditions while her third-
generation Japanese American family was more low-key about it: "I have more
challenges navigating my life in his family than he does in my family . . . they
have all these cultural customs . . . like for our wedding, they had all these cultural things that we had to do, which irritated me because it wasn't a part of any
wedding that I had been in, and you know, because I'm not Chinese . . . the only
custom we had was the dove and crane thing."

Stating that "it's really hard being married to a Chinese family," Sophie also
talked about conflicts arising from what she saw as her husband's subconscious
tendency to assert and value his ethnic culture and identity over hers. This
included her husband trying to teach Chinese to the kids because his Chinese is
slightly better than her Japanese, and though this is okay with her, she is annoyed
because she always has to remind the kids that that there is "another side." Their

conflict included fights, for example, over their different approaches to the value and use of money:

> The first fight we had was over money because my husband's [being Chinese] been raised to be aware [of] the value of money, whereas the way I grew up, I didn't have a checking account until I went to college. . . . And when I get upset, my husband would often say things to [the] kids like, "Oh, Mommy is just upset that she's not Chinese" and I told him that "You've got to quit saying that because the kids think being Chinese is better," and he's like "Well, it is," and I told him that if you thought that you should not have married me. . . . It's harder to be a non-Chinese in a Chinese culture than to be a non-Japanese in a Japanese culture.

Her husband, to the contrary, told me that he and his wife were trying to raise their children as "Asian American" and "not trying to push one culture over another." He, however, admitted:

> We want both sides to be represented equally, but what we do is not conscious sometimes. I would consciously try to do things [the] Chinese way, and my wife would protest, "But there is another half here!" And I admit I do say to [the] kids things like "Because you have Chinese blood, etc." and my wife says things like, "In Japanese culture, we do it like this, etc." So we do have a conflict over a way of doing things sometimes, but it's hard to talk about it, like how you do things in a certain way, even washing dishes . . . we don't really have a conversation about how we do little things, so if I teach one way and my wife another way, and I see [the] kids doing it another way, I'm like, "Oh, why are you doing it like that?" I don't even realize I'm doing that.

Sophie does realize, however, that despite this imbalance, she is able to transmit certain "ways of being Japanese," without even realizing she's passing [them] down; she refers to some of these cultural elements as "group centeredness," "thinking about other people first," "harmony," and "respect for elders." Sophie's description of the more intangible "ways of being" that are embodied by individuals and passed down at a subconscious level is reminiscent of Pierre Bourdieu's concept of "habitus."[12] Negotiating her dissatisfaction with the fact that her cultural side and family gets "ignored," and that her husband's family "doesn't really pay attention" to her family and its culture, her goal is to raise her kids as "Asian Americans," and to have a strong "Asian American identity," not just being a "Chinese kid or a Japanese kid."[13]

Shane, though a Chinese American, expressed concerns that his ethnic culture was being overshadowed by his more culturally fluent Vietnamese American wife Marie. Confessing that there is, from his perspective, "a lot of conflict" between them in terms of cultural negotiation, he said, "I'm fearful that the Chinese part won't be well represented, but that's something we both agree that we are going to work on."[14] One way in which he felt that his wife's side was overwhelming his was her strong emphasis on family; while that was a major point of his attraction to his wife, he sometimes became resentful of how closely knit her family was, which tended to dominate their family dynamic; this included Marie's strongly felt obligation to support her family. He remarked: "So in a way, I'm kind of defaulting to her. Because for me . . . I feel a lot more Americanized than her. My Chinese isn't very good. So I don't speak any Chinese, and . . . her parents live with us."

Though he hasn't been very "forceful" about pushing Chinese culture on his kids, Shane does want to at least "preserve some of that culture" with the kids. His wife Marie portrayed a slightly different picture; while it was clear that the kids were getting a bit more from the Vietnamese side, mostly because of Marie's parents' presence in the household, she did not see herself as particularly culturally fluent nor as pushing ethnicity too heavily. She also saw herself as giving their kids a lot of rope in terms of letting them choose what they want, saying, "whatever we can carry on, we can pass it on to them . . . but in the end, it's up to them."[15]

## Conflicts Avoided: Relying on the Spouse for Cultural Work or Taking the Practical Approach

In some cases, obversely, one spouse, especially if he/she was culturally dominant in the relationship, complained that the other did not do enough "cultural work" at home in regard to his/her own ethnic culture for the children. In these cases, it appeared that if one side became emphasized more, it was primarily due to the other partner's lackadaisical attitude toward his or her culture. For example, even though Chinese American Corinne admits that her ethnic side gets emphasized more, she expressed concern that the kids were not getting enough of her husband's Vietnamese culture and that it was she who had to do everything:

> I am actually the one pushing Vietnamese things, too, like telling [the] kids to call their Vietnamese grandma in Vietnamese. My husband is not teaching them anything, zippo. The only reason they know any Vietnamese is because of me. Because I feel like they *should* know; I don't want them growing up speaking only Chinese. . . . I don't think that my husband doesn't want to teach them; I just don't think he makes a conscious effort. I don't know why. So the thing we have thought about is that we should teach them Spanish rather than Chinese or Vietnamese, because Spanish is something we both know.

Stella, a Cambodian American married to Korean American Justin, commented, "Honestly, I think I embraced my husband's culture more than he did mine. He does like Korean food, but I'm always asking him, how do you say this in Korean, or that in Korean, and I've encouraged him to visit Korea when we went on a trip to Asia. I don't know if he lost his culture somewhere along the way, but I'm big on mine. I don't think he'll bring a lot of his culture."

Gloria, the Filipina American, expressed a similar situation with regard to her Korean American husband, Aaron, whom she observed did very little cultural work with their children: "And so my husband's Korean isn't the greatest, and he's not teaching them things. Like I used to watch them [the kids] brush their teeth and count in numbers, like one through ten in Filipino for top teeth, and in Spanish for bottom teeth. I tell my husband like you should at least teach them how to count to them in Korean, but he doesn't—he's busy, he's working. . . . He just doesn't introduce stuff to them. I at least try to teach Filipino language to them . . . like both of my parents speak English to my kids, so I'll say, 'Can you please speak to them in Filipino?'" Gloria attributed much of her husband's lack of passion about his culture both to his cultural incompetency and being too "busy": "I think it's too active of a thing to do, and I think he feels already spread too thin to have one more thing on his plate to worry about . . . he has to worry about work, he has to worry about finances . . . about his job."

Korean American Nora said about her Vietnamese American spouse:

> I think it's interesting. I don't know how much of a negotiation we are going to have to do with [our child] because I feel like Dennis is like not—I don't know if he's aware of this or not—but I don't feel like he's as invested in passing his culture on to her. Because I think for him, it's always kind of been this background thing. . . . And I'm like, well, why don't you speak your ethnic language with her? And he barely does . . . obviously English, he's more comfortable with it. . . . But I think the other thing is that maybe he feels like, "Oh my mom speaks it, it's enough." Like "She'll get it somehow" . . . and maybe like very subconsciously . . . maybe he doesn't want to. It's like, "I have this American kid now, born in the U.S., and I have an Asian American wife." I don't know . . . it's curious to me because I am like trying at every turn to like throw in Korean words and some Korean phrases. . . . And I just, for me, I just feel like I want to do this. I don't want her to grow up like a lot of other Korean Americans I know where they're like, "God, I wish my parents had taught me the language." Like, "I wish I had another realm in which I operated culturally" or felt some connection to, culturally.

The couples described here are illustrative of cases where there is something of a mismatch in attitudes toward and role in cultural transmission. The more apathetic partners either behave as if they do not care about ethnic cultural transmission, but even if they do, they seem to do very little about it, relying on their partners or hoping that the children will "get it somehow" by virtue of being Asian American or being around co-ethnics.

These participants indeed rarely contradicted the claims of their more concerned spouses, typically admitting that they were not doing much to push their
culture on the children. When asked what kinds of ethnic/cultural efforts he
makes toward his children, Gloria's husband, Aaron, said the kids do not get
much "culture" except to hang out with his relatives once in a while where
mostly English is spoken anyway. Framing his explanation with a "we," he added:

> Well, the answer is, we haven't like pushed certain cultures toward [our
> kids]. Well, like . . . we're not trying to get them to learn Korean language
> or Filipino language. My preference is that they learn Spanish and then—so
> from a cultural standpoint, to be honest with you, we don't really push cul-
> ture . . . you know, if people ask he's probably going to say he's half Korean,
> half Filipino, which is Asian, but we don't really try to push like one culture
> over the other.

Confessing that he would not be able to define what Korean "culture" is, Aaron
does, however, admit that he would like to teach things like "respecting other
people," but "not necessarily just with Asians" but "in general." Despite the fact
that his wife Gloria sees herself as making more of an effort with regard to Filipino culture, Aaron expresses a divergent perspective here that neither he nor
his wife do much to "push" ethnic cultures on the kids. This indeed may reflect
Aaron's highly lackadaisical attitude toward ethnic transmission that leads him to
project his beliefs onto his wife, or to discount his wife's efforts and concerns;
whatever the reason, such couples do not tend to see themselves in competition
with each other.

Some participants managed to avoid conflicts by attempting to take a practical approach to cultural negotiation. Jeremy, for instance, expressed a desire that
both Korean and Chinese cultures be passed down equally to his future children, despite his and his wife's "weak grasp" of Chinese and Korean cultures,
but thought that whichever culture that was most useful and practical could take
precedence:

> I want the child to be exposed to both, and I would be okay with even like
> the emphasis of more Chinese versus more Korean, but only to the extent
> that if there is something practical about the whole issue. . . . There are
> simply more resources for cultivating Chinese culture than there are for
> Korean culture [such as language classes offered] . . . so if we are strapped
> for time and money, at least give them a part of their culture. . . . If we have
> to make a practical decision, I'd probably go in the direction I just said; if it
> had to be greater emphasis on Chinese versus Korean, I'd be okay with that.

For those who lacked ethnic language skills, several participants stated they
preferred teaching another language—Spanish came up repeatedly—over the

languages of either parent. Again, such statements challenge the assumption that ethnic retention is necessarily highly and consciously valued for all interethnic couples, especially in the absence of cultural fluency, or that if ethnic retention is valued, it may be valued only on a selective basis.

## Inter-Asian Hierarchy?

The previous section brings an interesting issue of possible inter-Asian ethnic hierarchy relation to the process of family-making. Existing literature is replete with works that examine inequalities between the dominant "majority" cultures and "minority" cultures. A central theme within the study of race and ethnicity and immigration in the United States has been the dynamics and ramifications of an unequal power relationship among the majority Whites and minority groups of color. The literature, however, is relatively scant on the issue of hierarchies within the same ethnic or racial group, including among Asian Americans of different origins.[16]

Even though it may have appeared that the extent to which the spouses were more passive or active in maintaining ethnic culture was random, or that this was determined mostly by the cultural competence of the spouse involved, I have found that subtle dynamics of inter-Asian inequalities may be at play for some couples along the lines of national origins. First, there is no question that the different Asian groups, among themselves, have stereotypes about each other and perceive that there is a hierarchy among nations designated as Asian-Pacific. When asked if there are hierarchies among Asian groups, the answers from the participants were invariably as follows: Chinese or Japanese at the top, Koreans next, then perhaps Vietnamese, Asian-Indians, and Filipinos after that, and then other Southeast Asians.

In terms of stereotypes, the Chinese, for example, were commonly described by the participants as "frugal," and fixated on money matters, and ethnocentric about their culture. To my surprise, more than one Japanese American I spoke to was admonished by their parents and family to avoid marrying a person of Chinese descent because the Japanese culture may be "erased."[17] The Koreans were described as having rigid patriarchal social and familial systems, and the men as "angry," "bad tempered," "hard drinking" and the women as "materialistic." Chinese men were seen as less rigidly patriarchal—for example, more willing to cook and do housework—but Chinese women as "headstrong." Vietnamese were also stereotyped as materialistic but in a more "flashy, showy" way, with the implication that they were the least disciplined about money. Filipinos were viewed as being the least ethnocentric and most willing to out-marry with Whites, an observation that is supported by existing scholarly evidence. Japanese Americans were viewed as laid-back and more subtle about cultural assertions, as being "proper" "trying not to stand out," and having "tolerance, honor." They, however, also carried stereotypes of being "imperialistic" (references to the Japanese colonial past in Asia). One respondent related to me a familiar wisecrack that encapsulate some of these stereotypes: "Koreans are the ones with the big house and a nice car, Chinese are the ones with the big house and the small car, and Vietnamese have small houses and a big car."

Although the participants did not like to admit any inequalities or hierarchies in their marital or cultural dynamics, a cautious observation could be made that these potential inequalities may have played into some of the couples' dynamics. As mentioned, there was a detectable pattern in which spouses of both Japanese and Korean descent married to Chinese Americans, for example, expressed concerns that their heritage may get a short shrift if they do not make an extra effort. Recall that Sophie, the Japanese American married to a Chinese American expressed fear and her general perception that Chinese Americans in general are more assertive about their cultures than other groups, certainly more so than Japanese Americans, who she felt were quieter about showcasing their culture. Conversely, Aaron, the Korean American married to a Filipina, stated that he did not have much cultural conflict with his wife but admitted that the kids were much more surrounded by intraethnically or intermarried Korean friends and their kids than Filipinos, implying a possible dominance of his influence.

Aaron's wife Gloria confirmed both statements; she agreed that their closest social circles were made of Korean Americans and their spouses, but that there was not much dynamic of cultural inequality or conflict within their relationship. If any sort of imbalance existed, Gloria appeared to "resolve" the issue of any possible cultural power differential by taking the "default" position of raising the kids as "American" however possible. Indeed, when asked whether her kids identify more with the Filipino or the Korean side, she replied, "Probably both, I would say. We hang around with more Korean Americans and their children . . . but it's kind of like we are all Americanized, what we do and how we talk, and what we would eat." When queried how she would prefer her kids identify themselves when they grow up, Gloria responded, "I want them to identify themselves as like scholar-athlete type of kids. Kids who are smart, kids who play sports, kids who play well with others . . . no matter who they are or what they look like. I want them to be good kids . . . that's how I was raised. . . . I just want them to be, I guess, American."

Interestingly, despite her denial of any dynamic of inequality within her own marriage, Gloria made a matter-of-fact observation about the reality of hierarchy among Asian groups and went on to direct a pointed critique at Koreans in particular—which may hint at some internal power imbalance she may feel within her marriage—while her husband Aaron denied that he ever "sensed" any hierarchy among Asian groups. Using an example of a few times she attended a Korean ethnic church, she said:

> I think Korean Americans have—I don't know. It's like they may place themselves above others . . . it's very subtle. . . . So we were at a Korean

church and . . . I brought a couple of [Filipina] girlfriends to that church, and I don't think they saw it as a welcome church . . . you know, ironically, it's a church, right? It's supposed to be inclusive, welcoming people. But . . . there was a Korean sense about that and it was a Korean thing. . . . I don't know. There is like an exclusivity, where it's like an inside joke thing or like saying things in Korean. . . . So I kind of felt like there is a little, little bit [of hierarchy] there, but I never thought that about other groups, no.

Stella, the Cambodian American, commented that the stereotypes of Korean American men as being patriarchal are such that when she set out to marry her husband, her friends asked her, "Are you sure you want to do that?"

The Vietnamese American, Dennis, married to a Korean American confessed that he may not be doing such a great job of passing down his side of the culture compared to his wife, and frankly speculated that his more lackadaisical attitude about ethnic culture may partly stem from the fact that he was perhaps ashamed of being from Vietnam growing up: "Yeah, I look back now at what we went through just to get here, and I'm actually very proud of it, and I share that story with other people openly when they ask. But I think as a kid . . . I was more ashamed of it than I was proud and just did not reveal to anybody that I was from Vietnam and whatnot." He hopes the kids will identify as Asian American, or as a hyphenated American, and plans to put more effort to help make this happen.[18]

Pamela, the Korean American, describes this hierarchy in terms of her parents' reactions when finding out about her Vietnamese American partner: "It's funny because me dating a Vietnamese guy, my mom was like . . . of course Koreans have [a] stereotype for every single Asian ethnicity. I can't remember what she said about the Vietnamese; I want to say she said that they are stubborn. . . . I was like 'Whatever, Mom'. . . . But yeah, I'm finding that you know Koreans, Chinese . . . maybe Whites, and then everything else is below that." She elaborated:

> I'm trying to remember what their first questions was [sic]—I think it was "What does he do?" I said, "Doctor," and they said, "Go on." And my mom tries to guess, "Is he Korean?" I'm like, "No." "Is he Chinese?" "No." "Is he White?" "No." I'm like, "Keep guessing, Mom," and I think she said, "Is he Vietnamese?" and I'm like, "Yeah," and she was like "Aarggggh" . . . then she said a stereotypically negative thing. . . . My dad was more logical about it and asked me "What he is doing now?" . . . They met him, spoke to him. My dad got along well with him, but they of course had to find something negative about him; it came down to the way he talked, something about him not talking very clearly, which he does. . . . I hate to say that, but they are just happy that . . . I met someone. . . . Like, "Oh, my God, you're 36 years old," and I think they were really scared.

Pamela added that to her parents, it did not hurt that her partner was more "Chinese" looking than Vietnamese.

The issue of hierarchy is subtle and difficult to tease out, and requires further research. But there is a sense in which, for a number of the couples in my study, the side that is lower on the ethnic hierarchy may defer in some key ways to the one with the higher ranking. As mentioned earlier, Stella, even after admitting that her relatively "Americanized" Korean American husband does not do much to pass down his culture, confessed that she embraced his culture more than he did hers, and thinks that the kids would identify as Korean American rather than Cambodian American. This is curious given that she is the one who is more ethnic-culturally fluent in the marriage. In some cases, it may be that the greater cultural competency of one partner may override the possible consequences of any interethnic hierarchy, but the issue of inter-group power dynamics and how this may interact with the issue of cultural competence may be worth investigating further in future research.

Another clue to the possible relevance of this hierarchy is that inter-Asian hierarchy is most often voluntarily brought up by the individuals belonging to the group lower on the ranking. Jared, the Vietnamese American, said clearly, "Yes, there is definitely a 'pecking order' among the Asian groups." He then related a story about his brother who had married into a Korean American family and the mistreatment he received within that family. He said that his brother had a "really hard time" in that family for a long time and received a "fair amount of prejudice" from them, being forced to deal with "rude" comments like they had never seen a Vietnamese man as tall as he was: "They thought that was a compliment, but it was offensive." Complementing this view, Korean American Nora, when asked about the possible dynamic of the intercultural hierarchy issue within her marriage, first hesitated, then admitted that it is there in "some way," and she often feels "awkward" because she feels that her husband's Vietnamese family privileges her sometimes: "I feel like maybe they're [her husbands' family] drawing on certain Asian-ethnic hierarchies because I think a lot of people are now impressed with Korea, right? Korea being such an economic giant right now. Culturally, everybody is watching their dramas and movies. I almost feel like they look up to me sometimes."

## Conclusion

Despite the fact that the racial group referred to as "Asian American" is composed of a highly diverse range of nationalities/ethnicities, the pervasive image of Asian Americans as a culturally/racially monolithic group has hindered sociological explorations of the interethnic dynamics among Asian Americans. In this chapter, I have attempted to offer an inside look at these dynamics in the context of interethnic marital unions, particularly in terms of how different ethnic/national identities and cultures are negotiated and constructed within the context of interethnic marriage and family-making. Although most of the interethnically married couples believe that they share the Asian American identity, the constructed, negotiated, and shifting nature of "Asian American" is thrown into full relief when these couples struggle to define what being "Asian American" means in their creation of interethnic family lives and culture.

Although participants draw upon cultural elements from different sides, what was striking was the degree to which this "Asianness" was relatively devoid of much tangible cultural content because of the participants' lack of cultural fluency, and often, community/family cultural resources. Aside from their recitation of some "Confucian-type" cultural features as being common among all "Asian American" groups, these families are retaining rather thin, diluted, and disembedded forms of ethnic cultures that are made up as participants go along, and which some do not even see as all that Asian. Unexpectedly, the ethnic cultures being maintained here bear considerable similarities to the "symbolic" forms of ethnicity practiced by later generation European-ethnic groups.[19]

The situation of Asian Americans in this study is in no way the same as the earlier generation European-ethnics, however. As racialized, minoritized ethnics marked by their physiology and "foreignness," Asian Americans do not have the luxury of optionally practicing their ethnicity or blending into the dominant White group; because they cannot do so, interethnic couples strive to craft an identifiable Asian American culture and identity through which they can internally and externally signal an understanding of themselves. In constructing this identity, the participants struggled keenly to define "Asianness" as representing a distilled essence of what they are as a group, something which they felt connected all the national groups and could represent them as "Asian Americans."

An argument I make, however, is that this hybridized Asian American identity does not simply connote an oppositional group assertion nor a racial boundary closure against the majority White culture but involves both accommodation to and resistance against the mainstream.[20] Although the experiences of racism are very real for the participants, none of the interethnically married participants viewed their unions or family-making as a way of rejecting their Americanness.[21] Rather, they were struggling to find ways of making claims to social belonging from a position of marginalization and cultural/social exclusion. Asian interethnic marriage and the panethnic identity and culture created within it then can perhaps be seen an alternative, ethnically and racially based way of being American.

As we witnessed, however, the construction of this hybrid panethnic culture can be a fraught process with considerable interethnic tensions and conflict. This is because the hybridizing process, even if experienced as new and empowering, is inherently a disruptive process involving instabilities and deep dislocations. As Homi Bhabha puts it, such dislocations may include "dissonances that have to be crossed despite proximate relations; the disjunction of power or positions that have to be contested; the values, ethical and aesthetics, that have to be 'translated' but will not seamlessly transcend the process of transfer."[22] Creation of hybrid cultural forms are also often unsettling and uncertain processes as such cultural constructions are ongoing and offers no promise of closure.

## Notes

1. Parts of this chapter have appeared in Chong 2017.
2. See Chong 1998; Smith 1990; Song 2003, 118.
3. Tuan (1998) divides her respondents into three groups in terms of how cultural traditions were being retained. For her, the first, most active group, consists of older respondents. The second, largest group, are those who are similar to my largest group; they are those who "claim that culture is important but are at a loss to show how this is so in their lives" (113). The third group consists of those who claim little importance of retaining ethnic culture; I have found no correspondence to this group.
4. Cf. Tuan 1998; Kibria 2002; Guevarra 2012.
5. Jiménez 2010b, 122; also see Alba 1990; Waters 1990. Tuan (1998) describes something similar in her book; she also notes that eating ethnic foods was one of the few cultural elements that were observed with any regularity and that what was consumed was a hodgepodge of American and Asian-ethnic foods.
6. Espiritu 2003; Song 2003.
7. Cf. Vasquez 2017, 128; O'Brien 2008, 40–42.
8. Tuan (1998, 115) also notes that some of her respondents were unclear as to whether the "ethnic" values they purport to ascribe to were actually ethnic or just universal values, such as stress on education, working hard, and so on.
9. Unlike what has been uncovered in other studies, none of my interethnic couples expressed a refusal to transmit ethnic culture with the reason that they did not want their kids to be stigmatized as being "different." Tuan (1998, 64), for example, describes parents who intentionally "pick and choose" elements of ethnic culture that would not make their kids be viewed as too different, or choose not to pass down ethnic culture at all. For my participants, it is possible that there may be an unconscious process of ethnic cultural selection that keeps the participants and their families from standing out from the mainstream too much in a negative way. This lack of conscious wish to reject ethnic cultures may be reflective both of the strength of panethnic identity of the participants and the ascendance of multicultural ideology in the United States.
10. Tuan 1998, 58.
11. Tuan 1998, 67
12. Bourdieu 1984.
13. The generally "laid-back" nature of cultural transmission found in families of Japanese origin may have to do with the psychological legacy of the historical treatment of the Japanese in the United States, especially of the Japanese internment, which has led to self-silencing about racism in many families (especially the interned generation) and a desire to overcompensate by becoming "super" Americans and de-emphasizing Japanese cultural elements in family-making. See Tuan 1998, 66; Nagata 1993; Takezawa 2000. By the same token, Saenz et al. (1995)'s article on ethnic identity among children of interracially married couples reported that children of Anglo-Chinese couples are most likely to hold the strongest ethnic (Chinese or Asian) identity (least likely to have an Anglo identity) than children of other Anglo-Asian couple combinations.
14. At least one other study has reported a similar finding; Mia Tuan (Tuan 1998, 124) mentions a finding that "For respondents with interethnic and interracial children, their hope is to expose them to both sides of their cultural background even though, as some acknowledge, greater emphasis may be placed on one side." Her example suggests that the more culturally fluent spouse, or a spouse who has a stronger grandparent presence, may end up exerting more ethnic influence on the children.
15. This finding that the parents tend to see themselves as ultimately giving the "choice" to their children to decide how ethnic to be, or which ethnicity to emphasize, is also echoed in Tuan's work (1998, 125).

16. There are a few exceptions. One article that explicitly addresses the issue of inter-Asian hierarchy in the context of marital and dating preference is by Gin Yong Pang (1994). Nazli Kibria (2002, 174–75) also reports on inter-Asian preference of her informants in terms of dating and marital preference. Both studies discuss the inter-Asian nation-based rankings in a general way, and both of these rankings confirm my findings. See also Bonilla-Silva 2004, 938; Kasinitz et al. 2004, 10; Moran 2001; O'Brien 2008, 116; Spickard 1989; Tuan 1998.

17. Evidence suggests that in Hawaii, where the Japanese occupy the top of the ethnic and racial hierarchy, the situation is not quite the same; the general sense there is that the Japanese culture dominates others.

18. Ed, a Filipino American with a Korean American wife, pointed not so much to the lower placement of Filipinos in the ethnic/national hierarchy to explain the imbalance of ethnic transmission but to the lack of cultural leverage Filipinos may have because of less robust Filipino immigrant institutions: "Koreans have their churches, Sunday schools, but we don't as much." He felt that the only element of Filipino culture he could pass down was holidays.

19. Cf. Dhingra 2007, 122; Kim 2004; Tuan 1999.

20. Also see Lee 1996.

21. In contrast, some recent findings on Latinos, such as those by Jessica Vasquez (2017, 145), document how some endogamous or interethnc Latino marriages were predicated on rejection of whiteness.

22. Bhabha 1997 quoted in Hall 2000, 226.

# 7

# DOES GENDER MATTER?

Gender disparities in interracial marriage rates among Asian Americans are a long-established pattern, with more Asian-ethnic women than men marrying out with non-Asians, predominantly with Whites. These disparities are largely rooted in racialized images long attached to Asian-ethnic women and men; hyper-sexualized but submissive and docile stereotypes of Asian women as a focal point of their appeal to Western men, and the feminized and nerdy images of Asian males as central to their low placement in the U.S./global masculinity hierarchy. As noted in Chapter 2, gender-based disparity in interracial marriages diminishes in the second generation and later, suggesting that at least for the U.S.-raised/-born generation, Asian American men may not be as disadvantaged in terms of desirability as romantic partners to non-Asians than the first-generation. Indeed, particularly in the past 20 years or so, a discernable improvement in terms of societal and media images of Asian Americans—of men especially—suggests some shifts in the images of Asian Americans. At the same time, upward trends in interethnic marriages among the U.S.-raised/-born Asian-ethnics substantiate increased desirability of Asian Americans as dating/marital partners in relation to each other.

In view of possible changes in societal perceptions of Asian-ethnics, in tandem with changing self-perceptions of Asian Americans, does gender still matter for Asian-ethnic women and men in relation to romance and marriage? In what ways does gender still affect men and women in terms of their positionality and experiences in the dating/marriage market? In this chapter, I will address this issue, drawing both upon the responses of my participants and current media narratives by and about Asian Americans. I complement the analysis of my interview data with a textual analysis of present-day popular media images and narratives about Asian Americans because of the disproportionate and fundamental impact popular media historically have had, and still do, on the societal and self-perceptions of Asian Americans. In his study of Chinese American masculinities, Chan refers to this relationship as the "dialectical link between popular culture and individual male identity formations," and that "Without such changes, the fictional models of masculinities represented in popular culture control and limit the ways in which Chinese American men articulate their individual notions of masculinity."[1]

Based on my evidence, I contend that gender does still matter for Asian American men and women when it concerns their value and desirability in the dating/marriage market, with Asian-ethnic women still enjoying a relative "advantage." This is the case despite the evidence of subtle shifts in social discourses about and images of Asian-ethnic men in popular media venues. At the same time, I argue that the "advantage" of Asian-ethnic women in the cross-racial dating market should not be read as some grand testament to their position of gender-racial superiority relative to White women; in spite of their ostensibly favorable position in the marriage/dating market relative to Asian-ethnic men, Asian-ethnic women's romantic desirability is still tethered to their romantic and sexual capital as "exotic" sex objects and as paragons of conventional hyper-femininity.

## Changing Images of Asian Americans at the Dawn of the Twenty-First Century

In the twenty-first century, images of Asian Americans in the U.S. are undergoing unprecedented transformations. These changes are not dramatic enough to overturn historical stereotypes, but Asian Americans are now portrayed in popular culture in ways never before seen. First, coinciding with the rise of multiculturalist discourses and ideologies of diversity, the hitherto out-of-sight Asian-ethnics are simply more visible in the media. Along with history-making television shows and Hollywood films prominently featuring or casting Asian Americans in the post-2000 era, Asian-ethnics, since the 1990s or so, have been regularly represented in venues such as commercials and children's shows along with other people of color.

With the emergence of a critical mass of well-educated and politically conscious U.S.-raised/-born in the past two or three decades, Asian Americans have been gaining ground as a political and social force. Coming together through more effective political and social mobilization, Asian Americans are no longer sitting on the sidelines as the "quiet" and "docile" minority group but have begun to make their voices heard and flex their political muscle. Pertaining to the issue of changing images and stereotypes, activism by Asian-ethnic professionals in the media industry to improve representation of Asian Americans in television, film, and theater appears to have begun to bear some fruit.

The U.S. media industry, particularly Hollywood, has been notorious for their exclusion of Asian Americans in both executive positions and in media programming. They have been known for their discriminatory treatment of Asian

American actors and other media professionals, and for their role as primary purveyors of negative Asian stereotypes through repellent and racist depictions of Asians.[2] One watershed event in the struggle against this state of affairs was the organized protest against the first Broadway production of *Miss Saigon* in 1991, a protest revolving around the hiring of the Caucasian British actor Jonathan Pryce to play the role of the half-Vietnamese pimp referred to as the "Engineer" in the production, a role that the protestors felt should go to an Asian actor. The protest itself was ultimately unsuccessful in forcing the producer, Cameron Mackintosh, to use an Asian-ethnic actor, but it became a significant event in making clear that Asian Americans were no longer willing to sit idly by and allow the discriminatory treatment of Asian actors to continue. After the tenure of Jonathan Pryce, the role of Engineer has been played successfully by a string of Asian-ethnic stage actors whom the theater establishment originally claimed did not have the talent nor the singing ability to play the role.[3]

Although there is still a paucity of Asian American executives in important decision-making positions in Hollywood, Asian American actors since then have made noticeable inroads in terms of winning roles and bucking stereotypes, though they have by no means toppled the old stereotypes. Scathing criticisms of the film and television industry and the challenges Asian-ethnic actors face in it are still in full swing; at the time of this writing, the latest such criticisms were outlined in a *New York Times* article discussing contemporary Asian American actors vigorously mobilizing as "fierce advocates for their invisibility—and frank critics of their industry," organized around "Whitewashing" in Hollywood, calling out Hollywood for "taking Asian roles and stories and filling them with White actors."[4] That said, how *have* things been changing in the media? I will address the situation of Asian-ethnic women and men in turn.

One of the first second generation actors to crack the stale, time-worn stereotype of Asians as accented and foreign was the female actor Lucy Liu in her role as Ling Woo in the successful FOX television series Ally McBeal (1997–2001). Although it is debatable whether she was able to break out of the racialized-gendered typecasting as a "dragon lady" in a new guise, Lucy Liu became a breakout star through her portrayal of a feisty, far-from-docile attorney, who was also an unaccented "American." At the time of her appearance, Asian American characters were so invisible that the character Ling became the most significant representation of the Asian-ethnic female, or of any Asian-ethnic, on U.S. television. Since then, Lucy Liu has taken on other television and movie roles, roles that have been hit-and-miss in terms of stereotype-breaking; at the time of this writing, she has a starring role in the CBS popular prime-time television series, *Elementary*, where she reimagines the role of Watson opposite the British actor, Jonny Lee Miller as Sherlock Holmes.

In the area of comedy, brash and raunchy stand-up comedians/actors like Margaret Cho are some of the trailblazers of second generation Asian Americans who have challenged stereotypes. Cho is, however, also known for starring in the first-ever U.S. television show about an Asian American family, *All American Girl* (1994). This ill-fated, poorly crafted/produced show lasted just one season due to its superficial and inauthentic portrayal of a Korean American family and its inability to resonate with audiences; not surprisingly, the show featured no Asian American writers, directors, or producers. Since 2000s, Asian-ethnic female comics have been more successful in showcasing their unique talents on television. One example is Mindy Kaling, an Indian American comedian/actor with a popular romantic comedy television series *The Mindy Project* (2012–2017) on Fox and films such as *Late Night* (2019). Currently, other talented female comedians/writers/actors like Ali Wong are making an impact through their stand-up comedy and roles as writers and actors; Wong wrote for *Fresh Off the Boat*, the first-ever successful primetime television series about an Asian American family, which premiered on ABC in 2015. On that show, actor Constance Wu, who plays the mother Jessica Huang, has received attention as one of the few Asian-ethnic actresses to be cast on a primetime show.

In the 2000s, another Asian-ethnic actress who made a prominent mark is Sandra Oh, whose steady rise in the acting industry was propelled by her role as Cristina Yang in the ABC medical drama series *Grey's Anatomy* (2005–2014). She also won the 2019 Best Actress Golden Globe for her lead role in BBC America's drama series *Killing Eve*, the first lead actor Golden Globe award for a person of Asian descent. She also became the first Asian American actress to (co-) host the Golden Globes.[5] Around the same time, Constance Wu and Ali Wong have followed up their successes by starring in highly successful romantic comedy films about Asian Americans *Crazy Rich Asians* (2018) and *Always Be My Maybe* (2019), respectively.[6]

Male Asian-ethnic actors or figures who can be described in some way as "breakthroughs" in terms of challenging negative or stereotypical Asian male images appeared a bit later, mostly post-2000.[7] John Cho and Kal Penn, stars of the successful stoner comedy *Harold & Kumar* film franchise (2004, 2008, 2011), became the first-ever Asian American male leads in a major Hollywood film. In 2006, the Korean American Yul Kwon drew attention for winning the 2006 reality TV show *Survivor: Cook Islands*. His victory was widely attributed to his smarts, but he was also noticed for his good looks and career accomplishments. Another example is actor Rick Yune; although he has mostly played villains, several of his roles have been of an attractive, powerful, and fearless male, as in *The Fast and the Furious* film franchise. On television, actors Daniel Dae Kim and Ken Leung made a mark playing complex and multi-dimensional characters on the television series *Lost*. In addition to Daniel Dae Kim, another actor who has acquired substantial acting success in the 2000s is Steven Yeun, starting with his role as a skilled Zombie-killer in AMC's acclaimed *The Walking Dead*; he is also the love interest of a White female.[8]

More recently is the breakout hit *Fresh Off the Boat* (2015–), the first Asian American network family sitcom in 20 years (after the *All American Girl* debacle) that is based on restaurateur and writer Eddie Huang's memoir growing up in a Taiwanese American family. This is the first show about an Asian American family in U.S. television history to be renewed after its first season, starring Randall Park as an attractive and amiable loving father Louis Huang; many view the Huang character as transcending a one-dimensional caricature of the Asian dad.[9] Following that show, Korean American comedian Ken Jeong's sitcom *Dr. Ken* (2015–2017), a show where Jeong plays a funny, affable, All-American dad of two "typical" Korean American kids, became the second American network show about an Asian American family to be renewed beyond the first season. At the time of this writing, the actor who perhaps has had the most mainstream success with his own, groundbreaking show is the Indian American actor/comedian Aziz Ansari with his self-satirizing Netflix series *Master of None* (2015–), which has won awards and accolades including two Emmys and a Golden Globe for Ansari as Best Actor.[10]

Despite these improvements, Asian male stereotypes have in no way been upended. Asian Americans still predominantly occupy second fiddle and side-kick roles, with a few exceptions, and cannot entirely shake the emasculated nerd stereotype. Moreover, as will be discussed more fully later in the chapter, Asian American men seem to be cracking the unflattering stereotypes but may be relying on the model minority stereotype to elevate their romantic capital. In popular media, one such example is aforementioned Yul Kwon, a Stanford- and Yale-educated attorney, who showed that Asian American men can have muscles and charm, but never without brains and other "model" qualities like loyalty, responsibility, and perseverance. For all of chef and restaurateur Eddie Huang's braggadocio as a self-described "big-dick Asian," hip-hop enthusiast, and weed-dealing lawbreaker, he also won literary awards as an undergraduate, attended a selective law school, and became a corporate attorney and a wealthy businessman. And Ken Jeong, after his breakout role as a short, naked, and effeminate Chinese mobster in the box office hit *The Hangover* (a role that was highly controversial for reinforcing Asian male stereotypes for laughs), starred as a stereotypical Asian male doctor in *Dr. Ken*, a show loosely based on his real life as a licensed physician, making him a living model minority.

In sum, although some of these men, and some of my participants discussed later, have begun to challenge the damaging stereotypes of Asian-descent men, I contend that they are seen as appealing not for having entirely freed themselves of conventional Asian male stereotypes but for embodying the most "desirable" features of both the White hegemonic masculinity ideal and the conventional Asian-ethnic male, for example, being athletic, sociable, aggressive/competitive but also loyal/faithful, smart, responsible, and cooperative, the latter qualities representing the slices of the model minority features.

Within such a shifting environment, how are the external perceptions and self-perceptions of participants in my study changing? One consistent finding of my study is that while the participants are cognizant of some of the progress for Asian Americans, they are at best ambivalent and guarded about it, as well as about the prospects for the future of their children. Throughout this book, my participants' experiences of racist treatment and stereotyping over their lifetimes have been described at length. My evidence suggests that these experiences do substantially shape the self-understandings of the women and men, their sense of desirability as romantic partners, and their chances in the dating/marriage market, but that these differ considerably along the lines of gender.

## Asian American Women and Marriage/Dating

The lower barriers that the women in my study in general enjoy within the interracial marriage/dating market compared to the men stem, as discussed, from persisting image of Asian American women as exotic, submissive, yet hyper-sexualized. This situation has roots, as pointed out in Chapter 2, not only in the legal and ideological regulation of Asian-ethnic women's sexuality within the U.S. borders but from the ways in which "genealogy of the White man-Asian woman-dyad emerged largely from extraterritorial intimacies,"[11] that is, the permitting and flourishing of Asian female-White male intimacies in overseas locales—such as in areas of military conquest/involvement or colonial possessions—while such intimacies were outlawed within the United States. Within the United States at least, such exotified images of Asian-ethnic females on the part of many non-Asians appear to be alive and well, certainly in the societal imaginings and fantasies communicated via various media venues.

The women in my study, whether interracially or interethnically married, seem to perceive only a few hurdles due to their race within the dating/marriage market once they are adults. Most women are alert to their specific worth and value as sexual and romantic objects in the U.S. dating/marriage market as women of Asian-ethnic descent, although they may express ambivalent feelings about the "benefits," which stem from Western and colonialist/post-colonialist fantasies about Asian females. In adulthood, very few women related having trouble getting dates and encountered men of all races who found them appealing. It is also no coincidence, I believe, that even during their growing-up years, more women in my study than men mentioned feeling insulated to some extent from overt racist treatments because of their peers' perception of them as relatively physically attractive; recall the reflections of Sarah, the 41-year-old Korean American mentioned in Chapter 3, who believed that her Caucasian-like features, such as her large eyes, helped deflect racism. Sandra, the 36-year-old from the same chapter, also related that her pretty looks were rewarded with attention from boys and contributed to her relatively healthy self-esteem:

> People will give me affirmation like the boys I would have crushes on were like the popular boys and they weren't Korean but we liked each other. I remember in like the third grade, this one boy, everyone liked him. Yeah, so I liked him and he liked me and felt like, just growing up, I always felt like "Oh! He was a popular boy." So I don't think I had that many—I didn't have like those issues about like wanting to be someone different. It was probably just improving on whatever I have, like I want more clothes.

Indeed, both women and men in my study regularly mentioned how much easier Asian American women "had it" in the dating/marriage market compared to Asian American men.

In her study of Asian Americans and miscegenation, Susan Koshy aptly uses the term "sexual capital" to "capture the shifting value encoded in images of Asian American femininity within the United States over the course of the last century," particularly the movement from a "sexual commodity" (some of it as a war-time related commodity) prior to the 1960s to becoming, to a degree, the "possessor of the sexual capital," especially as the "sexual model minority" in the more contemporary era. Building on Bourdieu's concept of social and cultural capital, Koshy defines sexual capital as "the aggregate of attributes that index desirability within the field of romantic or marital relationships in a given culture and thereby influences the life-chances and opportunities of an individual."[12]

Furthermore, becoming a "sexual model minority," a process associated with the movement toward being the "possessor" of the sexual capital from being a sexual commodity, stems from a reconstruction of the Asian femininity image from the sexually licentious in the pre-WWII era to "domestically feminine" in the post-WWII era, as Asian wives of U.S. servicemen entered the U.S. and Asian-White intimacy was recontextualized as situated within marriage, which increased Asian-ethnic women's sexual capital.[13] Clearly, the societal perceptions and self-perceptions of Asian American women are that Asian-ethnic women have superior forms of "sexual capital" than Asian-ethnic men.

As shown throughout the book, however, this reality does not free all Asian-ethnic women from feelings of internalized inferiority, which speaks to the women's recognition of their generally subordinate position as members of a historically undesirable minority group. Nor does it free them from racism and the effects of White privilege, the latter especially in terms of beauty standards. Despite their status as a "sexual model minority," most women reported feelings of self-dislike at their peak during their growing-up years, and the participants who grew up surrounded by Whites experienced feelings of inferiority more intensely. These included, as discussed, feeling as if they were not as appealing as the White "cheerleader types," wondering if they could not get dates because they were of Asian descent, and not liking themselves because of the way they looked.

Even the women who interracially married related prior experiences with non-Asian men who made them feel that they were not "good enough" and did not measure up to the ideal American standards of beauty. One example is Pauline, the Indian American married to a White man, from Chapter 3 and 4. Pauline always felt that she knew her "limitations" regarding dating White guys when she was growing up because "I just knew I couldn't compete with the [White] girls so much prettier than me." She added, "If the White guys were really, really attractive, I knew I couldn't stand a chance with them. And I'm like, why am I bothering? I'm not going to waste my time and get hurt, and kind of feel like a fool." And even later in college years, when it became "cool" for Whites to date interracially, she believed White boys were interested mostly out of curiosity.

Even for such interracially married women, various degrees of internalized self-doubt appeared as an undercurrent in their narratives; this demonstrates that even Asian American women, despite their purported advantages in the dating/marriage market, are not exempt from the silent but pervasive psychological traumas stemming from racism. And as discussed in Chapter 2, much of this arises from the fact that being a "sexual model minority," especially as a fetishized embodiment of the "lost" traditional womanhood in the West, does not supplant normative White middle-class femininity, but serves as an alternative to "normative" hegemonic femininity:[14] "As a sexual model minority, the Asian American woman cannot entirely displace the White woman, whose appeal is reinforced by racial privilege and the power of embodying the norm, but she does, nevertheless, represent a powerfully seductive form of femininity that can function as a mode of crisis management in the cultural context over different meanings of American."[15]

## Grappling With Asian Fetish/Yellow Fever

Thus, despite their relative "success" in the dating/marriage market, the women in my study recognized, and talked about, the negative flipside of their popularity: the drawbacks of being an Asian American woman. Most significantly, the "deficits" they described centered on their awareness that their desirability as Asian-ethnic women may stem in large part from a process of exotification that objectifies them and reduces their humanity and individuality. As briefly discussed in Chapter 3, this acute awareness was demonstrated in one interesting way: the spontaneous mention or discussion of the phenomenon of the "Asian fetish" or the "yellow fever" from the majority of the women I interviewed, including women who are interracially married to White men.[16]

Most Asian American women in the U.S. are familiar with the concept of "Asian fetish" or "yellow fever," a set of attitudes and behavior perceived to be

held by a subset of non-Asian men who have an obsessive sexual/romantic interest exclusively in Asian-ethnic women. Lara, an interethnically married woman
who grew up in Hawaii, recalled her experiences upon coming to the East Coast
to attend a small predominantly White liberal arts college:

> I knew about discrimination [against Asians] but . . . I think for me, the
> biggest shock that I was unprepared for was the Asianophile. That was
> really—I talked to some of my college friends from Hawaii who went to
> that college with me also, and we were all very much guarded about that.
> Because at a liberal arts college like ours which is very White . . . we stood
> out, right? There is [sic] only like four or five of us. And the same guy . . .
> sought each of us out and when we compared notes, we're like, "Oh my
> God! That guy also found me too."

Vicky also stressed that she was "especially sensitive to that 'yellow fever' thing"
when dating White men because she did not want the guy to "just go out with
me" because of that. Her entire dating narrative was littered with questions and
doubts about the extent to which "yellow fever" figured into each man's attraction to her, and in the end, she wondered if they all had it to some extent. Kira,
recallng the time in  college that she first ran into "guys with Asian fetishes" said,
"I just remember seeing some of these guys in the dorm and just like needing to
run the other way because it just felt like . . . they were checking you out for no
other reason than the way you look."

While there are many White men and women, as well as non-White men
and women, who possess a personal preference for individuals belonging to
certain racial, ethnic, and national origins, it is not easy to distinguish between
men with "yellow fever" and those who supposedly love a woman for herself in a non-fetishistic way. Having to navigate and discern this fine line is
a difficult dilemma with which most participants, especially the interracially
married ones, appear to struggle, especially because it raises the question of
whether their own spouses are exempt from the "Asian fetish." For example,
recall Carla, the interracially married Chinese American in Chapter 3 who
talked about a prior White boyfriend whom she suspected of not wanting to
marry her because she did not have the right "genes" for producing physically
desirable offspring. Carla was now married to a man who apparently did not
have such concerns and who expressed happiness in having a spouse who represented "difference." Carla was also aware, however, that her husband, who
majored in Asian studies, spoke Chinese, lived in China for a while, and had
several Asian-ethnic girlfriends before her, so she did go through a period of
questioning whether her husband could be one of "those egg boys" (White
on the outside, yellow on the inside). In the end, Carla was satisfied with her
husband's explanation that since he had dated women of all races/ethnicities,
he did not have an Asian fetish; she instead attempted to appreciate the fact

that his cultural knowledge of and interest in Asia eased her marital life, such as his knowing how to treat her parents with respect.

Vicky also married a man who had a special interest in Chinese culture; despite her extended discussion of the Asian fetish, she seemed to exclude her husband from that category, or if she suspected him of harboring the Asian fetish, she did not admit it. On the other hand, some women, such as Joy, outrightly admitted that her spouse had yellow fever as she talked about the string of Asian-ethnic girlfriends he had before her. Joy, however, said that she chose to accept that fact and to not let it bother her, though it did bother her initially. In either case, what this discussion of yellow fever/Asian fetish demonstrates most centrally is that Asian-ethnic women have to contend with the possibility that their appeal to many non-Asian men, especially to White men, may be based on an unwanted and fantasy-based exotification of Asian females laden with colonialist and post-colonialist dynamics.

The women's struggles with this issue also involved engaging in battles against the Asian female stereotype. Admitting that she was especially sensitive to this issue, Vicky talked about how she consistently "overcompensated" in order to fight against the Asian female stereotype; this included doing everything she could to challenge the Chinese female stereotype, for example, by learning to be extra-assertive: "You can't be afraid. You have to be twice as assertive [to fight the stereotype], and I don't mean like bitchy or like pushy, but you've got to be strong." In fact, she fought the demure, submissive Asian female stereotype both in relation to non-Asian *and* Asian men because she felt objectified by both. But in the end, Vicky said she ended up with a White man because she felt that her White husband was not afraid of "strong women" like herself and was not as intimidated. She, on the other hand, did not feel as accepted by fellow Asian-ethnic men.[17]

Carla, as well, perhaps signifying her nagging doubt about yellow fever on the part of her husband, explained that early in their relationship, she went out of her way to disabuse her husband of any stereotypes he may have of Asian-ethnic women, especially by making sure he understood that she was not the submissive type. For instance, she tried hard to distinguish herself from her husband's previous Asian girlfriend, whom she thought did too much for him around the house, pronouncing, "You do your own—if you need something, you are doing it yourself. I made that very clear. 'Just so you know, that is the way it is, and it's the way it's always going to be.' And he said 'Okay I get that.' . . . So yeah . . . I don't know if it would be different if I married somebody who was Asian. . . . It's hard to know because you can't say that every Asian person is the same either."

Women from other racial minority groups also face the task of negotiating exotification and gendered stereotyping in cross-racial marriage and dating. Jessica Vasquez tells the story of Latina women whose motivations for marrying fellow Latino men were driven by the need to "avoid the distasteful stereotypes held by White men"—for example, the seeking of "Latina spice"—and sought "identity freedom through endogamy." As she also notes, these women are aware that being in an interracial marriage, one in which they could be viewed as "other" by their intimate partners, can stem from a situation in which the notion of "diversity" in the United States has been reduced to "cultural consumption by Whites who 'exoticize, criticize, trivialize, and compartmentalize people of color.'"[18] Although very few of my narratives contained explicit discussions of women consciously avoiding interracial marriage for the purpose of avoiding being othered and exoticized by non-Asian men, at least one interethnically married woman admitted, "at least I know my husband didn't marry me because I was exotic."

## Asian American Men and Marriage/Dating

The situation for Asian American men in the U.S. marriage/dating market, though seemingly improving, is more challenging; it is generally one of disadvantage and "deficit" in the minds and opinion of the majority of the participants.[19] Almost all participants agreed that, though "getting better," Asian-ethnic men still suffer from negative, emasculating stereotypes that affect their self-perception and chances in the dating/marriage markets. Throughout this book, the men express how the geek stereotypes have dogged them throughout their lives and the immense internal insecurity this generates in men regarding dating, especially across racial lines.

### *Internalized Inferiority and Romantic Desirability*

As I have illustrated throughout the book, feelings of internalized inferiority are rampant among men who grew up in predominantly White environments, regardless of whether they ended up interracially or interethnically married. Being subject to racial slurs, being made fun of for looking different, and being typecast as nerds were commonplace occurrences for most participants growing up, making them feel like they fell far short of ideal American masculinity. As interethnically married Vietnamese American Andrew opined about his growing years:

> When I was in high school, I always had crushes on White women . . . but I don't know why I didn't date White girls . . . but there wasn't a lot of reciprocity in terms of, like, attraction. . . . I was always attracted to the cheerleader types, but I was shy. . . . The negative stereotypes. . . . So I was like, well, what White girl's going to want to be with me, you know? . . . And I had to deal with, you know, the fact that I'm not tall.[20]

As discussed, such experiences may be much less intense and prevalent for those who grew up in Asian-dominated areas, many of whom seemed to have been somewhat insulated from incidences and effects of racism, though they were by no means immune. Although some men, particularly those who grew up in Asian-dominated areas, claimed to never have been attracted to any type of women other than Asian, most participants in this study, including the majority of interethnically married men, found women of various races attractive growing up but often felt that they could not pursue their desires because of the fear of being rejected romantically. Thus, it seems reasonable to speculate that some men did not even make an effort to pursue non-Asian women; that is, it is possible that these individuals may have opted out from cross-racial dating/marriage from the get go.[21] There is evidence from my participants that this may be the case; for example, interethnically married Jeff remarked that although he and most of his Asian-ethnic friends "gravitated" toward and exclusively dated Asian-ethnic women, if any of them managed to date a non-Asian, especially a White woman, this was viewed as a kind of "scoring":

> I think as I got older, I don't know if it's ingrained in me or locked in me that I was just expecting that I would find an Asian American girl to date. But it became a running joke with our group of friends because none of us had dated White girls. And so, it was just a joke. I mean, I don't think it was anything where I consciously said, "Oh, I want to date a White girl just because she's White." But it became the joke because, I guess, it's that—we always joked that it was an unattainable fruit. . .

For Jeff and his friends, although there was no question that they preferred Asian-ethnic women because of cultural comfort, commonality, and attraction, there was a sense in which dating non-Asians, especially White women, was still viewed as being somewhat out of reach. These narratives indicate that such feelings of internalized inferiority often lead to, and are based on, the idealization of White women as the standard bearers of beauty.

## Idealization of White Femininity

For both interracially or interethnically married men, insulating themselves from the onslaughts of the messages of the superiority of the White beauty standard seemed next to impossible. Idealizing White femininity as the pinnacle of attractiveness, at conscious or unconscious levels, appeared as a pattern for most of the men. Not surprisingly, interracially married men in particular tended to be highly assimilated and saw themselves as transcending negative stereotypes of Asian-ethnic men. Such assimilative tendencies often went hand in hand with a desire for women of the dominant group. Winning the approval and acceptance of White females as romantic partners provided men with a sense that they were successfully approximating the American middle-class hegemonic masculinity and winning societal acceptance. Some of this appeared in Chapter 3.[22] "Scoring" a White partner imbued many men with a sense of validation of their masculinity as well as social approval.[23] In some cases, the glorification of White femininity was expressed by way of an interesting logic; although White men desiring Asian-ethnic women can be viewed as a fetishistic fixation, the reverse did not hold true, since White women were bearers of the universal "standard of beauty" and thus it was "natural" for all men, including Asian men, to desire White women. One participant stated:

> My friends say they feel it odd to see an Asian woman with a White guy. I agree with them. . . . But you just don't think it's the other way around. . . . if you see an Asian guy who only dates White women, that's different because a lot of guys like to date White women. . . . The White woman is kind of a standard even in Asian cultures, in many Asian cultures of beauty.

With this observation, not only does this participant deny the possible interpretation that White women, or women of a dominant group, can become the object of fetishization by men of a subordinate group—a prime example of "colonization of consciousness" that results in racialized desires for the females of the "superior" race—he also implicitly testifies to the inferior status of Asian-ethnic women in relation to White women.

The concept that an Asian man dating a White woman does not represent fetishism while the reverse is true is echoed by an Asian-ethnic blogger who promotes Asian men as the "dream" marriage material for non-Asian women:

> The Asian male and White female (AM/WF) couple have [sic] been the poster boys/girls for interracial dating —and for good reasons. Now I'm not trying to knock off White Male/Asian Female (WM/AF) couples but in the case of AM/WF, there's a beauty that exists between the two. Unlike WM/AF couples, which too often include a White male with an Asian fetish, the relationship between an AM/WF is completely balanced. No fetishes, no objectification.
>
> Between the Asian male and White female there's a sense of equality in power. No specific gender wears the pants [permanently] and there's a divine sense of understanding. From my experience, 100% of the White girls that I know who are interested in Asian guys are ALL highly cultured, open minded, beautiful, and intelligent women. Some have traveled the world while others possess the intellect to crush Professor Xavier [from movie and graphic novel X-Men].[24]

With the idea that White men interested in Asian women may likely be deviant as fetishists while the reverse is not true, the narrative slavishly idealizes the White female, in fact, it idealizes her, especially the women who like Asian men.[25]

## *Negotiating Hegemonic Masculinity*

So how do Asian-ethnic men in my study deal with this situation? Anthony Chen's widely read article on Asian American masculinity describes the various ways in which Asian-ethnic men handle internalized inferiority.[26] Chen outlines four major "gender strategies" specifically used by Chinese American men to "achieve manhood" by way of a "hegemonic bargain" struck with White American masculinity. Chen found that the men in his study either compensated for this negative image ("compensators") by trying to conform to the White hegemonic ideal as much as possible (being athletic, fun, aggressive, sociable) or deflected ("deflectors") attention from the negative stereotypes by trying to be as successful in conventional ways, such as by fulfilling the model minority stereotype. Some men also dealt with the situation through denial ("deniers"), whereby they perceived that these stereotypes did not apply to them as they were "White," and finally, through repudiation ("repudiators"), by rejecting the negative images and being proud of being an Asian-ethnic.

In general, findings in my study indicate that interracially married Asian American men, because most of these men were likely to be the most assimilated, tended to engage in either a strategy of denial or compensation, at least in the early part of their lives, or utilized a mix of both. These strategies can change and vary over a lifetime. Matt, for instance, was a clear example of someone who as a youth practiced ethnic distancing regarding dating/marriage, engaging in compensation for and denial of his "Asianness." Although he knew he could not climb to the top of the masculinity ladder, he tried to challenge the nerdy stereotype by attempting to become sociable, attractive, athletic, and, at the same time, accomplished. Indeed, according to Jachison Chan, "On the one hand, the desire to identify with a normative heteromasculine model of masculinity is fueled by an urgent need to disinherit emasculating representations. On the other hand, succumbing to those same norms reflect a willingness to adhere to a predominantly White model of masculinity."[27] Matt was attracted to and dated almost exclusively White women, and professed that he did not find Asian–ethnic women all that appealing. The birth of his mixed-race children, however, motivated him to increasingly embrace his ethnicity, steering him away from these ethnic-distancing strategies.

Another example of a compensation and/or denial strategy by Asian American men is provided by Carla through her intriguing comment about a Chinese American guy in college who was "very handsome, very athletic, very tall." But she observed that he was the "type of boy who is not dating an Asian girl. He only dated very blond girls at school." This boy was clearly highly "Americanized," engaged in ethnic-distancing, and only pursued relationships with girls belonging to the dominant racial group: "I would say that he was very non-Asian and he never participated in any of the Asian American student association events at all. I would say that he was completely assimilated." In her view, some Asian men were able to approximate the ideal hegemonic American masculinity if they tried, but it appears that achieving the hegemonic ideal through compensation typically went hand in hand with almost complete assimilation and Anglo-conformity, including using their superior physical capital to exclusively date White women and reject Asian women. Although interracially married Asian American women in this study were generally highly assimilated as well, I believe my observations support the findings elsewhere that the assimilation bar may also be higher for Asian American men than it is for Asian American women who wish to cross the racial line in terms of romance, sex, and marriage.[28]

Men who were interethnically married tended to utilize more of the repudiation strategy in recognizable ways. Lewis and Jared, for example, explicitly described how their evolving racial awareness enabled them to repudiate the dominant hegemonic masculinity ideals and to embrace their ethnicity/race and who they truly were, and to stop trying to compensate or constantly hold themselves to the standards of White masculinity. For some of them, this included favoring Asian-ethnic women over White women.

The men in my study often employed some combination of the four strategies, sometimes simultaneously, sometimes throughout different periods of their lives. For example, just because some men primarily utilized the repudiation strategy and proudly embraced their ethnicity did not mean that they did not attempt to compensate for their perceived deficits in some way. Jared, the Vietnamese American from Chapter 5, admitted, for example, that despite his high degree of racial consciousness and efforts to accept and be proud of himself as an Asian-ethnic man (a repudiator), he nonetheless was keenly aware of the fact that he to some degree needed to challenge and subvert the "nerdy" and "weak" Asian male stereotypes in order to win societal respect (a compensator).

Jared hence spoke proudly of his tall, muscular (read: un-Asian) physique and his assertive, aggressive social manner, which he used to disarm people: "So, there is [sic] a lot of stereotypes about the kind of diminutive or quiet or reserved, asexual, unathletic Asian American. And because I think I'm a little bigger, and taller, because I play a lot of sports, because I'm very loud and because I hold pretty strong philosophical, political views and I'm not shy about expressing them, I surprise people." Conversely, men who can primarily be compensators or deniers can also simultaneously use the repudiation strategy. This can be seen most clearly among interracially married men such as Matt, Ted, and Kyle, who tried later in their lives to embrace their ethnicity, especially to actively forestall ethnic loss in their children.

## Deploying the Sexual Model Minority Capital

As mentioned earlier, my study finds, though, that despite their efforts to break out of the stereotypical molds, Asian-ethnic men, regardless of which of the four strategies or combinations they utilize, appear to end up appropriating the model minority stereotype in some way, consciously or subconsciously, to elevate themselves in the masculinity hierarchy. That is to say, whether they are compensators, deniers, deflectors, or repudiators, men in my study recycle and incorporate the model minority stereotype in their attempt to construct a new kind of "Asian American" masculinity to differentiate themselves from and compete with the men who are the bearers of White hegemonic masculinity. In this sense, Asian American men also have come to parallel Asian American women's status as the "sexual model minority," with similar and different resources to draw upon for their "sexual capital." That is, while Asian-ethnic women and men are both associated with "model minority" traits of intelligence, industriousness, and docility, Asian-ethnic men may draw more on the stable and reliable economic-provider stereotype as part of their "sexual model minority" appeal.[29]

Although it is easiest to see how the deflectors, or even repudiators, of hegemonic White masculinity might be the ones least likely to be rejecting of the model minority aspects of their ethnic identity, I find that some of the compensators who ostensibly attempted to approximate White hegemonic masculinity were also appropriating the perception of Asian-ethnic men as smart, responsible, and economically successful to enhance their appeal to women. Consider the following narrative by Korean American George, who discusses what he sees as the appeal of Asian-ethnic men to White women as stemming from a "combination" of the traits of the White hegemonic masculinity (such as being tall, athletic, sociable, and even aggressive) and a slew of conventional model minority traits associated with Asian-ethnic males:

> What they [non-Asian women] like about Asian men is that Asian men are very considerate and have soft edges—now, I'm sounding stereotypical—but that's what they think. And physically they like that we don't have body hair. . . . I talked to other Asian guys that have Caucasian girlfriends, and they all say the same thing. They like the fact that we're hairless. . . . They like the fact that . . . we're well-educated. I think some of the stereotypes are true because they're just the dynamic of being Asian. One thing I hate to say is that they like tall Asian men. . . . They also like Asian men because they're smart . . . kind edges, smart . . . what else? . . . And a lot of Asian guys know how to cook, though I'd like to say, it's mostly the Chinese guys.

Reflecting on his past relationship with a White woman, Andrew remarked that his former White girlfriend's parents did not have many "issues" with an Asian like him dating their daughter, in contrast to her previous boyfriend who was Black. He recalled, "I don't think they were racist, per se, but because we [Asian American men] have that good stereotype, we're, you know, hardworking, the whole educated, respectful-of-elders type of deal." Reflecting further on why his White girlfriends, more than Asian-ethnic women, tended to see him as being "gentler" than White men, he remarked: "Part of me thinks it's

got to be, you know, that White girls are used to such a high level of obnoxious-
ness or confidence, or whatever, coming from a White guy, that they think Asian
men may be like White men *except* in these ways. And to them, that's attractive."
His narrative clearly expresses the fact that Asian American men are perceived to
have exceeded White men in being "hard-working" and "educated" and, owing
to "Confucian-influenced" parenting, diverge culturally from White men, such
as when they show respect to elders.[30]

The irony of course is that the views that Asian American women have
of their co-ethnic men, which can include such descriptors as "chauvinistic,"
"patriarchal," "emotionally unavailable," and "mama's boy," starkly contrast with
White and other non-Asian women's model minority notions of Asian-ethnic
men.[31] Andrew tried to explain this discrepancy by speculating that it is perhaps
because "Asian women are more focused on the negative part." He explains,
"They [White women] go, well, my mate or my [Asian-ethnic] boyfriend . . .
is compassionate or whatever, instead of focusing on the 'Man, he yells just like
my uncle . . . or that's very sexist [as Asian women often think]."[32] Nonetheless, the above narratives overall point to changing societal perceptions of Asian
American men as moving beyond an image as the most unattractive, undesirable, and patriarchal, to one that is more sexually desirable and an ideal marriage
material.[33]

## Conclusion

Gender still makes a difference in the marriage/dating market in terms of how the
wider society constructs and imagines the romantic/sexual desirability of Asian-
ethnic men and women. As I have discussed in Chapter 2 and in this chapter, the
images and stereotypes of both Asian-ethnic women and men have undergone
changes, even radical reversals, in the United States over the last century and a
half. The dominant view of Asian-ethnic women as the deviant, morally corrupt
prostitute during the 1800s was transformed into a more docile and domesticated
"lotus-blossom" stereotype in the post-WWII era, albeit still hypersexualized, a
view that has remained relatively stable into the present time and has contributed
to the rise in Asian-ethnic women's sexual capital and their "advantage" in the
dating/marriage market relative to Asian-ethnic men. The image of Asian-ethnic
men has arguably undergone a more radical transformation, from a highly sexually threatening "lascivious and predatory" stereotype (especially as predators of
White women) that prevailed in the 1800s and into the early twentieth century,
to an asexual, romantically undesirable stereotype, more recently reinforced by
the nerdy aspects of the "model minority" image. Although these images appear
to be the opposite, what the views of Asian-ethnic women and men have in
common is that they are both constructed as the exotic "other" in relation to the
dominant, normative White hegemonic femininity and masculinity, and both
images exist to buttress White male superiority.

There is some evidence that these time-worn stereotypes may be changing, especially for Asian-ethnic men. At least in the mass media, these changes include efforts to overturn the nerdy, emasculated images of Asian-ethnic men and to present them as embodying certain features of hegemonic masculinity. At the least, many Asian-ethnic men, according to my research, appear to be engaged in a struggle to define and craft their own version of a distinctive "Asian American" masculinity, often one that combines the elements of White hegemonic masculinity with what are considered some of the masculinity ideals found in "Asian" ethnic cultures.[34] In this tentative effort, Asian-ethnic men may be trying to elevate their standing in the current masculinity hierarchy and reduce their marginalized, invisible, feminized status. Certainly, such efforts can be observed in their maneuverings in interracial romance and marriage; Asian-ethnic men, especially the second generation and later, seem to be successful in projecting more appeal in the romance and marriage market, both interracial and interethnic, than in the past, especially as a softer-edged, more reliable, less aggressive masculine alternative to the White hegemonic masculine ideal.

For both Asian-ethnic men and women, however, such increases in their respective sexual capital do not necessarily translate into a liberation from their marginalized gender status, nor from their status as the foreign "other." For Asian-ethnic men, in "performing" this new kind of alternative masculinity, especially by incorporating the model minority traits of the smart, dependable, industrious, and economically successful man into the dominant White masculinity ideal, they may not so much be ascending the masculinity hierarchy as much as reinforcing the model minority stereotype. Indeed, in one internet blog about Asian American masculinity, Asian American men lament about a key contemporary model minority-related stereotype of Asian-ethnic masculinity, that of the economically successful "provider" type:

> In our society, there is one young Asian masculinity that gets ample recognition . . . the rich young businessman or the rich young lawyer. . . . It's all about the green. No other form of Asian masculinity gets much respect. And even then, it's not perfect sailing for the rich Asian man either because above him at the highest level, there still exists a hierarchy.[35]

The outcome of this may be a perpetuation of Asian-ethnic men's marginalized masculinity status and even their cooptation in preserving the conventional patriarchal structures via their role as the "sexual model minority." As for the women, despite their purported "advantage" in the dating/marriage market, they cannot escape that this benefit may be based largely on the hyper-sexualized fetishization of Asian-ethnic women as the exotic other who can never displace normative White femininity but serve as the obverse and inferior alternative. Like the men, the women also can hardly avoid the injuries of race stemming from the process of racialization of Asian-ethnics.

It is hard to tell what the future holds in terms of the relative racialized-gendered positionality of Asian-ethnic women and men. At least for the men, things seem to be continuing to head in the right direction; there has been, at the time of this writing, quite a buzz over how the Asian male leads in recent blockbuster movies such as the *Crazy Rich Asians* or in the successful Canadian Korean American family sitcom *Kim's Convenience* (2016–) may be impacting the image of the Asian male. *Crazy Rich Asians* has received particular attention for its potential to overturn Asian stereotypes in general, both male and female. The possible impact of the growing global appeal of "soft pan-Asian masculinity"—a form of soft and highly aestheticized masculinity that is increasingly becoming globally associated with Asian-ethnic men through transnational flows of popular culture and media – is also being debated, or at least its role in laying the ground for alternative Asian masculinities.[36] Although these recent developments must be recognized as milestones for the Asian-ethnic community, the jury is still out on their real-life impact. For the time being, it is likely that the gender inequalities in the interracial dating/marriage market will continue.

One final subject matter of interest is the future of the relationship between Asian-ethnic men and women; one notable pattern from my study is that unlike Black women who are known to complain bitterly about out-marriages of eligible Black men, particularly to White women, Asian American men in my study, on the whole, do not speak of out marriage of Asian-ethnic women to White men in equally bitter tones, although a few do grouse about some Asian American women's preference for non-Asian men and demean the "lower quality" of White men who pursue Asian-ethnic women.[37] Nonetheless, the Asian American community has not been without tensions between Asian American women and men, especially between women espousing a feminist position that is critical of sexism, a position that has also been expressed by some women in this study, as well as men who charge Asian American women with betraying Asian-ethnic men and benefitting from their hyper-sexualization at the expense of Asian-ethnic men.[38]

Similar to the long-troubled male/female dynamic within Black and other communities of color, this tension represents the historical conflict between the race-centered and/or "cultural nationalist" position embraced by many men as a way to combat their racialization and social exclusion, and, on the other hand, Asian-ethnic feminist concerns surrounding Asian patriarchal structures. But feminist concerns and struggles against racism need not be at loggerheads. As Asian American men struggle with a redefinition of masculinity that avoids patriarchy and heteronormativity, Asian American women may increasingly be drawing upon an awareness of their bond with Asian American men over common experiences of racism and marginalization, if the recent growth of interethnic marriages and panethnic sentiments can be taken as a measure.[39]

Those Asian-ethnic men who still keenly feel and experience the deficits in the romance/marriage market within the U.S. increasingly view areas outside the

U.S., or the globe as a whole, as a stage in which to flex their sexual capital and even exercise patriarchal privilege, particularly through transnational movement to and from the "homeland." Indeed, as Yen Espiritu notes in her study of Filipino Americans, the second generation and later are not exempt from partaking in transnational activities, which she conceptualizes as a "disruptive strategy": transnationalism is "the process by which immigrant groups forge and sustain strong sentimental and material links with their countries of origin—as a disruptive strategy, enacted by immigrants to challenge binary modes of thinking about time and space and to resist their differential inclusion in the United States as subordinate residents and citizens."[40] While I believe that it is important not to overstate the degree of transnational activities,[41] I do agree that Asian American men's (and all Asian-ethnics') yearning for "home" is thus in part a response to their "enforced homelessness" and social exclusion, such that "homeland" becomes a site for migrants from the "margins" to reestablish a sense of parity—to reinforce or raise their social standing.[42] The danger is the possibility of the re-inscription of male dominance and gender hierarchies, one that is authorized in this case both by the hegemonic White and ethnic/national-specific patriarchies that become complicit in maintaining the subordination Asian-ethnic women, and of women in general.[43]

## Notes

1. Chan 2001, 11–12; Yuen 2017.
2. Chan 2001; Chou 2012; Eng 2001; Shimizu 2012; Yuen 2017; Wong 1978; Zia 2000.
3. This despite that a worldwide search was conducted specifically for the Asian American *female* lead for the original Broadway production to act alongside Jonathan Pryce, which ended up going to a newcomer, Lea Salonga, a talented Filipina singer and actress.
4. Hess 2016; also see Chow 2016.
5. Oh won a Golden Globe for Best Supporting Actress for *Grey's Anatomy* and has other awards under her belt for her acting (and has been nominated for many), including the Screen Actors Guild and People's Choice Awards. She was also nominated for an Emmy for *Killing Eve* in 2018. During her acceptance speech at the 2019 Golden Globes, she prominently thanked Lucy Liu for blazing the trails for Asian-ethnic actresses.
6. Ali Wong also co-wrote this Netflix film; Randall Park co-wrote and plays the male romantic lead. Daniel Dae Kim also co-stars.
7. Some parts of the media-related discussion on Asian-ethnic men in this paper was co-written with Nadia Y. Kim.
8. Cho, Kim, Yune, and Leung have persistently invoked their responsibility to improve and complicate representations of Asian Americans, especially men, whenever the significance of their career and choice of roles arose as a point of discussion.
9. His character, as that of others on the show, has also stirred controversy for reinforcing prevailing stereotypes as they rupture them, such as Louis as part sexually desirable and part sexually neutered (www.newyorker.com/magazine/2015/03/09/home-cook ing-television-emily-nussbaum). Eddie Huang bemoans the television dad as completely neutered, "what White people think about Asian American dads: goofy, inept, emasculated, kind of a bitch" (www.theguardian.com/tv-and-radio/2015/jan/23/ eddie-huang-tv-fresh-off-the-boat). Other characters on recent television shows,

especially Han Lee on *Two Broke Girls* (played by Matthew Moy) and, to a lesser extent, Dong on *The Unbreakable Kimmy Schmidt* (played by Ki Hong Lee) have been excoriated for serving as a retread of the sexless, emasculated, foreign man with whom America is all too familiar. Examples of popular discussion of Randall Park include www.latimes. com/entertainment/movies/la-et-mn-randall-park-interview-20141216-story. html#page=1, www.rollingstone.com/tv/features/randall-parks-long-road-to-comedy-gold-20150304, www.thedailybeast.com/articles/2015/01/30/randall-park-from-kim-jong-un-to-the-brave-new-asian American-sitcom.html, www.wsj.com/articles/ran dall-park-on-abcs-new-fresh-off-the-boat-1423067322

10. In sports, one breakthrough star worth mentioning is Jeremy Lin, the celebrated New York Knicks' point guard and the originator of the "Linsanity" frenzy, whose athletic prowess in the hyper-masculine game of basketball is credited with helping challenge the conventional belief that Asian guys "can't ball." As an athlete and a person, Lin was described as being "nerdy cool," a "relatively low-key yet evident swagger," and a "substantial yet unfreakish build"; it was also said that "[a]mid all the hoopla, he's utterly unafraid to be himself—which, in the end, is the only form of masculinity a mother truly wants for her son." See Fei 2015.

11. Koshy 2004, 13. One can argue that, in contrast, the Asian man-White woman dyad was produced primarily through domestic sexual prohibitions.

12. Koshy 2004, 15.

13. Koshy 2004, 12.

14. It is important to note that serving as a "sexual model minority" is not the only form of racialized feminine sexuality available to Asian-ethnic women, but it is one of the major useful concepts to capture the social-sexual position inhabited by Asian-ethnic women in U.S. society and perhaps even globally.

15. Koshy 2004, 17.

16. Cf. Chou et al. 2015.

17. Cf. DasGupta and DasGupta 1996.

18. Vasquez 2017, 141–42.

19. Cf. Chou et al. 2015; Robnett and Feliciano 2011; Kao et al. 2018; Muro and Martinez 2018.

20. See Espiritu (2003, 189–90) for strikingly similar narratives by Filipino American young men.

21. See Tuan 1998. Tuan similarly relates a respondent who "narrowed his field of potential dating and spousal partners because of the pressures his mother placed on him as well as a belief that White women were out of his league" (59).

22. See Nemoto 2009.

23. Indian American women in my study, such as Pauline, complained in particular of Indian American men's desire to pursue White women for dating.

24. The Falco 2010.

25. Not surprisingly, another interesting theme that arose in my interviews was the presence of "submerged gratitude" expressed by some interracially married men toward their wives or White women they have dated, especially for their open-mindedness and appreciation of the Asian-ethnic men.

26. Chen 1999.

27. Chan 2001, 13.

28. See Okamoto 2007.

29. To be sure, Chou (2012, 111–12) has found that some Asian American men are self-confidently appropriating and redefining "the model minority man" or "king of geekdom" through studying, avoiding sports or partying, and being passive to circumvent the mimicry of hegemonic masculinity which often demands engaging in physical, often violent, altercations (Chou 2012). This also is not to deny the response of "bad boy posturing" among some Asian American men, a masculinity associated

with working-class White men or men of color. Modeled as an East or Southeast Asian gangster, these men were regulars on Asianave.com, a website dedicated to guns, cars, and distinct styling, such as spiked hair and black jackets, representing overt rebellion against the normalized "hegemonic" masculinity described by Chou and others. Other formulations include Asian American men emulating "gangsta rap," "gangsta hip-hop culture," and other enactments of impoverished inner-city life or of ostentatious displays of wealth in more recent mainstream hip-hop culture (Chou 2012).

30. Cf. Chua and Fujno 1999; Lu and Wong 2013.
31. Chou 2012; Chow 2000; Nemoto 2009; Chan 2001. It is important to note, however, that not all Asian American women harbor negative stereotypes of Asian-ethnic men.
32. See Louie 2003; 2017; Ng 2018; Suh 2016.
33. A number of studies have similarly documented non-White women 's perceptions of Asian-ethnic men as a kind of "dependable," "intelligent," "stable," gentle" model minority marriage material. See Bystydzienski 2011, 53; Fong and Yong 2000, 60; Nemoto 2009; Diggs 2001, 11; Sung 1990, 53.
34. Salesses 2013; Shimizu 2012.
35. big WOWO 2011. Koshy (2004) also states that "sexual capital" for Asian American men is closely associated with economic power (166: FN 43).
36. See Sun Jung 2010; Louie 2003; 2017; Ng 2018; Suh 2016. In attempting to explain the prominence of the "soft" and "gentle" masculinity trope, one can certainly point to the long legacy of feminization of Asian-descent men in the U.S., but perhaps also to the impact on the present Western perception of what Sun Jung (2010) calls "pan-east Asian soft masculinity," a form of highly aestheticized, soft masculinity becoming globally associated with Asian men through transnational flows of popular culture (some recent prominent examples of this being Korean TV dramas and K-pop stars), a trend which may imply both benefits and costs for Asian-descent men around the world.
37. Also see Chow 2000.
38. See Kim 1990; Lowe 1996; Espiritu 2008, 117–212; Shimizu 2012, 8. This tension traces back to the publishing of the landmark anthology of Asian American writing *Aiiieeeee! An Anthology of Asian American Writers* in 1974, and the ensuing critiques against the masculinist position of the editors. On the flip side, ground-breaking Asian American female writers such as Maxine Hong Kingston and Amy Tan have been bitterly criticized by various Asian American men for purportedly perpetuating the emasculated image of Asian-ethnic men (see Chan 2001).
39. Works by scholars such as Jachinson Chan (2001) affirm my findings; in his review of Chinese American writers, he also concludes that in their struggle to redefine a Chinese or Asian American masculinity during what he refers to as a "crisis of masculinity" to which Asian American men are currently subject, they yet "do not have a unified definition of a Chinese American masculinity . . ." (137). See also Shimizu (2012) for her discussion of "ethical manhood" as an alternative vision of Asian American manhood.
40. Espiritu 2003, 70.
41. Espiritu (2003, 213) does state that while significant segments of foreign-born Filipinos regularly engage in transnational activities, most Filipino migrants do not live transnational "circuits" but are intent on settling permanently in the U.S.
42. Espiritu 2003, 86.
43. Espiritu puts it this way (2003, 214): "In sum, transnationalism must be understood as a contradictory process—one that has the potential to break down borders and traditions and create new cultures and hybrid ways of life but also to fortify traditional hierarchies, homogenize diverse cultural practices, and obscure intragroup differences and differential relationships. In this sense . . . transnationalism is at best a compromise—a "choice" made and lived in a context of scarce options."

# 8

# CONCLUSION

## Asian American Intermarriage: Being in and From the Racial Middle

Marriages do not simply denote a private realm of individual desires, emotions, and interactions but are also the sites of the interplay of larger social forces that provide a look into the "complex interconnection between cultural, economic, interpersonal, and emotional realms of experience."[1] Studying intermarriage, traditionally a domain of illicit love, desire, and intimacy, thus provides an excellent opportunity for social analysis, as it offers significant insights into the larger politics of race and gender as these are played out, negotiated, and contested in the realm of the personal. This study has focused on interracial and interethnic marriages among U.S.-born/-raised Asian Americans to explore how such individuals negotiate structural and cultural forces impinging upon them and what this reveals about their social/racial positioning, ethnic/racial identity construction, and the nature of current racial/ethnic hierarchies.

The findings presented in this book are a study about the unique circumstances of a group occupying an ambiguous racial-middle position within U.S. society and globally, a position that I argue has rendered the experiences of Asian Americans distinctive and complex but relatively invisible. Along with the greater fine-tuning of assimilationist theories, a number of assumptions and speculations have been made about Asian-ethnics, particularly with regard to their racial-middle social and structural positionality. The interpretations of Asian American experience have, however, been far from uniform, particularly with regard to their current model minority status.

A main point of contention has been whether Asian Americans can parlay the purported "benefits" associated with their model minority status to overcome the liabilities of their denigrated racial status that have rendered Asian Americans unfit to be considered fully "American," especially as physically differentiated "perpetual foreigners." Although the dominant view seems to be that the U.S.

boundaries of "White" will not likely expand any time soon to include Asian-ethnics on equal terms with Euro-ethnics and that Asian Americans' experiences are and will likely remain distinctive as those of a racialized group, underlying assumption is that Asian-ethnics, despite the shameful history of the U.S.'s mistreatment of them, will at least bypass African Americans in achieving cultural and social assimilation into the dominant White middle-class culture in some manner, perhaps along with many Latinos. Indeed, Asian Americans' high outmarriage trends with Whites are commonly referenced as one indicator of this possibility.

Due to the scarcity of studies focusing on the internal dynamics of Asian American intermarriages, we do not have a full picture as to what extent Asian Americans are on track to cultural and social assimilation. Although classic assimilation theories and literature on race relations presume that interracial marriages signify an ongoing attenuation of ethnic culture and an intensified identification with mainstream culture, this is an open question with regard to Asian Americans. By unpacking the black box of intermarriage dynamics among Asian Americans and examining how the partners in these marriages think and feel about identity, ethnic culture, race, and issues of cultural and social belonging, this study explores the complexity of the social, cultural, and subjective location of Asian Americans in the present day, and what intermarriage indicates about social integration of Asian-ethnics in the U.S.

## Intermarriage and Race: How Race Matters for the Model Minority

One of the major insights revealed by this study of intermarriage is that even as a non-Black, racial-middle group persistently glorified as the model minority, the issue of race is anything but irrelevant to Asian American intermarriages and in the lives of Asian Americans. For all of the participants in this study, both interracially and interethnically married, the present system of racial hierarchy constitutes the dominant social and ideological framework that constrains their subjectivities and social lives, more specifically, in developing their identities, corralling and taming romantic desires, and exploring socioeconomic possibilities. To be sure, the individuals in this study are afforded some space to maneuver and exercise agency in forging their distinctive identities, cultures, and family lives against the dominant mainstream White norms/culture, but these choices must be exercised within the dictates of the "White racial frame."[2] For example, this White racial frame includes multiculturalist or colorblind ideologies, two contemporary racial discursive frameworks that supposedly aim to transcend racism and within which most of the participants operate to a degree. These ideological frames, however, do not negate racism but ultimately maintain its logic and pernicious effects in key ways: multiculturalism, by celebrating and commodifying racial difference, thereby neutralizing a critical stance against racism, and colorblind ideology, by evading the real-life significance and effects of a racial system.

One useful way to see the way race matters in the lives of Asian Americans in this study is to explicitly compare Asian American intermarriages to Black intermarriages. As discussed, one of the key insights provided by in-depth studies of contemporary Black-White intermarriages in the United States is that despite a decline in its importance as a barrier to intermarriages, race still matters. Studies of Black-White marriages show intermarriage to be anything but a simple indicator of social/racial acceptance of Blacks or the lessening of social distance between Whites and Blacks, but reveal the extent to which race and racial boundaries continue to persist in the United States. Even in this historical moment of celebratory "post-racialism," it is when individuals attempt to cross racial divides through love or marriage that such racial borders become explicitly visible and relevant. For Black-White couples, the ongoing significance of race and of the Black-White racial divide is particularly highlighted by the unfavorable reactions many of these couples still receive from their immediate families and communities at large, both Black and White.

For Asian American interracial couples in this book, race appears to matter in somewhat different ways in the context of intermarriage. The most central difference pivots around the ambiguities that surround the social/cultural acceptability of Asian-ethnics, including a higher level of acceptability than Blacks as marriage partners to Whites. These ambiguities incite a complicated relationship on the part of Asian-ethnics to whiteness that often renders the matters of race more opaque, including for Asian-ethnics themselves. For interracial couples in particular, one finding of note is that expressions of social disapproval from the White community against intermarriage with Asian-ethnics appear generally more muted. While a few participants in my study did experience overt opposition by parents/families of White partners that was clearly motivated by racism, most experienced a higher level of acceptance. In the latter case, what appears to be a greater level of social acceptance, or social assimilation, of Asian-ethnics is often accompanied by declarations from both White partners and their families of the acceptability of Asian-ethnics due to their more middle-class socioeconomic status and high educational profiles, as well as "cultural" status associated with being a model minority that may help to paper over racial differences between Whites and Asians-ethnics.

Experiences of racism and "othering," however, were by no means absent in the lives of Asian-ethnics in this study, as disclosed through a number of strikingly similar and recurring narrative tropes. All participants struggled with racialization, racist treatments, and internalized racism during their growing-up years. Growing-up years in particular were marked by yearning for White, mainstream society acceptance. This desire is understandable in light of the fact that the participants were U.S.-raised/-born and socialized in White-dominated institutions and culture and thus did not see themselves as dramatically different from the racial majority in the way that they thought and felt. For almost all participants, experiences of racialization and racism continued into adulthood, encountered in the domain of everyday interactions and in certain forms of institutional discrimination, such as discriminatory treatment in the labor market.[3]

Given the elusiveness of full social acceptance for Asian Americans, what this study found is that interracial marriages—while considered increasingly acceptable by both Asian-ethnics and Whites and even as access to White privilege by some Asian-ethnics—can ironically generate sharper racial consciousness for Asian-ethnics once it becomes clear that individual acceptance as marital partners does not necessarily signify achievement of group equality. Speaking of intermarriages, multiracial/multicultural family formation, and their implications for social change, Kimberly DaCosta observes:

> Empathy is limited in its capacity to bring about needed social change, since people can cultivate empathy for specific individuals while keeping intact their basic (negative) beliefs about the categories of people from which those individuals come. This is why assertions that people in intermarriages . . . are less prejudiced . . . are problematic. It is easy to make exceptions for one's kin, marking them as the exception to the negative rule for others of a particular group, thus leaving the lines of demarcations intact.[4]

For many Asian-ethnics in this study, their own cross-racial marriages were therefore not uncritically accepted as a waystation to racial inequality but often became a field of struggle in which unequal racial dynamics were made visible and realities of racial inequalities negotiated.

For interracially marrieds in particular, the appearance of children often becomes a key catalyst for racial/ethnic awakening and assertion, once the realization sets in that their own subordinate racial minority status in society puts them at the risk of ethnic cultural/identity loss or absorption. These dynamics of larger social/racial inequality frequently play out in the participants' private marital and family lives, including the various ways the Asian-ethnic parent must help their mixed-race children negotiate the issues of racial inequality and racism.[5] This, combined with the participants' need to negotiate the racial privilege of their White spouses, who are often immersed in colorblind ideology, leads to a reassessment of the Asian-ethnic parent's own ethnic/racial identity and identification. Joane Nagel calls this phenomenon a "reverse cultural transmission," a process whereby the need to pass down ethnic culture and history to children may prompt the weakly ethnically identified parent to learn about his or her own cultural heritage/traditions and take on a new level of ethnic self-awareness.[6] Armed with a new racial awareness, the Asian-ethnic participants in this study attempt to exercise agency in crafting a home culture where Asian-ethnic elements can be incorporated and ethnic identities kept alive, with varying degrees of success.

## Parenting With or Without the Privilege of Whiteness

One of the notable findings of this study relates to the White spouses' behavior and attitudes within the interracial marital context as compared to the Asian-ethnic participant, which spotlights the power of the White racial frame and White privilege that can permeate interracial marriages and child-raising. Extant literature on Asian American interracial unions tends to focus on ethnic identity/ cultural issues of the minority group members. However, insofar as interracial unions involve two parties whose engagements with each other lead to a more complete picture of how the two cultures and identities are negotiated and how cultural transformations may occur, this study examines the responses of both White and Asian-ethnic spouses.

In terms of interracial marriage, the findings of this study differ somewhat from other recent studies of minority-majority intermarriage that highlight how the White partner can actively participate in adapting to, and in preserving, the minority partner's culture to produce a kind of blended "biculturalism."[7] My study has shown that this kind of "cultural migration" of the majority partner into the minority partner's ethnic space does certainly happen along with the heightening of the White partner's awareness of their own White privilege. However, the hegemonic norm of whiteness and the ideology of White supremacy primarily remain a pervasive backdrop for many of these interracial marriages, and this can be seen in the White privileged parenting enjoyed by the White spouse. That is, by and large, the White partner remains embedded in a perspective in which whiteness is presumed as the superior norm, a stance which is frequently cloaked in the discourses of colorblind ideology and celebratory multiculturalism.

This privilege often includes the White parents' liberty to frame race as irrelevant in their children's or family's lives, particularly to deny or downplay that racism might be affecting their mixed-race children.[8] Even if the White spouses agree to incorporating the Asian-ethnic partner's ethnic culture and identification into their family lives in the name of multicultural celebration of difference, this carries with it the freedom to frame the minority spouse's ethnic cultural and identificational elements as "colorful" and "fun" additions that add "interest" to their lives. In this process, whiteness and White middle-class culture firmly remain the unstated and invisible standard.[9] In fact, this attitude dovetails with findings in existing literature that reveal some White Americans' belief that being a real "American" signifies White people who "lack" culture, in contrast to ethnic/racial minorities who perhaps have "too much" culture; as Renato Rosaldo stated, "full citizenship and cultural visibility appear to be inversely related. When one increases, the other decreases. Full citizens lack culture and those most culturally endowed lack full citizenship."[10] Furthermore, most White spouses were willing to participate in maintaining the ethnic cultures of their Asian-ethnic spouses only if the latter took the lead. All of this points to the fact that parenting children of color does not automatically translate into racial enlightenment nor obviate the effects of White privilege, let alone lead to "cultural migration" of the majority partner.[11]

For the Asian-ethnic partner, on the other hand, even if operating within the multicultural discursive framework, the issue of race becomes an even greater focal point of concern, especially as such concerns are triggered by the experiences of their mixed-race children. These concerns of the Asian-ethnic parents, especially as they relate to their fear of ethnic cultural loss or absorption into the dominant culture, should hardly be surprising.[12] Studies show, for one thing, that since the "one-drop" hypodescent rule does not apply to mixed Asian-ethnics as it does to Blacks, Asian mixed-raced persons in the United States, therefore, are more likely to identify as White or multiracial than Blacks and have that identification be accepted by others.[13]

As discussed earlier, the main challenge for the Asian American parent is not so much the struggle for directly counteracting assimilation but the navigating of tensions between the forces that produce desires for assimilation and the need to assert racial and/or cultural distinctiveness, tensions that figure in complicated ways into the business of family- and identity-making. Insofar as the superiority of whiteness still constitutes the dominant cultural frame in which the non-White participants must negotiate, the process of identity-making for Asian Americans involves negotiating their complex relationship to whiteness throughout their lives, whether in the form of the desire for whiteness, rejection of it, or both. Indeed, while Asian-ethnics can engage in any one of these various responses to whiteness, it is the deeply ambivalent relationship to whiteness they develop that is most striking.

In many ways my participants' situations resemble those who are positioned within what has been referred as the "minority culture of mobility," a culture inhabited by middle-class minorities with specific and distinct problems attendant to being middle class and minority, including "knowledge and behavioural strategies that help to negotiate the competing demands of the White mainstream and the minority community."[14] These problems, which arise from necessary contacts with Whites, include the "demand for conformity to White middle-class speech patterns and interactional styles in school, work and other public settings" and having to "encounter prejudice and discrimination more often than poorer co-ethnics" because middle-class individuals have to navigate White-dominated areas more intensively.

One consequence of these problems is the "psychological burden of loneliness and isolation, as well as social disadvantages such as exclusion from information networks and the exaggerated visibility of the token, as well as economic loss."[15] I argue therefore that as a putative "honorary White" racial-middle group located at the juncture of majority social acceptance and rejection, middle-class Asian-ethnics not only come to realize that socioeconomic mobility and model minority status for them does not automatically translate into social or racial privilege but also that they are subject to a particular kind of racial quandary, a situation in which they can be seduced into believing that they can be rid of their stigmatized racial status through assimilation such as interracial marriage.

Indeed, the possibility of being seduced into the fantasy of acceptance as an "honorary White" group through paths such as interracial marriage remains a key concern and temptation that besets a middle-class racial-middle group homogenized with the stereotype of model minority. As Ruth Hsu critically observes:

> For now, Asian American desires are too imbricated with those of the American nation-state. The political and economic leverage that Asian Americans have wrested from the power elite has served to draw us deeper into a complicitous relationship with the existing socio-economic structure. Unfortunately, this community's stolid trek toward and among the circuitous pathways of the American middle-class is ultimately assimilative without necessarily being transformative in terms of the enormous social injustices that capitalism has set up.[16]

Such desires to be incorporated into the "American" society, particularly through interracial marriage with Whites—while at the same time not viewing interracial marriage to Blacks as a path to making one similarly "American"—not only exposes the commonplace assumption that assimilation in the U.S. context signifies becoming a part of the White majority society and partaking in the benefits of White privilege, but that interracial marriage to Whites serves to ultimately uphold the twin ideologies of White supremacy and anti-Black racism. While illustrating the reality and dangers of such temptations, this book also explores the ways in which many Asian Americans, even interracially married ones, manage to contest these assimilative and accommodating impulses through the development of greater racial consciousness and cognizance of social/cultural marginalization of Asian Americans, including forming a self-critical eye and skepticism about intermarriage in the course of their everyday family and married lives.[17]

## The Construction of "Asian American": Constraints and Agency

If the Asian-ethnic participants' identity formations as observed in this study are fields of struggle that are characterized by contradictions, ambivalences, and resistances with regard to hegemonic whiteness, then interethnic marriage seems to represent a distinct kind of response to this challenge. At first glance, Asian interethnic marriages seem to be a more straightforward form of struggle against whitening and the threat of cultural/ethnic erasure by the White culture, as interethnic marriage involves crossing ethnic boundaries and transcending ethnic divisions to construct a new panethnic formation. What I have argued in this book, however, is that despite this construction of racial/panethnic solidarity and identity of "Asian American" as a form of distinctive group and cultural assertion, akin to what Gayatri Spivak has called "strategic essentialism,"[18] its construction also represents an intimate negotiation with White middle-class culture and identity, as well as a particular way of being and making claims to being American. First, it is important to note that insofar as Asian panethnic formation is an individual (negotiating new personal identities) as well as a group phenomenon (reconstructing communities, institutions, cultures, histories),[19] all Asian-ethnic individuals in this study, whether interethnically or interracially married, are, in their own ways, engaged in helping to construct racial/panethnic identity as "Asian Americans" within the context of their marriages. Examining how interethnically married individuals engage the Asian American identity helps show particularly clearly how this panethnic concept, category, and culture is evolving on the ground and helping to transform the content and meaning of "Asian American."

As discussed earlier, the category of "Asian American" has been historically highly controversial, no less among Asian-ethnics themselves. Although it has been embraced since the 1960s as a group identity in the service of political mobilization, particularly by young, U.S.-born college-educated activists, its beginnings as an externally imposed category that "lumps" or homogenizes diverse peoples of Asian-ethnic origins has been viewed as problematic. It has been viewed as a particularly problematic label by groups who are not of northeast Asian origins, such as Filipinos and Asian Indians, many of whom do not feel that they should be placed in the same category as northeast, or even southeast Asians, and feel that they are marginalized within the emergent Asian American community.[20] Nonetheless, this panethnic/racial label has increasingly gained acceptance and in effect has created a new racial category within the U.S. racial landscape.

Thus, as an identity, the "Asian American" label, even if contested, is a panethnic identification and a form of racial ethnogenesis that Asian-ethnic groups have used to build bridges with one another. To be sure, individuals and groups identify with this label to differing degrees both along ethnic/national lines and within a particular ethnic/national grouping. Moreover, the kind of identity individuals choose to emphasize—ethnic/national, panethnic, or American—differs depending on the situation and the context in which the participants find themselves; that is, individuals often "code switch" their identities depending on the situation. However, even though one can say that racial or panethnic identity such as "Asian American" is a "choice" among various different identities the participants can embrace or choose to emphasize, it is becoming a compelling method of self-identification or a way of being "American" for groups who must negotiate society's continued racialization of them.

Adopting the "Asian American" identity, then, can be seen as a form of accommodation to a racialized social structure, while, as a "choice," it can simultaneously be viewed as contestation against the same racist social structure because it allows individuals to recuperate racial identity as a vehicle of political and identity mobilization. The contradictory phenomenon of ethnic renewal "creates new racial subjects while conforming to the pre-existing U.S. racial order, as it provides a crucial consciousness-raising tool with which to make demands on the state."[21] For interethnically married participants in particular, the act of coupling with another Asian-ethnic in itself becomes a process of forging and constructing a common pan-Asian identity/culture and racial connection that may lead to intensified racial consciousness, even if the individuals continue to be concerned about their competing feelings of allegiance to individual ethnic/national identities and the larger pan-Asian identity.

Within these marriages, there is no question that new, hybridized cultural forms are emerging, forms that connect and integrate various elements of different national and ethnic cultural elements. These hybrid panethnic cultural and identity formations, though they do not occur seamlessly and without conflict, can in many ways be viewed as a meaningful "third space" of hybridity for many of the participants—new cultures being forged at the junction of disparate cultural realms that may provide diasporic subjects with unique ways of being and consciousness.[22] Although ethnic identities/cultures being constructed among the U.S.-born/-raised in this study are an outcome of negotiations between multiple cultural domains that include the family, the ethnic community, as well as the dominant culture, these new cultural spaces have provided the participants with contestatory potential against the majority culture, including the possibilities of disrupting the majority culture's representations of Asian Americans and perhaps even of gradually transforming the dominant culture.

One of my main arguments, however, has been that insofar as the majority culture remains the referential norm, the choices of the interethnically married participants—who at first glance seem to have chosen a path of repudiation of whiteness by marrying within racial boundaries and producing Asian-ethnic children—do not represent a liberation from the power of whiteness. That is to say, their positionality does not signify an outright rejection of whiteness but rather a tense struggle to balance their desire for whiteness/White middle-class culture, which they still recognize as being equated with "American" with their commitment to ethnic identities and cultures. This ongoing tension between Americanness and the desire for ethnic/racial assertion is due to the fact that Asian-ethnics, similarly to many Latinos, are subject to *both* a process of racialization *and* whitening.[23] Thus, I propose that recognizing the contestatory potential of hybridized cultures/identities or "third spaces," particularly through a focus on the fluidity and inventiveness of identity-/culture-making, should not obscure the limitations placed on the disruptive agency of ethnic/racial minorities.

One of the interesting questions to consider is to what extent this new "Asian American" culture is distinctive from the "symbolic" ethnicity of Euro American culture. Some scholars have argued that this Asian American culture is more similar to "symbolic" than expected. I do find that in many ways, the cultural practices and content of my participants resemble that of "symbolic" ethnicity in that they are surprisingly thin and based on a very limited number of practices such as ethnic food consumption and engagement with occasional holiday rituals, and most of it modified at that. However, what I also find is that Asian Americans do not have the luxury of simply jettisoning their ethnicity or asserting a purely symbolic type ethnicity but are compelled to perform their ethnicity for the benefit of the larger culture because their Asian-ethnic racialness is externally imposed. As long as ethnic/racial boundaries remain intact for a group, ethnicity is inherently less symbolic, less optional, and a more consequential dimension of the group's identity, despite any structural assimilation. As Bandana Purskayastha writes, whether racial minorities have to "contend with externally imposed boundaries or whether their assertion of ethnicity is a free choice delineates their position in relation to their White peers in contemporary middle-class America."[24] Moreover, exercising ethnicity, no matter how symbolic it may seem, is far from costless for Asian-ethnics as ethnic-cultural performance always demarcates a place of "othered" racial and cultural difference.

## Asian Americans and Assimilation: Subordinated Incorporation

An important question remains about where Asian Americans, as a distinctive racial group, will fit into the future American racial landscape and American society. Some scholars have maintained that America is moving toward a new kind of biracial or bi-modal hierarchy that is a non-Black/Black divide rather than the old White/non-White dichotomy, with Asian-ethnics being incorporated, for the most part, into the "White" category;[25] others have proposed a future of triracial hierarchy, with certain higher-socioeconomic-status Asian Americans and lighter-skinned Latinos serving as a "buffer" race in the middle between the White and the "collective Black" population, the latter comprised of Blacks plus darker-skinned Latinos and Asian-ethnics.[26]

It is hard to predict what the future racial-social positioning of Asian Americans is likely to be. I view it as unlikely that the "White" category will be expanded any time soon to accept Asian Americans as it had for earlier European-ethnic groups such as Southern and Eastern Europeans. As long as the European nations continue to be situated at the top of the global/inter-national economic and political power structure, the present racial structure and ideology that asserts the superiority of the "White" races at the apex will persist, and "White" groups, and those who are accepted as such, will do all they can to uphold and maintain this racial hierarchy. This global and post-colonialist racial structure and ideology is the dominant framework within which domestic racial politics and inequalities are shaped, and race relations within the U.S. borders will continue to reflect these global racial dynamics.

If this is the case, the most likely scenario that I anticipate is that Asian Americans, perhaps along with other higher socioeconomic and light-skinned Latinos, will continue to occupy the racial-middle status within the United States as "honorary Whites." It approximates the model of triracial hierarchy advanced by Eduardo Bonilla-Silva, although I am not as much in agreement about this hierarchy being built upon Latin American-type pigmentary logic, especially as it applies to Asian-ethnics.[27] I believe that even "darker-skinned" Asian immigrants such as Laotians, Thais, Vietnamese, or Cambodians who are predicted to be in the category of the "collective Black" will, as long as they can attain middle-class social status over time, likely join the racial-middle, "honorary White" strata along with the East-Asian origin groups such as Chinese, Japanese, and Korean Americans. In fact, the children of Vietnamese immigrants as a whole, for example, are already doing much better educa-tionally than expected given many of their original lower socioeconomic and refugee status, and recent studies show that interracial marriage rates of Whites with Southeast Asians, whatever this phenomenon may signify in terms of assimilation, are quite high, higher than marriage rates between White and East Asian-ethnics.

On the other hand, I do not believe that this racial-middle, "honorary White" status signifies full-fledged acceptance into the White category nor successful "whitening" but will continue to denote a denigrated racial status in which Asian-ethnics remain racially marked and are not fully included as American, that "their standing will depend upon Whites' wishes and practices": as Bonilla-Silva writes, " 'Honorary' means they will remain secondary, will still face discrimina-tion, and will not receive equal treatment in society . . . albeit substantial segments of the Asian American community may become 'honorary White,' they will also continue to suffer from discrimination and be regarded in many quarters as 'per-petual foreigners.'"[28]

Indeed, as has been the case historically, I believe that the pivotal role of racially middle strata of "honorary Whites" is to continue to serve as the "buffer" group in racial conflict to ensure that Whites maintain their racial supremacy. This secondary status is evidenced by the most recent research that, despite Asian Americans' purported "structural assimilation" as the model minority (mainstream educational, labor market, residential incorporation), race presents a formidable barrier in achieving reduction of full "social distance" between Asian-ethnics and the dominant White majority.[29] For example, recent studies show that U.S. native Whites, while they are generally open to structural relationships with immigrant-origin individuals (e.g., as friends and neighbors), simultaneously view all non-White peoples as dissimilar, based on race, a perception which is linked to avoidance and lack of full social acceptance."[30] As long as such perceptions of dissimilarity along racial lines as a defining source of difference persist, full social incorporation may not be attained for even middle-class Asian Americans, even if acculturation and a substantial degree of "structural assimilation," coupled with social mobility, occur.

In terms of an assimilation path, what this will probably signify is that Asian-ethnics will, as the case has been made for Latinos, "assimilate" as a distinct but subordinate racial group, similar to a process which some scholars have referred to as "racialized assimilation."[31] Not offered the privileges of full social/cultural incorporation into the U.S. citizenry, most Asian Americans, whether interracially or interethnically married, will likely be most comfortable embracing a hyphenated American identity rather than an unhyphenated "American identity," the significance of hyphenated identity being that it reflects both the effects of partial social belonging and racial subordination at the same time that it can serve as a vehicle for asserting and performing ethnic/racial distinctiveness. In terms of intermarriage, this means that "assimilation" for Asian Americans may be considered as possible not only through interracial marriage with Whites, but through integration into panethnicity by way of interethnic marriage, further consolidating a distinct racial identity.[32]

However, insofar as Asian Americans, and other groups of color, are being incorporated as a distinct but subordinate racial group within a racially hierarchical system, it may then be worthwhile to consider whether there is any utility at all of using the term "assimilation" in these discussions. I suggest that it may be more sensible to eschew the term "assimilation" altogether when talking about the racialized integrative experiences of minority groups, given the term's historical connotation of full absorption into the majority. To describe the racialized integrative paths of groups such as Asian Americans, and other groups of color, I instead suggest the term "subordinated incorporation." This term is useful because "incorporation" does not imply a one-way absorption or disappearance into the majority culture as "assimilation" does, and the term emphasizes the significance of "subordination" in this process of distinct, racialized integration within the context of a persistent racial hierarchy in U.S. society.

The future of Asian American incorporation is uncertain. Among many factors, what will also surely affect the future integrative path of Asian Americans are the shifts in the inter-state power relations and global racial power structure. Another interesting question in this integrative journey is whether the kind of racial consciousness reflected in the rise of panethnic identification, a response to society's racialization of Asian-ethnics, can foster the development of a kind of "pan-minority identity" in the future, where Asian-ethnics will move toward a greater sense of solidarity with other minorities of color and strive for social change toward greater social and racial equality, rather than seeking for assimilation into the majority White culture and attempting to partake in White privilege.

## A Preliminary Comparison With Latinos

An investigation of Asian American intermarriage and assimilation leads to the question: are there any major differences in the integrative experiences between Asian Americans and those of Latinos, the other racial-middle group? I will respond to this question briefly and tentatively here, primarily addressing some recent findings on Mexican Americans in particular. Even though Latinos and Asian Americans are considered the racial-middle minority, much of the existing evidence on Asian Americans and Latinos suggests that the integrative experiences of the two groups may vary; one objective indicator of this is the differences in intermarriage rates between the two groups for the later generations as discussed earlier in the book. The central question here is: what are the key factors that account for this difference in the contemporary period? I propose that race plays a key role in the different integrative experiences of two groups, underscoring the centrality of White racial privilege in the United States.

A recent book on Mexican Americans by Tomás Jiménez finds that even though racialization for Mexican Americans is central, even down to the later generations, as to why Mexican Americans remain a distinctive ethnic group with greater tendencies to retain ethnic culture, it is the "replenishment" by the new waves of Mexican immigration that is the more important explanation for this cultural maintenance than society's racialization of Mexican Americans: "race matters in the Mexican American experience but not for the reasons that others have asserted. In the present context, immigration informs the meaning attached to race . . . instances in which race matters in the lives of Mexican Americans are virtually always linked to notions of Mexicans as foreigners."[33] In other words, although being "othered" as foreigners is central to the continued racialization of Mexican Americans, as has been argued for Asian Americans, Jiménez views this situation as being caused more by continuous waves of immigration that reinforce the foreign stereotype than by any biologically based racism against Mexican Americans per se. This reading of the Mexican American situation is also accompanied by the suggestion that were it not for immigrant replenishment that provides the "raw materials" for the identity/cultural strengthening and retention among the Mexican American community, the assimilation trajectory for Mexican Americans, despite their history as a colonized minority in the U.S., would likely be more similar to earlier European-ethnic groups who progressively "Whitened." In short, race is not irrelevant, but rather what renders race relevant is immigration.

I believe that my findings on Asian Americans in this book offer an interesting and subtle contrast to Jiménez's argument about Mexican American assimilation experience, though the two groups share some similarities. Most significantly, I believe that although the situation of post-1965 immigrant replenishment for Asian Americans certainly has had some similar effects on the Asian American community, most centrally in contributing to a slowing down of the speed of assimilation for the second and later generation by reinforcing the "foreigner" stereotypes, I do not believe that the immigration replenishment and race is tied in a similar way for Asian Americans. I assert that for Asian Americans, ongoing racism based on physiological difference, regardless of immigration, is the most important factor in their continued racialization that leads to the distinctive assimilation experiences of Asian Americans.

The evidence from existing studies of Asian American intermarriage as discussed in Chapter 2 bears this out. As discussed, he likelihood of interracial marriage is lower, and the likelihood of endogamy or interethnic unions greater, for later generations of Asian Americans than it is for later-generation Latinos. Jiménez's study itself marshals considerable evidence that for Mexican Americans as well, the later generations have achieved a great deal of assimilation, including high rates of intermarriage with non-Mexicans and the lessoning importance of race and ethnicity in choosing a partner, accompanied by significant intergenerational socioeconomic progress.[34] This journey down the assimilative path would have continued were it not for continued immigration from Mexico. Based on their assessment of high rates of intermarriage among Mexican Americans in the last few decades, Waters and Jiménez go even further to state that "Despite the growth of the Mexican population and the related increase in the number of eligible Mexican marriage partners . . . social barriers between Mexican Americans and Whites are thin."[35] Again, the view here is that despite the importance of race, the discrimination in the Mexican Americans' experience is primarily a function of contemporary immigration than legacies of colonization, and that while Mexican Americans may be viewed as foreign because of the presence of immigrants which limits the extent to which Mexican Americans feel comfortably situated in the American mainstream, "Mexican Americans are *not* forever foreigners [like Asian Americans] [italics mine]."[36]

I would argue that for Asian Americans, to the contrary, struggles with the "forever foreigner" image remain primary because discrimination that continues to characterize their experiences is most importantly a function of their difference

resulting from physiology, and that their continued racialization as a phenotypi-
cally distinctive and undesirable minority group defines, and will continue to
define, their experiences into the foreseeable future. Recent studies on the Mexican middle class, such as by Jody Agius Vallejo, provide even further support for
this perspective. Vallejo finds that despite the variation in assimilative paths for
different sectors of the Mexican American middle-class individuals in her study,
there are many who are able to completely cross the White racial boundary if
they are culturally assimilated to White middle-class culture and/or are closer to
Whites in appearance and color.

For these "Whitewashed" Mexican Americans who are able to pass for White
and singularly identify as "American" if they chose, ethnicity is more or less voluntary and optional. She writes, "not all of the Mexican American population
is persistently viewed as a racialized ethnic group . . . some Mexican Americans
have the option of choosing a White racial identity," and "That some Mexican Americans claim they are Whitewashed is institutionally supported by the
fact that Mexicans are federally defined as an ethnic group and can be of any
race, including White." Furthermore, she surmises that "a [middle-class Mexican
American] minority pathway to mobility may be a bump in the road experienced
by the socially mobile while their children might incorporate closer to middle-
class Whites." Asian Americans are not likely to enjoy such racial privilege.[37]

One irony, however, is that precisely because of ethnic cultural replenishment
brought by new immigrants, the Latino community offers its later generation
the option of remaining robustly connected to their cultural heritage. In the
United States, it has been observed that the pull of ethnic affiliation for groups
like Mexican Americans may be buttressed by the popularity of Mexican American culture, which has made it an "in thing," something "cool," which "reduces
the stigma of being Mexican American and even give[s] it a certain cachet."[38]
Not only does this increasing Mexicanization of U.S. culture foster greater desires
for ethnic retention and racial/ethnic pride for many members, but it even produces pressures for younger or later generation members to prove their cultural
"authenticity" to the ethnic community, for example, by demonstrating fluency
in Spanish.[39] This level of ethnic cultural normalization, which does not as yet
exist for Asian Americans in my view, also results in certain key differences in the
two groups' integrative experiences.

The cachet of Asian American culture, though increasing within the U.S.
and certainly globally, is not equivalent to that of Latino culture within the
U.S. borders, and the stigma attached to being Asian and foreign still appears
to override any societal trends toward greater acceptance of and familiariza-
tion with Asian-origin cultures. I thus argue that for Asian American participants, the revitalized desire for ethnic retention stems less from the inherent
appeal of the immigrant culture than from the effects of continued racism
and racialization that lead to "othering" of Asian-ethnics in the wider society.

Furthermore, while the rapidly expanding numbers of Latinos and of Mexican Americans in the United States encourage cultural pride and identification with ethnicity for the Latino group—"To be a Mexican American youth . . . is to be part of [a] growing majority"[40]—the relatively smaller population size of Asian Americans does not seem to offer them the similar luxury of drawing upon the psychological and cultural advantages stemming from the strength in numbers.

It is not surprising, then, that a subtle contrast I noticed between Asian Americans in my study and Mexican Americans is the greater level of ethnic-distancing that seems to be practiced by the native-born Asian Americans from their foreign-born counterparts, which suggests a sharper contradiction experienced by many Asian Americans between their assimilative desires and the inability to assimilate or "Whiten" within the context of the dominance of American mainstream culture.[41] This ethnic-distancing seems to be coupled with a weaker level of authority exercised by the immigrant population as arbiters of cultural authenticity over the later generation as compared to the Mexican Americans.

Indeed, struggles for ethnic "cultural authenticity" to "prove" ethnic belonging rarely emerged as an important issue in the narratives of my participants, although such struggles have been documented in studies of particular Asian American groups, such as Indian Americans.[42] Even though the participants in my study wished to maintain certain aspects of their ethnic cultures, they were under no illusion that what they were trying to sustain would in any way be "authentic," nor did they feel that they were under any significant pressures from the ethnic communities to adhere to any strict standards of cultural authenticity (for example, fluency in the ethnic group's language) in their efforts to construct ethnic cultures within their families. In fact, some studies have pointed out that challenges to prove ethnic authenticity for Asian Americans come more from non-Asians than fellow Asian-ethnics.[43] In short, when faced with situations of racism and discrimination, the ethnic-distancing actions of many Asian Americans are akin to what Andreas Wimmer refers to as "boundary contraction," wherein the actors distance themselves from the group category to which they are assigned by the larger society and draw narrower boundaries around themselves; in this case, this means dis-identifying with the immigrant population and signaling themselves as part of the U.S.-born Americans.[44]

To be sure, Asian Americans in my book are not simply trying to claim an affiliation with the dominant majority while completely rejecting their ethnic identity, but, like many Mexican Americans and other minorities, are engaged in a subtle balancing that allows them to proclaim their ethnic affiliations while affirming that they are Americans. However, I suggest that the emergence of the "Asian American" category and my participants' identification with it, insofar as they have been motivated primarily by racism and racialization of Asian Americans, constitutes more of a kind of "defensive" ethnicity than a voluntary form of ethnic retention and assertion aided by revitalization of ethnic resources, at least as compared to Mexican Americans.[45] Again, one of the clearest findings in this study is the tension the participants feel between their "assimilative" desires," that is, the desire to be accepted by the White majority as equals and their inability to do so because of social stigmatization of Asian-ethnics as culturally and racially different. Thus, the participants' embracement of the Asian American label is not simply motivated by their revitalized pride in and desire to maintain ethnic identity but because of the continuing social-cultural exclusion of Asian-ethnics that make it necessary to embrace this difference.[46]

As discussed, the ethnic revival movement that precipitated a shift in ideology from Americanization to multiculturalism since the 1960s assists in maintaining ethnicity's appeal, fervor, and strength. For Mexican Americans at least, it appears that multiculturalism provides the legitimacy necessary for building a more robust ethnic identity. For younger cohorts who have come of age in this multiculturalist age, multiculturalism provides tangible incentives that inspire the youths to sustain an attachment to an ethnic identity, including embracing "difference" as a positive value. Although this multiculturalist valuing of "difference" exists for both interracially and interethnically married Asian Americans in this study, as does evidence that the participants can develop a pride-driven wish to strengthen ethnic identity/culture, I contend that even for Asian Americans belonging to the middle class, one cannot underestimate the extent to which the motivation to sustain ethnic culture and identity may be borne out of racialization experiences.

## Notes

1. Padilla et al. 2007, ix.
2. According to Chang (2016), the key elements of "White racial frame" are "racial hierarchy, stereotypes, loaded language and concepts that make up race today . . . made by elite Whites . . . to rationalize White superiority and justify the extreme oppression of non-White peoples" (35). Also see Chou and Feagin 2015.
3. Fong 2008. There is a great deal of evidence that Asian-ethnics, for example, receive fewer returns for similar levels of education as compared to Whites. For example, see Kim and Zao 2014; Sakamoto et al. 2009.
4. DaCosta 2007, 187.
5. There is growing literature on identity negotiation of mixed-race individuals (part of critical mixed-race studies). For examples, see Rocha and Fozdar 2017; King-O'Riain et al. 2014; Matthews 2007.
6. Nagel 1996, 11. See also Song 2003; Dhingra 2007.
7. See Vasquez 2014.

8. Cf. Chang 2016, Chap. 5.
9. Dyer 1997.
10. Rosaldo 1989, 198.
11. Cf. Chang 2016, 126.
12. Bonilla-Silva 1999, 940. See also Lee 2015; Waters 1990. It is worth noting that, throughout history, many conquered ethnic/racial groups eventually have disappeared or have been annihilated through biological intermixing with the conquerors, whether by rape or interracial unions and marriage, such as numerous native American tribes (Nagel 1996).
13. The issue of ethnic identification for any mixed-Asian multiracial individuals, however, is a highly complex matter. See DaCosta 2007; Xie and Goyette 1997.
14. Neckerman et al. 1999, 949.
15. Neckerman et al. 1999, 950.
16. Hsu 2008, 308.
17. Cf. O'Brien (2008), especially her section on "racial progressives." O'Brien also finds that among racial progressives, ethnic identification with Latino or Asian Americans does *not* decrease with intermarriage to Whites (165).
18. Spivak 1988.
19. Nagel 1996, 10.
20. Cf. Ocampo 2016; Purkayastha 2005.
21. DaCosta 2007, 184.
22. Bhabha 1990.
23. Davilla 2008, 12.
24. Purkayastha 2005, 4. Although scholars like Roger Sanjek have gone as far as to propose that there may exist a kind of "race-to-ethnicity" conversion for Latinos and Asians, I do not see such conversion happening anytime soon for Asian Americans (Sanjek 1994).
25. Gans 1999; Lee and Bean 2004; Yancey 2003.
26. Bonilla-Silva 1999.
27. Bonilla-Silva 1999.
28. Bonilla-Silva 1999, 944.
29. See Healey and Stepnick 2017, 35.
30. See Schachter 2016, 982. Also see Roth 2012. Roth points to a need to distinguish between structural assimilation and racial incorporation.
31. Flores-Gonzales 1999; Golash-Boza 2006; Lee and Kye 2016.
32. Rosenfeld 2001. Also see Kasinitz et al. 2004, 9; Qian and Lichter 2001; Qian et al. 2001; Okamoto 2007.
33. Jiménez 2010b, 250.
34. Jiménez 2010b, 86, 254.
35. Waters and Jiménez 2005, 110.
36. Jiménez 2010b, 176, 265. Also see Vallejo 2012.
37. Vallejo 2012, 180, 182, 178, 181. Also see Kasinitz et al. 2004, 10–11.
38. Jiménez 2010b, 132, 209–14.
39. Jiménez 2010b, 166.
40. Jiménez 2010b, 210.
41. Cf. Kasinitz et al. 2004, 6–7.
42. For examples, see Maira 2002; DasGupta and DasGupta 1996.
43. Tuan 1998. Kasinitz et al. (2004) also finds that language retention/bilingualism is particularly difficult for the Asian American second generation and beyond (9).
44. Wimmer 2008. Wimmer refers to an opposite process as "transvaluation," whereby actors respond to racism by aligning themselves with immigrants and standing up for immigrant co-ethnics.

45. See Portes and Rumbaut 2001; Chong 1998.
46. This is not to deny that cultural resources generated by recent immigrant replenishment are playing a role in shaping Asian American ethnic identity and culture by contributing material cultural building blocks for sustained panethnic expressions (for example, food, music, language, traditions, and so on) that can move beyond mere symbolic ethnic expressions.

# APPENDIX A

## List of Interview Participants

Name, Age, Ethnicity/Race, Degree

### Interracial Couples

| Husband | Wife |
| --- | --- |
| 1  Albert, 35, White, College | Zoe, 33, Filipina Am, College |
| 2  Allen, 31, White, MD | Jade, 31, Korean Am, MD |
| 3  Barry, 40, Korean Am | Jackie, 33, White, JD |
| 4  Calvin, 45, White, MBA | Carla, 43, Chinese-Am, MBA |
| 5  Cameron, 51, White, College | Pauline, 42, Indian Am, MD |
| 6  Chinese Am, 44, MBA (Not interviewed) | Ellen, 45, White, College |
| 7  Dalton, 42, White, MBA | Carol, 44, Chinese Am, MBA |
| 8  Fred, 47, Black mixed-race, College | Janet, 40, Korean Am, College |
| 9  Kyle, 38, Chinese Am/White, MA | Shaye, 39, White Hispanic, College |
| 10  Lance, 41, Chinese Am, MBA | Helen, 42, White, College |
| 11  Larry, 39, Chinese Am, Ph.D | Selena, 47, White, Ph.D. |
| 12  Luke, 44, White, College | Kira, 39, Chinese Am, MA |
| 13  Mannie, 42, White, College | Vicky, 39, Chinese Am, JD |
| 14  Marshall, 37, White, MA | Joy, 33, Korean Am, MA |
| 15  Matt, 41, Chinese Am, JD | Susan, 42, White, College |
| 16  Max, 40, White, JD | Sonia, 38, Indian Am, MD |
| 17  Perry, 57, White, MA | Lily, 53, Chinese Am, JD |
| 18  Sam, 43, White, MA | Sarah, 41, Chinese Am, MD |
| 19  Seth, 52, White, College | Sage, 44, Korean Am, College |
| 20  Ted, 38, Vietnamese Am, MD | Molly, 39, White, MD |
| 21  White, 36, BA (Not interviewed) | Sandra, 36, Korean Am, MD |
| 22  White, 38, MA (Not interviewed) | Monica, 40, Korean-Am, JD |

(19 couples: 38 people) +3 = 41 people

## Interethnic Couples

| Husband | Wife |
|---|---|
| 1  Aaron, 37, Korean Am, College | Gloria, 37, Filipina-A, College |
| 2  Andrew, 34, Vietnamese-A, JD | Pamela, 36, Korean Am, MD |
| 3  Bart, 31, Chinese Am, College | Sadie, 31, Korean Am, College |
| 4  Carter, 44, Asian Mixed Ethnicity, College | Samantha, 41, Asian Mixed Ethnicity, College |
| 5  Charlie, 52, Chinese Am, College | Jane, Japanese-A, 49, College |
| 6  Cooper, 49, Chinese Am, College | Sophie, 45, Japanese-A, College |
| 7  Daniel, 38, Korean Am, College | 38, Indian-A, College (not interviewed) |
| 8  Dennis, 39, Vietnamese-A, MA | Nora, 39, Korean Am, JD |
| 9  Douglas, 35, Korean Am, JD | Lucy, 35, Filipina-A, MD |
| 10  Ed, 34, Filipino-A, JD | 34, Korean Am, MA (not interviewed) |
| 11  James, 38, Taiwanese-A, MA | Rachel, 39, Japanese-A, College |
| 12  Jared, 40, Vietnamese-A, Ph.D | Corinne, 40, Chinese Am, MA |
| 13  Jeff, 35, Korean Am, College | Becky, 34, Taiwanese-A, MBA |
| 14  Jeremy, 39, Korean Am, Ph.D | Claire, 42, Chinese Am, MD |
| 15  Justin, 39, Korean Am, MA | Stella, 34, Cambodian-A, MA |
| 16  Lewis, 48, Chinese Am, Ph.D | Alice, 44, Asian Mixed-Race, MA |
| 17  Miles, 35, Korean Am, College | 35, Chinese Am, Ph.D. (not interviewed) |
| 18  Oliver, 42, Laotian-A, College | Lara, 45, Chinese Am/White, College |
| 19  Shane, 34, Taiwanese-A, MD | Marie, 34, Vietnamese-A, MA |
| 20  Wade, 32, Taiwanese-A, College | Polly, 32, Korean Am, MD |

(17 couples: 34 people) + 3 = 37 people

## Intraethnic Couples

| Husband | Wife |
|---|---|
| 1  Edmund, 35, Korean Am, College | Jamie, 28, Korean Am, College |
| 2  George, 37, Korean Am, MD | Linda, 36, Korean Am, JD |
| 3  Harold, 39, Korean Am, College | 41, Korean Am, JD (not interviewed) |
| 4  Mack, 40, Korean Am, Ph.D | Kacy, 31, Korean Am, College |
| 5  Marvin, 41, Korean Am, JD | Shannon, 36, Korean Am, MA |
| 6  Parker, 30, Korean Am, MA | Laila, 36, Indian-A, JD |
| 7  Sawyer, 37, Indian-A, JD | Shirley, 36, Korean Am, College |

(6 couples: 12 people) + 1 = 13 people

## Single Participants

1. Daisy, 38, Taiwanese-A, JD (F)
2. Eugene, 22, Chinese Am, College (M)
3. Hailey, 28, Taiwanese-A, College (F)
4. Hilary, 40, Korean Am, College (F)

5. Jada, 27, Chinese Am, College (F)
6. Jana, 32, Korean Am, JD (F)
7. Jasmin, 39, Korean Am, College (F)
8. Shaun, 25, Chinese Am, College (M)
9. Sherman, 35, Korean Am, College (M)

# APPENDIX B

## Interviewing

All spouses were interviewed individually to ensure that they felt the freedom to speak freely and frankly; in some cases, the couples were interviewed together afterward if they consented and had time. Interviewing the couples together, when feasible, allowed for an observation of relational dynamics between the couples, particularly with respect to power dynamics along the lines of race, ethnicity, and gender. It also allowed for an observation of how the couples managed self-presentations with regard to each other and to the interviewer, allowing a view of the difference between the participants' subjective and intersubjective selves and how their individual self-presentations and narratives squared with their presentations as couples. The interviews typically lasted from one and a half to four hours, with limited follow-up interviews. The majority of interviews were carried out in the interviewees' homes (sometimes in the presence of their children) and in a few instances in their places of business; in cases where travel to another part of the country was not possible, interviews were conducted by phone or Skype. Almost all interviews were tape-recorded, transcribed, and thematically coded and analyzed. All data were coded first with open/substantive coding that helped identify major concepts and categories, then with axial coding, which helped find connections between the categories.[1] The data were analyzed and coded simultaneously during the collection and analysis phases, which allowed the interviewer to remain open to emerging themes and to adjust questions and analytical categories as the data collection and analysis proceeded. This approach enabled the interviewer to be maximally interactive with the data during all phases of research and in generating concepts, categories, and theories.

This study utilizes the grounded theory method, which is designed to generate original insights, concepts, hypotheses, and theories from data during both the collection and analysis phases, especially through careful attention to the participant's own narratives and perspectives. Individual interviews typically began with a set of semi-structured questions about the participant's background, including childhood history, family and social environment, educational background, and general experiences growing up. The interviewer detailed questions about dating history and events leading up to their marriages, including factors that informed their spousal choices. Respondents were asked to reflect on their experiences as racialized ethnics, including any experiences of racism and discrimination while growing up and as adults, including in the workplace. Specific questions were asked about the respondents' parental influences on their lives and choices, and the evolution of their ethnic-racial identities. Each person was also asked how they identified themselves, especially, how they identified along the spectrum of American to hyphenated-ethnic and panethnic labels.

A set of questions focused on the respondents' family and marital life, starting with relationships with spouses and children; in particular, the participants were asked to discuss issues regarding their children's ethnic identity development, and these questions typically prompted discourses on the respondents' child-raising philosophies, their personal feelings about ethnicity and ethnic culture, and their assessment of their children's experiences as mixed-racial children. They were also asked questions regarding power dynamics within their marriages, especially in relation to the negotiations of ethnic identity and culture within the family. Although the respondents were approached with a set of prepared questions, it was important to try to leave the interviews open-ended whenever possible to allow the participants to discuss topics that were most meaningful to them. When couples were interviewed together after the individual interviews, the discussion was left mostly open-ended; this enabled the interviewer to see what subjects were of most significance to the couples and to observe the relationship dynamics.

Most participants were highly forthcoming and open about their experiences. For Asian American participants in particular, this may have been due to their perception that the researcher, as a U.S.-raised Asian American, could relate to many of their experiences, but non-Asian-ethnic participants were open as well. The men interviewed were generally as forthcoming as the women. The only interesting difference of note was that on the whole, the interracially married participants seemed, at least initially, more enthusiastic about participating in this project and to talk to me about their experiences, while interethnically married participants, though not all, seemed a bit more laid back. I realized as the interviews went on that one of the reasons for this was that interracially married participants felt they had a lot of interesting experiences to relate due to being in a mixed-race relationship in which there were a lot more perceived "differences" to negotiate, whereas many interethnically married participants had perceptions that somehow their marriages and family lives were not as interesting or worthy of discussion because they were simply part of a same-race and culturally similar couplings. Of course, their experiences were interesting, and as they were prodded with questions, they revealed a great deal of compelling information and reflections that even surprised the participants themselves. Setting aside the benefits accruing from panethnic identification, I felt that this was a testament to how the society's efforts to culturally and racially homogenize Asian-ethnics under the banner of "Asian Americans" affects the self-perception of Asian-ethnics, that is, as too similar to each other to be worthy of notice. As a final note, this study focuses on marital relations and parenting issues within the context of family-making and does not deal directly with the experiences of the participants' children except insofar as it emerged as a topic of discussion among the parents.

## Note

1. Strauss and Corbin 1990.

# BIBLIOGRAPHY

Abelmann, Nancy and John Lie. 1995. *Blue Dreams*. Cambridge, MA: Harvard University Press.

Abu-Lughod, Lila and Catherine Lutz. 1990. *Language and the Politics of Emotion*. Cambridge, MA: Maison des Sciences de l'Homme and University of Cambridge Press.

Aguirre, Benigno E., Rogelio Saenz, and Sean-Shong Hwang. 1995. "Remarriage and Intermarriage of Asians in the United States of America." *Journal of Comparative Family Studies*. 26: 207–15.

Aguirre, Benigno E., Rogelio Saenz, and Sean-Shong Hwang. 1990. "Discrimination and the Assimilation and Ethnic Competition Perspectives." *Social Science Quarterly*. 70 (3): 594–606.

Alba, Richard. 1999. "Immigration and the American Realities of Assimilation and Multiculturalism." *Social Forum*. 14 (1): 3–25. Cambridge, MA: Harvard University Press.

Alba, Richard. 1990. *Ethnic Identity: The Transformation of White America*. New Haven, CT: Yale University Press.

Alba, Richard and Victor Nee. 2003. *Remaking the American Mainstream: Assimilation and Contemporary Immigration*. Cambridge, MA: Harvard University Press.

Ancheta, Angelo. 1998. *Race, Rights, and the Asian American Experience*. New Brunswick, NJ: Rutgers University Press.

Anzaldua, Gloria. [1987] 2007. *Borderlands/La Frontera: The New Mestiza*, 3rd ed. San Francisco: Aunt Lute Books.

Appadurai, Arjun. 2004. "Disjuncture and Difference in the Global Cultural Economy." Pp. 100–8 in *The Globalization Reader*, edited by Frank J. Lechner and John Boli. Malden, MA: Blackwell Publishing.

Ashcroft, Bill, Gareth Griffiths, and Helen Tiffin (eds.). 2006. *The Post-Colonial Studies Reader*, 2nd ed. London: Routledge.

Axtmann, Roland. 1995. "Collective Identity and the Democratic Nation-State in the Age of Globalization." Pp. 33–54 in *Articulating the Global and the Local*, edited by Ann Cvetkovich and Douglas Kellner. Boulder, CO: Westview Press.

Bacon, Jean. 1997. *Life Lines: Community, Family and Assimilation Among Chicago's Asian Indians*. New York, NY: Oxford University Press.

Barron, Milton L. (ed.). 1972. *The Blending American: Patterns of Intermarriage*. Chicago: Quadrangle Books.

Batur-VanderLippe, Pinar and Joe Feagin. 1999. "Racial and Ethnic Inequality and Struggle from the Colonial Era to the Present: Drawing the Global Color Line." *Research in Politics and Society*. 6: 3–21.

Beall, Anne E. and Robert J. Sternberg. 1995. "The Social Construction of Love." *Journal of Social and Personal Relationships*. 12 (3): 417–38.

de Beauvoir, Simone. 1971. *The Second Sex*. New York, NY: Knopf.

Benjamin, Jessica. 1988. *Bonds of Love*. New York, NY: Pantheon.

Bhabha, Homi. 1994. *The Location of Culture*. London: Routledge.

Bhabha, Homi. 1990. "The Third Space." Pp. 207–21 in *Identity: Community, Culture, Difference*, edited by Jonathan Rutherford. London: Lawrence & Wishart.

Bhattacharyya, Gargi, John Gariel, and Stephen Small. 2002. *Race and Power: Global Racism in the Twenty-First Century*. London: Routledge.

bigWOWO. 2011. "Asian American Masculinity." February 23. [www.bigwowo.com/2011/02/asian-american-masculinity/]

Blau, Peter M. 1977. *Inequality and Heterogeneity*. New York, NY: The Free Press.

Blau, Peter M., C. Beeker, and K.M. Fitzpatrick. 1984. "Intersecting Social Affiliations and Intermarriage." *American Sociological Review*. 47: 45–62.

Blau, Peter M., T.C. Blum, and J.E. Schwartz. 1982. "Heterogeneity and Intermarriage." *American Sociological Review*. 47: 25–62.

Blau, Peter M. and J.E. Schwartz. 1984. *Crosscutting Social Circles: Testing Macrostructural Theory of Intergroup Relations*. New York, NY: Academic Press.

Blauner, Robert. 1972. *Racial Oppression in America*. New York, NY: Harper & Row.

Bogardis, Emory. 1967. *A Forty Year Racial Distance Study*. Los Angeles: University of Southern California.

Bonacich, Edna. 1973. "A Theory of Middleman Minorities." *American Sociological Review*. 38 (5): 583–94.

Bonilla-Silva, Eduardo. 2014. *Racism Without Racists: Color-Blind Racism and the Persistence of Racial Inequality in the United States*, 4th ed. Lanham, MD: Rowman and Littlefield.

Bonilla-Silva, Eduardo. 2004. "From Bi-Racial to Tri-Racial: Towards a New System of Racial Stratification in the USA." *Ethnic and Racial Studies*. 27 (6): 931–50.

Bonilla-Silva, Eduardo. 2001. *White Supremacy and Racism in the Post-Civil Rights Era*. Boulder, CO: Lynne Rienner Publishers.

Bonilla-Silva, Eduardo. 1999. "'This Is a White Country': The Racial Ideology of the Western Nations of the World-System." *Research in Politics and Society*. 6: 85–101.

Bourdieu, Pierre. 1984. *Distinction: A Social Critique of the Judgement of Taste*. Cambridge, MA: Harvard University Press.

Breger, Rosemary and Rosanna Hill (eds.). 1998. *Cross-Cultural Marriage: Identity and Choice*. Oxford, UK: Berg.

Butler, Judith. 1990. *Gender Trouble*. London: Routledge.

Butler, Judith. 1987. *Subjects of Desire: Hegelian Reflections on Twentieth Century France*. New York, NY: Columbia University Press.

Butterfield, Sherri-Ann P. 2004. "'We're Just Black': The Racial and Ethnic Identities of Second-Generation West Indians in New York." Pp. 288–312 in *Becoming New Yorkers: Ethnographies of the New Second Generation*, edited by Philip Kasinitz, John H. Mollenkopf, and Mary C. Waters. New York, NY: Russell Sage Foundation.

Bystydzienski, Jill M. 2011. *Intercultural Couples: Crossing Boundaries, Negotiating Difference*. New York, NY: New York University Press.

Cancian, Francesca. 1990. *Love in America*. Cambridge, UK: Oxford University Press.

Canclini, Nestor Garcia. 1995. *Hybrid Cultures: Strategies for Entering and Leaving Modernity*. Minneapolis, MN: University of Minnesota Press.

Carr, Leslie. 1997. *Colorblind Racism*. Thousand Oaks, CA: Sage Publications.

Cauce, Ana Mari, Yuma Hiraga, Craig Mason, Tanya Aguilar, Nydia Ordonez, and Nancy Gonzales. 1992. "Between a Rock and a Hard Place: Social Adjustment of Biracial Youth." Pp. 207–22 in *Racially Mixed People in America*, edited by Maria P. Root. Newbury Park, CA: Sage Publications.

Chan, Jachinson. 2001. *Chinese American Masculinities: From Fu Manchu to Bruce Lee*. New York, NY: Routledge.

Chang, Sharon H. 2016. *Raising Mixed Race: Multiracial Asian Children in a Post-Racial World*. New York, NY: Routledge.

Chaudhary, A.R. 2015. "Racialized Incorporation: The Effects of Race and Generational Status on Self-Employment and Industry-Sector Prestige in the United States." *International Migration Rev.* 49 (2): 318–54.

Chen, Anthony. 1999. "Lives at the Center of the Periphery, Lives at the Periphery of the Center: Chinese American Masculinities and Bargaining with Hegemony." *Gender & Society*. 13 (4): 584–607.

Chen, Juan and David T. Takeuchi. 2011. "Intermarriage, Ethnic Identity, and Perceived Social Standing Among Asian Women in the United States." *Journal of Marriage and Family*. 73 (4): 876–88.

Cheng, Anne A. 2001. *The Melancholy of Race*. New York, NY: Oxford University Press.

Cheng, Sealing. 2010. *On the Move for Love: Migrant Entertainers and the U.S. Military in South Korea*. Philadelphia, PA: University of Pennsylvania Press.

Childs, Erica Chito. 2005. *Navigating Interracial Borders: Black-White Couples and Their Social Worlds*. New Brunswick, NJ: Rutgers University Press.

Chin, Frank and J.P. Chan. 1972. "Racist Love." Pp. 65–79 in *Seeing Through Shuck*. New York, NY: Ballantine.

Chin, Frank, Jeffery Oayl Chan, Lawson Fusao Inada, and Shawn Wong (eds.). 1974. *Aiieeeee! An Anthology of Asian-American Writers*. Washington, DC: Howard University Press.

Chong, Kelly H. 2017. "'Asianness Under Construction': The Contours and Negotiation of Panethnic Identity/Culture Among Interethnically Married Asian Americans." *Sociological Perspectives*. 60 (1): 52–76.

Chong, Kelly H. 2013. "The Relevance of Race: Children and the Shifting Engagement with Racial/Ethnic Identity Among Second Generation Interracially Married Asian Americans." *Journal of Asian American Studies*. 16 (2): 189–221.

Chong, Kelly H. 1998. "What It Means to Be Christian: The Role of Religion in the Construction of Ethnic Identity and Boundary Among Second-Generation Korean-Americans." *Sociology of Religion*. 59 (3): 259–86.

Chou, Rosalind S. 2012. *Asian American Sexual Politics: The Construction of Race, Gender, and Sexuality*. Lanham, MD: Rowman and Littlefield.

Chou, Rosalind S. and Joe R. Feagin. 2015. *The Myth of the Model Minority: Asian Americans Facing Racism*. Boulder, CO: Paradigm Publishers.

Chou, Rosalind S., Kristin Lee, and Simon Ho. 2015. "Love Is (Color) Blind: Asian Americans and White Institutional Space at the Elite University." *Sociology of Race and Ethnicity*. 1 (2): 302–16.

Chow, Keith. 2016. "Why Won't Hollywood Cast Asian Actors?" *New York Times*. April 22. [www.nytimes.com/2016/04/23/opinion/why-wont-hollywood-cast-asian-actors.html]

Chow, Sue. 2000. "The Significance of Race in the Private Sphere: Asian Americans and Spousal Preferences." *Sociological Inquiry*. 70 (1): 1–29.

Chua, Peter and Diana C. Fujino. 1999. "Negotiating New Asian-American Masculinities: Attitudes and Gender Expectations." *The Journal of Men's Studies*. 7: 391–413.

Collins, Patricia Hill. 1990. *Black Feminist Thought: Knowledge, Consciousness, and the Politics of Empowerment*. New York, NY: Routledge.

Connell, R.W. 2005. "Hegemonic Masculinity: Rethinking the Concept." *Gender & Society*. 19 (16): 829–59.

Connell, R.W. 1995. *Masculinities*. Berkeley, CA: University of California Press.

Connell, R.W. and James W. Messerschmidt. 2005. "Hegemonic Masculinity: Rethinking the Concept." *Gender & Society*. 19 (6): 829–859.

Constable, Nicole. 2005. *Cross-Border Marriages: Gender and Mobility in Transnational Asia*, edited by Nicole Constable. Pennsylvania, PA: University of Pennsylvania Press.

Constable, Nicole. 1995. *Romance on a Global Stage: Pen Pals, Virtual Ethnography, and "Mail Order" Marriages*. Berkeley, CA: University of California Press.

Cooley, Charles Horton. 1902. *Human Nature and the Social Order*. New York, NY: Scribner's.

Cornell, Stephen. 1996. "The Variable Ties That Bind: Contents and Circumstances in Ethnic Processes." *Ethnic and Racial Studies*. 19: 265–89.

Cornell, Stephen and Douglas Hartmann. 1998. *Ethnicity and Race: Making Identities in a Changing World*. Thousand Oaks, CA: Pine Forge Press.

DaCosta, Kimberly McClain. 2007. *Making Multiracials: State, Family, and Market in the Redrawing of the Color Line*. Stanford, CA: Stanford University Press.

Dalmage, Heather M. 2000. *Tripping on the Color Line: Black-White Multiracial Families in a Racially Divided World*. New Brunswick, NJ: Rutgers University.

DasGupta, Sayantani and Shamita DasGupta. 1996. "Women in Exile: Gender Relations in the Asian Indian Community." In *Contours of the Heart: South Asians Map North America*, edited by Sunaina Maira and Rajini Srikanth. New York, NY: Asian American Writers' Workshop.

Davilla, Arlene. 2008. *Latino Spin: Public Image and the Whitewashing of Race*. New York, NY: New York University Press.

Dhingra, Pawan. 2007. *Managing Multicultural Lives: Asian American Professionals and the Challenge of Multiple Identities*. Stanford, CA: Stanford University Press.

Diggs, Nancy Brown. 2001. *Looking Beyond the Mask: When American Women Marry Japanese Men*. Albany, NY: State University of New York Press.

Doane, Ashley "Woody." 2003. "Rethinking Whiteness Studies." Pp. 3–18 in *White Out: The Continuing Significance of Racism*, edited by Ashley "Woody" Doane and Eduardo Bonilla-Silva. New York, NY: Routledge.

Du Bois, W.E.B. [1986] 1990. *The Souls of Black Folk*. New York, NY: Vintage Books and Library of America.

Dyer, Richard. 1997. *White: Essays in Race and Culture*. New York, NY: Routledge.

Ellman, Yisrael. 1987. "Intermarriage in the United States: A Comparative Study of Jews and Other Ethnic and Religious Groups." *Jewish Social Studies*. 49: 1–26.

Emeka, A. and J.A. Vallejo. 2011. "Non-Hispanics with Latin American Ancestry: Assimilation, Race, and Identity Among Latin American Descendants in the US." *Social Science Research*. 40 (6): 1547–63.

Eng, David. 2001. *Racial Castration: Managing Masculinity in Asian America*. Durham, NC: Duke University Press.

Espiritu, Yen Le. 2008. *Asian American Women and Men: Labor, Laws, and Love*. Lanham, MD: Rowman and Littlefield.

Espiritu, Yen Le. 2003. *Homebound: Filipino American Lives Across Cultures, Communities, and Countries.* Berkeley, CA: University of California Press.

Espiritu, Yen Le. 1992. *Asian-American Panethnicity: Bridging Institutions and Identities.* Philadelphia: Temple University Press.

Espiritu, Yen Le and Diane L. Wolf. 2001. "Paradox of Assimilation: Children of Filipino Immigrants in San Diego." In *Ethnicities: Children of Immigrants in America,* edited by Ruben G. Rumbaut and Alejandro Portes. Berkeley, CA and New York, NY: University of California Press and Russell Sage Foundation.

Faier, Lieba. 2009. *Intimate Encounters: Filipina Women and the Remaking of Rural Japan.* Berkeley, CA: University of California Press.

The Falco. 2010. "Interracial Dating: Are Asian Guys the Perfect Boyfriends?" July 8. [https://ranierm.wordpress.com/2010/07/08/interracial-dating-are-asian-guys-the-perfect-boyfriends/. Retrieved July 23, 2015]

Fanon, Frantz. 2004. *The Wretched of the Earth.* New York, NY: Grove Press.

Fanon, Frantz. 1967. *Black Skin, White Masks.* New York, NY: Grove Press.

Fei, Deanna. 2015. "The Real Lesson of Linsanity." *Huffington Post.* April 27. [www.huffingtonpost.com/deanna-fei/jeremy-lin-asian-americans_b_1281916.html]

Feliciano, Cynthia. 2001. "Assimilation or Enduring Racial Boundaries? Generational Differences in Intermarriage Among Asians and Latinos in the United States." *Race and Society.* 4: 27–45.

Fernandez-Kelly, Patricia and Richard Schauffler. 1994. "Divided Fates: Immigrant Children in a Restructured U.S. Economy." *International Migration Review.* 29 (4): 662–89.

Firestone, Shulamith. 1970. *The Dialectic of Sex: The Case for Feminist Revolution.* New York, NY: William Morrow.

Flores-Gonzales, Nilda. 1999. "The Racialization of Latinos: The Meaning of Latino Identity for the Second Generation." *Latino Studies Journal.* 10 (3): 3–31.

Fong, Coleen and Judy Yung. 2000. "In Search of the Right Spouse: Interracial Marriage Among Chinese and Japanese Americans." In *Contemporary Asian America: A Multidisciplinary Reader,* edited by Min Zhou and James V. Gatewood. New York, NY: New York University.

Fong, Timothy P. 2008. *The Contemporary Asian American Experience: Beyond the Model Minority,* 3rd ed. Upper Saddle River, NJ: Pearson.

Frankenberg, Ruth. 1993. *White Women, Race Matters: The Social Construction of Whiteness.* Minneapolis, MN: University of Minnesota Press.

Freud, Sigmund. [1921] 1991. *Group Psychology and the Analysis of the Ego, in Civilization, Society, and Religion, Vol. 12 Selected Works.* Harmondsworth: Penguin.

Fu, Vincent Kang. 2001. "How Many Melting Pots? Intermarriage, Pan Ethnicity, and the Black/Non-Black Divide in the United States." *Demography.* 38: 147–59.

Fu, Xuanning and Melanie Hatfield. 2008. "Intermarriage and Segmented Assimilation: U.S. Born Asians in 2000." *Journal of Asian American Studies.* 11 (3): 249–77.

Gambol, Brenda. 2016. "Changing Racial Boundaries and Mixed Unions: The Case of Second-Generation Filipino Americans." *Ethnic and Racial Studies.* 39 (14): 2621–40.

Gandhi, Leela. 1998. *Postcolonial Theory: A Critical Introduction.* New York, NY: Columbia University Press.

Gans, Herbert. 1999. "The Possibility of a New Racial Hierarchy in the Twenty-First Century United States." Pp. 371–90 in *The Cultural Territories of Race: Black and White Boundaries,* edited by Michèle Lamont. Chicago, IL: University of Chicago Press; New York, NY: Russell Sage Foundation.

Gans, Herbert. 1997. "Toward a Reconciliation of 'Assimilation' and 'Pluralism': The Interplay of Acculturation and Ethnic Retention." *International Migration Review*. 31 (4): 875–92.

Gans, Herbert. 1992. "Comment: Ethnic Invention and Acculturation, a Bumpy-Line Approach." *Journal of American Ethnic History*. 12 (1): 42–52.

Gans, Herbert. 1979. "Symbolic Ethnicity: The Future of Ethnic Groups and Cultures in America." *Ethnic and Racial Studies*. 2: 1–30.

Gans, Herbert. 1973. "Introduction." In *Ethnic Identity and Assimilation: The Polish Community*, edited by Neil Sandberg. New York, NY: Praeger.

Gibson, Margaret. 1988. *Accommodation Without Assimilation: Sikh Immigrants in an American High School*. Ithaca, NY: Cornell University Press.

Gilroy, Paul. 1993. *Small Acts: Thoughts on Politics of Black Cultures*. New York, NY: Serpant's Tail.

Glazer, Barney G. and Anselm L. Strauss. 1967. *Discovery of Grounded Theory: Strategies for Qualitative Research*. Chicago: Aldine Publishers.

Glazer, Nathan and Daniel P. Moynihan. 1970. *Beyond the Melting Pot: The Negroes, Puerto Ricans, Jews, Italians, and Irish of New York City*. Cambridge, MA: MIT Press.

Glenn, Evelyn N. 2011. "Constructing Citizenship: Exclusion, Subordination, and Resistance." *American Sociological Review*. 76 (1): 1–24.

Glenn, Evelyn N. 2002. *Unequal Freedom: How Race and Gender Shaped American Citizenship and Labor*. Cambridge, MA: Harvard University Press.

Glick Schiller, Nina. 1999. "Transmigrants and Nation-States: Something Old and Something New in the U.S. Immigrant Experience." Pp. 94–119 in *The Handbook of International Migration: The American Experience*, edited by Charles Hirschman, Philip Kasinitz, and Josh DeWind. New York, NY: Russell Sage Foundation.

Goar, Carla, Jenny L. Davis, and Bianca Manago. 2017. "Discursive Entwinement: How White Transracially Adoptive Parents Navigate Race." *Sociology of Race &Ethnicity*. 3 (3): 338–54.

Golash-Boza, Tanya. 2006. "Dropping the Hyphen? Becoming Latino(a) Through Racialized Assimilation." *Social Forces*. 85 (1): 27–55.

Goldberg, Theo. 2002. *The Racial State*. Malden, MA: Blackwell Publishers.

Goldberg, Theo (ed.). 1990. *Anatomy of Racism*. Minneapolis, MN: University of Minnesota Press.

Goldberg, Theo and Ato Quayson (eds.). 2002. *Relocating Postcolonialism*. Oxford, UK: Blackwell Publishers.

Gordon, Avery F. and Christopher Newfield (eds.). 1996. *Mapping Multiculturalism*. Minneapolis, MN: University of Minneapolis Press.

Gordon, Milton. 1964. *Assimilation in American Life*. New York, NY: Oxford University Press.

Gowen, Annie. 2009. "Immigrants' Children Look Closer for Love: More Young Adults Are Seeking Partner of Same Ethnicity." *The Washington Post*. March 9.

Gregory, Steven and Roger Sanjek (eds.). 1994. *Race*. New Brunswick, NJ: Rutgers University Press.

Grewal, Inderpal. 2005. *Transnational America: Feminisms, Diasporas, Neoliberalisms*. Durham, NC: Duke University Press.

Grewal, Inderpal and Caren Kaplan (eds.). 1994. *Scattered Hegemonies: Postmodernity and Transnational Feminist Practices*. Minneapolis, MN: University of Minnesota Press.

Guevarra, Rudy. 2012. *Becoming Mexipino: Multiethnic Identities and Communities in San Diego*. New Brunswick, NJ: Rutgers University Press.

Hall, Stuart. 2000. "Conclusion; The Multi-Cultural Question." In *Un/Settled Multicultur-alisms: Diasporas, Entanglements, Transruptions*, edited by Barnor Hesse. New York, NY: Zed Books.

Hall, Stuart. 1996a. "Introduction: Who Needs Identity?" Pp. 1–17 in *Questions of Cultural Identity*, edited by Stuart Hall and Paul DuGay. New York: Sage Publications.

Hall, Stuart. 1996b. "On Postmodernism and Articulation: An Interview with Stuart Hall." "Gramsci's Relevance for the Study of Race and Ethnicity." "New Ethnicities." In *Stuart Hall: Critical Dialogues in Cultural Studies*, edited by David Morley and Kuan-Hsing Chen. New York, NY: Routledge.

Hall, Stuart. 1992. "Ethnicities." In *Race, Culture and Difference*, edited by James Donald and Ali Rattansi. Newbury Park, CA: Sage Publications.

Hall, Stuart. 1991. "The Local and the Global: Globalization and Ethnicity." "Old and New Identities, Old and New Ethnicities." In *Culture, Globalization and the World-System: Contemporary Conditions for the Representation of Identity*, edited by Anthony D. King. Binghamton, NY: State of University of New York at Binghamton.

Hall, Stuart. 1980. "Race, Articulation, and Societies Structured in Dominance." In *Socio-logical Theories: Race and Colonialism*, edited by UNESCO. Paris: United Nations Edu-cational, Scientific, and Cultural Organization.

Hall, Stuart, David Held, and Tony McGrew (eds.). 1992. *Modernity and Its Futures*. Cam-bridge and Oxford, UK: Polity Press.

Harding, Jennifer and E. Deirdre Pribram. 2009. *Emotions: A Cultural Studies Reader*. New York, NY: Routledge.

Hardt, Michael and Antonio Negri. 2000. *Empire*. Cambridge, MA: Harvard University Press.

Harvey, David. 2003. *The New Imperialism*. Oxford, UK: Oxford University Press.

Healey, Joseph F. and Andy Stepnick. 2017. *Diversity and Society: Race, Ethnicity, and Gen-der*. Thousand Oaks, CA: Sage Publications.

Henriques, Julian, Wendy Holloway, Cathy Urwin, Couze Venn, and Valerie Walkerdine. 1984. *Changing the Subject: Psychology, Social Regulation, and Subjectivity*. New York, NY: Routledge.

Hess, Amanda. 2016. "Asian-American Actors Are Fighting for Visibility. They Will Not Be Ignored." *New York Times*. May 25. [www.nytimes.com/2016/05/29/mov-ies/asian-american-actors-are-fighting-for-visibility-they-will-not-be-ignored. html?smid=twnytimes&smtyp=cur&_r=1&smtyp=cur&_r=0http:/www.nytimes. com/2016/05/29/movies/asian-american-actors-are-fighting-for-visibility-they-will-not-be-ignored.html?smid=tw-nytimes&smtyp=cur&_r=0. Retrieved June 14, 2016]

Hobsbawm, Eric and Terence Ranger (eds.). 1983. *The Invention of Tradition*. New York, NY: Cambridge University Press.

Hochschild, Arlie. [1983] 2003. *Managed Heart: The Commercialization of Human Feeling*. Berkeley, CA: University of California Press.

Hodes, Martha (ed.). 1999. *Sex, Love, Race: Crossing Boundaries in North American History*. New York, NY: New York University Press.

Hollway, Wendy. 1984. "Gender Difference and the Production of Subjectivity." In *Chang-ing the Subject: Psychology, Social Regulation and Subjectivity*, edited by Julian Henriquez, Wendy Hollway, Caty Urwin, Couze Venn, and Valerie Walkerdine. New York, NY: Routledge.

Hongdagneu-Sotelo, P. and Michael Messner. 1994. "Gender Displays and Men's Power: The 'New Man' and the Mexican Immigrant Man." In *Theorizing Masculinities*, edited by H. Brod and M. Kaufman. Thousand Oaks, CA: Sage Publications.

Hsu, Ruth. 2008. "The Concept of Hybridity in Asian American Literary and Cultural Studies: Towards a Geography of Difference." Pp. 295–329 in *Hybrid Americas: Contacts, Contrasts, and Confluences in New World Literatures and Cultures*, edited by Josef Raab and Martin Butler. Berlin: Lit Verlag.

Hughey, Matthew. 2012. "Color Capital, White Debt, and the Paradox of Strong White Racial Identities." *Du Bois Review: Social Science Research on Race*. 9 (1): 169–200.

Hurh, Won Moo and Kwang Chung Kim. 1984. *Korean Immigrants in America: A Structural Analysis of Ethnic Confinement and Adhesive Adaptation*. Rutherford, NJ: Fairleigh Dickinson University.

Hwang, Sean-Shong and Steven Murdoch. 1991. "Ethnic Closure or Ethnic Competition: Ethnic Identification Among Hispanics in Texas." *The Sociological Quarterly*. 32 (3): 469–76.

Hwang, Sean-Shong and Rogelio Saenz. 1990. "The Problems Posed by Immigrants Married Abroad on Intermarriage Research: The Case of Asian Americans." *International Migration Review*. 24: 563–76.

Hwang, Sean-Shong, Rogelio Saenz, and Benigno E. Aguirre. 1997. "Structural and Assimilationist Explanations of Asian American Intermarriage." *Journal of Marriage and Family*. 59: 579–772.

Hwang, Sean-Shong, Rogelio Saenz, and Benigno E. Aguirre. 1995. "The SES Selectivity of Interracially Married Asians." *International Migration Review*. 29 (2): 469–91.

Hwang, Sean-Shong, Rogelio Saenz, and Benigno E. Aguirre. 1994. "Structural and Individual Determinants of Outmarriage Among Chinese-, Filipino-, and Japanese-Americans in California." *Sociological Inquiry*. 64: 396–414.

Ingraham, Chrys. 2008. *White Weddings: Romancing Heterosexuality in Popular Culture*, 2nd ed. New York, NY: Routledge.

Jackson, Stevi. 1993. "Even Sociologists Fall in Love: An Exploration in the Sociology of Emotions." *Sociology*. 27 (2): 201–20.

Jacobs, Jerry A. and Theresa G. Labov. 2002. "Gender Differentials in Intermarriage Among Sixteen Race and Ethnic Groups." *Sociological Forum*. 17: 621–46.

Jiménez, Tomás R. 2010a. "Affiliative Identity: A More Elastic Link Between Ethnic Ancestry and Culture." *Ethnic and Racial Studies*. 33 (10): 1756–75.

Jiménez, Tomás R. 2010b. *Replenished Ethnicity: Mexican Americans, Immigration, and Identity*. Berkeley, CA: University of California Press.

Johnson, Walter R. and Michael D. Warren (eds.). 1994. *Inside the Mixed Marriage: Accounts of Changing Attitudes, Patterns, and Perceptions of Cross-Cultural and Interracial Marriages*. Lanham, MD: University Press of America.

Joyner, K. and Grace Kao. 2000. "School Racial Composition of Adolescent Racial Homophily." *Social Science Quarterly*. 81: 810–25.

Jung, Sun. 2010. "Chogukjeok Pan-East Asian Soft Masculinity: Reading Boys Over Flowers, Coffee Prince and Shinhwa Fan Fiction." Pp. 1–17 in *Complicated Currents: Media Flows, Soft Power and East Asia*, edited by Daniel Black, Stephen Epstein, and Alison Tokita. Victoria, Australia: Monash University ePress.

Kalmijn, Matthijs. 2010. "Consequences of Racial Intermarriage for Children's Social Integration." *Sociological Perspectives*. 53 (2): 271–86.

Kalmijn, Matthijs. 1998. "Intermarriage and Homogamy: Causes, Patterns, and Trends." *Annual Review of Sociology*. 24: 395–421.

Kalmijn, Matthijs. 1993. "Trends in Black/White Intermarriage." *Social Forces*. 72: 119–46.

Kalmijn, Matthijs and Frank Van Tubergen. 2010. "Comparative Perspective on Intermarriage: Explaining Differences Among National-Origin Groups in the United States." *Demography*. 47 (2): 459–79.

Kao, Grace, Kelly S. Ballestri, and Kara Joyner. 2018. "Asian American Men in Romantic Dating Markets." *Contexts*. 7 (4, Fall): 48–53.

Karis, Terri A. 2003. "How Race Matters and Does Not Matter for White Women in Relationships with Black Men." Pp. 23–40 in *Clinical Issues with Interracial Couples: Theories and Research*. New York, NY: Haworth Press.

Kasinitz, Philip, John H. Mollenkopf, and Mary C. Waters (eds.). 2004. *Becoming New Yorkers: Ethnographies of the New Second Generation*. New York, NY: Russell Sage Foundation.

Kelsky, Karen. 2006 [2001]. *Women on the Verge: Japanese Women, Western Dreams*. Durham, NC: Duke University Press.

Kennedy, Randall. 2003. *Interracial Intimacies: Sex, Marriage, Identity and Adoption*. New York, NY: Pantheon Books.

Kibria, Nazli. 2002. *Becoming Asian American: Second-Generation Chinese and Korean American Identities*. Baltimore, MD: Johns Hopkins University Press.

Kibria, Nazli. 1999. "College and Notions of 'Asian-American:' Second-Generation Chinese and Korean Americans Negotiate Race and Identity." *Amerasia Journal*. 25 (1): 29–51.

Kibria, Nazli. 1997. "The Construction of 'Asian American': Reflections on Intermarriage and Ethnic Identity Among Second-Generation Chinese and Korean Americans." *Ethnic and Racial Studies*. 20 (3): 523–44.

Kibria, Nazli. 1990. "Power, Patriarchy and Gender Conflict in the Vietnamese Immigrant Community." *Gender & Society*. 4: 9–24.

Kikumura, A. and H.H.L. Kitano. 1973. "Intermarriage: A Picture of the Japanese-Americans." *Journal of Social Issues*. 29: 67–81.

Killian, Kyle D. 2003. "Homogamy Outlaws: Interracial Couples' Strategic Responses to Racism and to Partner Differences." Pp. 3–21 in *Clinical Issues with Interracial Couples: Theories and Research*. New York, NY: Haworth Press.

Kim, Chang Hwan and Yang Zao. 2014. "Are Asian American Women Advantaged? Labor Market Performance of College Educated Female Workers." *Social Forces*. 93 (2): 623–52.

Kim, Claire Jean. 1999. "The Racial Triangulation of Asian Americans." *Politics & Society*. 27 (1): 105–38.

Kim, Dae Young. 2004: "Leaving the Ethnic Economy: The Rapid Integration of Second-Generation Korean Americans in New York." Pp. 154–88 in *Becoming New Yorkers: Ethnographies of the New Second Generation*, edited by Philip Kasinitz, John H. Mollenkopf, and Mary C. Waters. New York, NY: Russell Sage Foundation.

Kim, Elaine. 1993. "Home Is Where the Han Is: A K-A Perspective on the LA Upheavals." In *Reading Rodney King/Reading Urban Uprising*, edited by Robert Gooding-Williams. New York, NY: Routledge.

Kim, Elaine. 1990. "'Such Opposite Creatures': Men and Women in Asian American Literature." *Michigan Quarterly Review*. 29: 68–93.

Kim, Nadia. 2008. *Imperial Citizens: Koreans and Race from Seoul to L.A.* Stanford, CA: Stanford University Press.

Kim, Nadia. 2007. "Critical Thoughts on Asian American Assimilation in the Whitening Literature." *Social Forces*. 86 (2): 561–74.

King-O'Riain, Rebecca C., Stephen Small, Minelle Mahtani, Miri Song, and Paul Spickard (eds.). 2014. *Global Mixed Race*. New York, NY: New York University Press.

Kitano, Harry H.L. and Lynn Chai. 1982. "Korean Interracial Marriage." *Marriage and Family Review*. 5: 75–89.

Kitano, Harry H.L. and Roger Daniels. 1988. *Asian Americans: Emerging Minorities*. Englewood Cliffs, NJ: Prentice Hall.

Kitano, Harry H.L. and Wai-Tang Yeung. 1982. "Chinese Interracial Marriage." *Marriage and Family Review*. 5: 35–48.

Kitano, Harry H.L., Wai-Tsang Yeung, Lynn Chai, and Herbert Hatanaka. 1984. "Asian-American Intermarriage." *Journal of Marriage and Family*. 46 (1): 179–90.

Koshy, Susan. 2004. *Sexual Naturalization: Asian Americans and Miscegenation*. Stanford, CA: Stanford University Press.

Lacan, Jacques. 1977. "The Mirror Stage as the Formative of the Function I as Revealed in the Psychoanalytic Experience." In *Ecrits: A Selection*, translated by Alan Sheridan. New York, NY: W.W. Norton.

Lai, Eric and Dennis Arguelles (eds.). 2003. *The New Face of Asian Pacific America: Numbers, Diversity and Change in the 21st Century*. San Francisco and Los Angeles: Asian-Week and University of California, Los Angeles, Asian American Studies Center Press.

Lamont, Michele and Virag Molnar. 2002. "The Study of Boundaries in the Social Sciences." *Annual Review of Sociology*. 28: 167–95.

Le, C.N. 2013. "Interracial Dating and Marriage: U.S. Raised Asian-Americans." *Asian Nation: The Landscape of Asian America*. October 3. [http//www.asian-nation.org/interracial2.shtml].

Lee, Jennifer. 2015. "From Undesirable to Marriageable: Hyper-Selectivity and the Racial Mobility of Asian Americans." *ANNALS of the American Academy of Political and Social Science*. 662 (1): 79–93.

Lee, Jennifer and Frank D. Bean. 2004. "America's Changing Color Lines: Immigration, Race/Ethnicity, and Multiracial Identification." *Annual Review of Sociology*. 30: 221–42.

Lee, Jennifer and Samuel Kye. 2016. "Racialized Assimilation of Asian Americans." *Annual Review of Sociology*. 42: 253–73.

Lee, Jennifer and Min Zhou (eds.). 2004. *Asian American Youth: Culture, Identity, and Ethnicity*. New York, NY: Routledge. (Own)

Lee, Robert G. 1999. *Orientals: Asian Americans in Popular Culture*. Philadelphia, PA: Temple University Press.

Lee, Sara. 2004. "Marriage Dilemmas: Partner Choices and Constraints for Korean Americans in New York City." Pp. 285–98 in *Asian American Youth: Culture, Identity, and Ethnicity*. New York, NY: Routledge.

Lee, Sharon. 1989. "Asian Immigration and American Race-Relations: From Exclusion to Acceptance?" *Ethnic and Racial Studies*. 12 (3): 368–90.

Lee, Sharon and Marilyn Fernandez. 1998. "Trends in Asian American Racial/Ethnic Intermarriage: A Comparison of 1980 and 1990 Census Data." *Sociological Perspectives*. 41: 323–42.

Lee, Sharon and Keiko Yamanaka. 1990. "Patterns of Asian American Intermarriage and Marital Assimilation." *Journal of Comparative Family Studies*. 21 (2): 287–305.

Lee, Stacey. 1996. *Unraveling the 'Model Minority' Stereotype: Listening to Asian-American Youth*. New York, NY: Teachers College Press.

Lee, Susan. 1996. "Racial Construction Through Citizenship in the US." *Asian American Policy Review*. 4: 89–116.

Leung, Russell (ed.). 1996. *Asian-American Sexualities: Dimensions of the Gay and Lesbian Experience*. New York, NY: Routledge.

Liang, Z. and N. Ito. 1999. "Intermarriage of Asian Americans in the New York City Region: Contemporary Patterns and Future Prospects." *International Migration Review*. 33: 876–900.

Lieberson, Stanley and Mary Waters. 1988. *From Many Strands: Ethnic and Racial Groups in Contemporary America*. New York, NY: Russell Sage Foundation.

Light, Ivan and Edna Bonacich. 1988. *Immigrant Entrepreneurs: Koreans in Los Angeles, 1965–1982.* Berkeley, CA: University of California Press.

Lopez, David and Yen Espiritu. 1990. "Panethnicity in the Unites States: A Theoretical Framework." *Ethnic and Racial Studies.* 13 (2): 198–224.

Louie, Kam. 2017. "Asian Masculinity Studies in the West: From Minority Status to Soft Power." *Asia Study Perspectives: A Publication for the Center for Asia Pacific Studies,* University of San Francisco. [www.usfca.edu/center-asia-pacific/perspectives/v15n1/louie]

Louie, Kam. 2003. "Chinese, Japanese and Global Masculine Identities." Pp. 1–15 in *Asian Masculinities: The Meaning and Practice of Manhood in China and Japan,* edited by K. Louie and M. Low. London: Routledge Curzon.

Louie, Vivian. 2004. "'Being Practical' or 'Doing What I Want': The Role of Parents in the Academic Choices of Chinese Americans." Pp. 79–109 in *Becoming New Yorkers: Ethnographies of the New Second Generation,* edited by Philip Kasinitz, John H. Mollenkopf, and Mary C. Waters. New York, NY: Russell Sage Foundation.

Lowe, Lisa. 1996. *Immigrant Acts: Asian American Cultural Politics.* Durham, NC: Duke University Press.

Lu, Alexander and Y. Joel Wong. 2013. "Stressful Experiences of Masculinity Among U.S.-Born and Immigrant Asian-American Men." *Gender & Society.* 27 (3): 345–71.

Luhmann, N. 1986. *Love as Passion.* Cambridge, UK: Polity Press.

Ma, Sheng-Mei. 1998. *Immigrant Subjectivities in Asian American and Asian Diaspora Literatures.* Albany, NY: SUNY Press.

Mahler, Sara J. and P. Pessar. 2001. "Gendered Geographies of Power: Analyzing Gender Across Transnational Spaces." *Identities: Global Studies in Culture and Power.* 7 (4): 441–59.

Maira, Sunaina. 2002. *Desis in the House: Indian American Youth Culture in New York City.* Philadelphia, PA: Temple University Press.

Manalansan, Martin F. 2000. *Cultural Compass: Ethnographic Explorations of Asian America.* Philadelphia, PA: Temple University Press.

Mass, Amy Iwasaki. 1992. "Interracial Japanese Americans: The Best of Both Worlds or the End of the Japanese American Community?" Pp. 265–79 in *Racially Mixed People in America,* edited by Maria P. Root. Newbury Park, CA: Sage Publications.

Matthews, Julie. 2007. "Eurasian Persuasions: Mixed Race, Performativity, and Cosmopolitanism." *Journal of Intercultural Studies.* 28 (1): 41–54.

McFerson, Hazel M. 2006. *Blacks and Asians.* Durham, NC: Carolina Academic Press.

McGavin, Kirsten and Farida Fozdar (eds.). 2017. *Mixed Identities in Australia, New Zealand, and the Pacific Islands.* New York, NY: Routledge.

McKinney, Karyn D. and Joe R. Feagin. 2003. "Diverse Perspectives on Doing Antiracism: The Younger Generation." Pp. 233–51 in *White Out: The Continuing Significance of Racism,* edited by Ashley "Woody" Doane and Eduardo Bonilla-Silva. New York, NY: Routledge.

Memmi, Albert. 2000. *Racism.* Minneapolis, MN: University of Minnesota Press.

Memmi, Albert. 1965. *The Colonizer and the Colonized.* New York, NY: Orion Press.

Min, Pyong Gap (ed.). 2002. *The Second Generation: Ethnic Identity Among Asian Americans.* Walnut Creek, CA: Alta Mira Press.

Min, Pyong Gap and Chigon Kim. 2009. "Patterns of Intermarriages and Cross-Generational In-Marriages Among Native-Born Asian Americans." *International Migration Review.* 43 (3): 447–70.

Min, Pyong Gap and Rose Kim. 2000. "Formation of Ethnic and Racial Identities: Narratives by Young Asian-American Professionals." *Ethnic and Racial Studies.* 23 (4): 735–60.

Mok, Teresa A. 1999. "Asian American Dating: Important Factors in Partner Choice." *Cultural Diversity and Ethnic Minority Psychology.* 5 (2): 103–17.

Moran, Rachel F. 2001. *Interracial Intimacy: The Regulation of Race and Romance.* Chicago: University of Chicago Press.

Murguia, Edward. 1982. *Chicano Intermarriage: A Theoretical and Empirical Study.* San Antonio, TX: Trinity University Press.

Muro, Jazmin A. and Lisa Martinez. 2018. "Is Love Color-Blind? Racial Blind Spots and Latinas' Romantic Relationships." *Sociology and Race and Ethnicity.* 4 (4): 527–40.

Nagata, Donna. 1993. *Legacy of Injustice: Exploring the Cross-Generational Impact of the Japanese-American Internment.* New York, NY: Plenum Press.

Nagel, Joane. 2003. *Race, Ethnicity, and Sexuality: Intimate Intersections, Forbidden Frontiers.* New York, NY: Oxford University Press.

Nagel, Joane. 1996. *American Indian Ethnic Renewal: Red Power and the Resurgence of Identity and Culture.* New York, NY: Oxford University Press.

Nagel, Joane. 1994. "Constructing Ethnicity: Creating and Recreating Ethnic Identity and Culture." *Social Problems.* 41 (1): 152–76.

Neckerman, Kathryn M., Prudence Carter, and Jennifer Lee. 1999. "Segmented Assimilation and Minority Cultures of Mobility." *Ethnic and Racial Studies.* 22 (6): 945–65.

Nederveen Pieterse, Jan. 1995. "Globalization as Hybridization." Pp. 45–68 in *Global Modernities,* edited by Mike Featherstone, Scott Lash, and Roland Robertson. London: SAGE.

Nederveen Pieterse, Jan. 2004. *Globalization and Culture: Global Melange.* Lanham, MD: Rowman and Littlefield.

Nemoto, Kumiko. 2009. *Racing Romance: Love, Power, and Desire Among Asian American/White Couples.* New Brunswick, NJ: Rutgers University Press.

Ng, Franklin, Judy Yung, Stephen S. Fugita, and Elaine H. Kim. 1994. *New Visions in Asian American Issues: Diversity, Community, Power.* Pullman, WA: Washington State University Press.

Ng, Natalie. 2018. "Asian Masculinity vs. 'Western' Masculinity by Shadowsweep and Natalie Ng." June 4. [https://medium.com/@natalie_ng/asian-masculinity-vs-western-masculinity-by-shadowsweep-and-natalie-ng-85cdfd1b2457]

O'Brien, Eileen. 2008. *The Racial Middle: Latinos and Asian Americans Living Beyond the Racial Divide.* New York, NY: New York University Press.

Ocampo, Anthony C. 2016. *Latinos of Asia: How Filipino Americans Break the Rules of Race.* Stanford, CA: Stanford University Press.

Okamoto, Dina G. 2007. "Marrying Out: A Boundary Approach to Understanding the Marital Integration of Asian Americans." *Social Science Research.* (36): 1391–414.

Okamoto, Dina G. 2003. "Toward a Theory of Panethnicity: Explaining Asian American Collective Action." *American Sociological Review.* 68: 811–42.

Okihiro, Gary Y. 1994. *Margins and Mainstreams: Asians in American History and Culture.* Seattle, WA: University of Washington Press.

Olzak, S. 1992. *The Dynamics of Ethnic Competition and Conflict.* Stanford, CA: Stanford University Press.

Omi, Michael and Howard Winant. 1994. *Racial Formation in the US: From the 1960s to the 1990s,* 2nd ed. New York, NY: Routledge.

Ong, Aihwa. 1999. *Flexible Citizenship: The Cultural Logics of Transnationality.* Durham, NC: Duke University Press.

Ong, Aihwa. 1996. "Cultural Citizenship as Subject-Making: Immigrants Negotiate Racial and Cultural Boundaries in the United States." *Current Anthropology.* 37 (5): 737–51.

Ong, Paul M. and Tania Azores. 1994. "Asian Immigrants in Los Angeles: Diversity and Divisions." Pp. 100–29. *The New Asian Immigration in Los Angeles and Global Restructuring*, edited by Paul M. Ong, Edna Bonacich, and Lucie Cheng. Philadelphia, PA: Temple University Press.

Onishi, N. 1996. "New Sense of Race Arises Among Asian-Americans." *New York Times*, p. A1.

Osajima, Keith. 1993. "Hidden Injuries of Race." In *Bearing Dreams, Shaping Visions: Asian Pacific American Perspectives*, edited by Gail Nomura, Shawn Wong, Linda Revilla, and Shirley Hune. Pullman, WA: Washington University Press.

Osajima, Keith. 1988. "Asians Americans as Model Minority: An Analysis of the Popular Press Image in the 1960s and 1980s." In *Reflections on the Shattered Windows: Promises and Prospects for Asian-American Studies*, edited by Gary Okihiro, John Liu, Arthur Hansen, and Shirley Hune. Pullman, WA: Washington State University Press.

Outlaw, Lucius. 1990. "Toward a Critical Theory of 'Race'." Pp. 58–92 in *Anatomy of Racism*, edited by Theo Goldberg. Minneapolis, MN: University of Minnesota Press.

Padilla, Felix. 1985. *Latino Ethnic Consciousness: The Case of Mexicans and Puerto Ricans in Chicago*. Notre Dame: University of Notre Dame Press.

Padilla, Mark B., Jennifer S. Hirsch, Miguel Munoz-Laboy, Robert E. Sember, and Richard G. Parker. 2007. *Love and Globalization: Transformation of Intimacy in the Contemporary World*. Nashville, TN: Vanderbilt University Press.

Palriwala, Rajni and Patricia Uberoi (eds.). 2008. *Marriage, Migration, and Gender*. New Delhi, India: Sage Publications.

Palumbo-Liu, David. 1999. *Asian/American: Historical Crossings of a Racial Frontier*. Stanford, CA: Stanford University Press.

Pang, Gin Yong. 1994. "Attitudes Toward Interracial and Interethnic Relationships and Intermarriage Among Korean Americans: The Intersections of Race, Gender, and Class Inequality." Pp. 112–19 in *New Visions in Asian American Studies: Diversity, Community, Power*, edited by Franklin Ng, Judy Yung, Stephen Fugita, and Elain Kim. Pullman, WA: Washington State University Press.

Parekh, Bhikhu. 1991. "British Citizenship and Cultural Difference." In *Citizenship*, edited by Geoff Andrews. London: Lawrence and Wishart.

Park, Robert E. 1950. *Race and Culture*. Glencoe, IL: Free Press.

Park, Robert E. and Earnest W. Burgess. 1924. *Introduction to the Science of Sociology*, 2nd ed. Chicago, IL: University of Chicago Press.

Pew Research Center. 2013a. "Second Generation Americans: A Portrait of the Adult Children of Immigrants." February 7. Pew Research Center, Washington, DC.

Pew Research Center. 2013b. "The Rise of Asian Americans." April 4. Pew Research Center, Washington, DC.

Pew Research Center. 2010. "Marrying Out: One-in-Seven New U.S. Marriages Is Interracial or Interethnic." June 4. Pew Research Center, Washington, DC.

Phinney, Jean. 1990. "Ethnic Identity in Adolescents and Adults: Review of Research." *Psychological Bulletin*. 108 (3): 499–514.

Portes, Alejandro. 1984. "The Rise of Ethnicity: Determinants of Ethnic Perception Among Cuban Exiles in Miami." *American Sociological Review*. 49: 383–97.

Portes, Alejandro and R. Rumbaut. 2001. *Ethnicities: Children of Immigrants in America*. Berkeley, CA and New York, NY: University of California Press and Russell Sage Foundation.

Portes, Alejandro and R. Rumbaut. 1993. *Legacies: The Stories of the Immigrant Second Generation*. Berkeley, CA: University of California Press.

Portes, Alejandro and Min Zhou. 1993. "The New Second Generation: Segmented Assimilation and Its Variants." *The Annals of the American Academy of Political and Social Sciences*. 530: 74–96.

Purkayastha, Bandana. 2005. *Negotiating Ethnicity: Second-Generation South Asian Americans Traverse a Transnational World*. New Brunswick, NJ: Rutgers University Press.

Pyke, Karen D. 2007. "Defying the Taboo on the Study of Internalized Racial Oppression." Pp. 101–20 in *Migration and Immigration, Social Change, and Cultural Transformation*, edited by Emory Elliott, Jasmine Payne, and Patricia Ploesch. New York, NY: Palgrave Macmillan.

Pyke, Karen D. and Tran Dang. 2003. "'FOB' and 'Whitewashed': Identity and Internalized Racism Among Second Generation Asian Americans." *Qualitative Sociology*. 26 (2): 147–72.

Pyke, Karen D. and Denise L. Johnson. 2003. "Asian American Women and Racialized Femininities: 'Doing' Gender Across Cultural Worlds." *Gender & Society*. 17 (1): 33–53.

Qian, Zhenchao. 2005. "Breaking the Last Taboo: Interracial Marriage in America." *Contexts*. 4 (4): 33–37.

Qian, Zhenchao. 2002. "Race and Social Distance: Intermarriage with Non-Latino Whites." *Race & Society*. 5 (1): 33–47.

Qian, Zhenchao. 1997. "Breaking the Racial Barriers: Variations in Interracial Marriage Between 1980 and 1990." *Demography*. 34 (2): 263–76.

Qian, Zhenchao, S.L. Blair, and S. Ruf. 2001. "Asian American Interracial and Interethnic Marriages: Differences by Education and Nativity." *International Migration Review*. 35: 557–86.

Qian, Zhenchao and Daniel T. Lichter. 2007. "Social Boundaries and Marital Assimilation: Interpreting Trends in Racial and Ethnic Intermarriage." *American Sociological Review*. 72 (February): 68–94.

Qian, Zhenchao and Daniel T. Lichter. 2001. "Measuring Marital Assimilation: Intermarriage among Natives and Immigrants." *Social Science Research*. 30: 289–312.

Raab, Josef and Martin Butler (eds.). 2008. *Hybrid Americas: Contacts, Contrasts, and Confluences in New World Literatures and Cultures*. Berlin: Lit Verlag.

Reddy, M.T. 1994. *Crossing the Color Line: Race, Parenting, and Culture*. New Brunswick, NJ: Rutgers University Press.

Rich, Adrienne. 1980. "Compulsory Heterosexuality and Lesbian Existence." *Signs*. 5 (4): 631–60.

Robnett, Belinda and Cynthia Feliciano. 2011. "Patterns of Racial-Ethnic Exclusion by Internet Daters." *Social Forces*. 89 (3): 807–28.

Rocha, Zarine L. and Farida Fozdar (eds.). 2017. *Mixed Race in Asia: Past, Present, and Future*. New York, NY: Routledge.

Rofel, Lisa. 2007. *Desiring China: Experiments in Neoliberalism, Sexuality, and Public Culture*. Durham, NC: Duke University Press.

Romano, Dungan. 1988. *Intercultural Marriage: Promises and Pitfalls*. Yarmouth, ME: Intercultural Press.

Romano, Renee. 2003. *Race Mixing: Black-White Marriage in Postwar America*. Cambridge, MA: Harvard University Press.

Root, Maria P.P. 2001. *Love's Revolution: Interracial Marriage*. Philadelphia, PA: Temple University Press.

Roozens, Eugeen E. 1989. *Creating Ethnicity: The Process of Ethnogenesis*. Newbury Park, CA: Sage Publications.

Rosaldo, Michele. 1984. "Towards an Anthropology of Self and Feeling." In *Cultural Theory*, edited by R.A. Shweder and R.A. Levine. Cambridge: Cambridge University Press.

Rosaldo, Renato. 1997. "Cultural Citizenship, Inequality, and Multiculturalism." Pp. 27–38 in *Latino Cultural Citizenship: Claiming Identity, Space and Rights*, edited by William V. Flores and Rina Benjayor. Boston, MA: Beacon Press.

Rosaldo, Renato. 1989. *Culture and Truth*. Boston, MA: Beacon Press.

Rosenblatt, Paul C., Terri A. Karis, and Richard Powell. 1995. *Multiracial Couples: Black and White Voices*. New York, NY: Sage Publications.

Rosenfeld, Michael. 2001. "The Salience of Pan-National Hispanic and Asian Identities in U.S. Marriage Markets." *Demography*. 38: 161–75.

Roth, Wendy. 2012. *Race Migrations: Latinos and the Cultural Transformation of Race*. Stanford, CA: Stanford University Press.

Rudrappa, Sharmila. 2004. *Ethnic Routes to Becoming American: Indian Immigrants and the Cultures of Citizenship*. New Brunswick, NJ: Rutgers University Press.

Rumbaut, Ruben. 1997. "Paradoxes (and Orthodoxies) of Assimilation." *Sociological Perspectives*. 40 (3): 483–511.

Rumbaut, Ruben. 1994. "The Crucible Within: Ethnic Identity, Self-Esteem, and Segmented Assimilation Among Children of Immigrants." *International Migration Review*. 28 (4): 748–94.

Saenz, Rogelio, Sean-Shong Hwang, Benigno E. Aguirre, and Robert N. Anderson. 1995. "Persistence and Change in Asian Identity Among Children of Intermarried Couples." *Sociological Perspectives*. 38 (2): 175–94.

Said, Edward. 1978. *Orientalism*. New York, NY: Pantheon Books.

Sakamoto, Arthur, Kimberly A. Goyette, and Chang Hwan Kim. 2009. "The Socioeconomic Attainments of Asian Americans." *Annual Review of Sociology*. 35: 255–76.

Salesses, Matthew. 2013. "A Conversation About Asian-American Men and Masculinity." *A-List Magazine*. January 3. [http://alist-magazine.com/home/a-conversation-on-asian-american-men-and-masculinity/]

Salgado de Snyder, Nelly, Cynthia M. Lopez, and Amado M. Padilla. 1982. "Ethnic Identity and Cultural Awareness Among the Offspring of Mexican Interethnic Marriages." *Journal of Early Adolescence*. 2 (3): 277–82.

Sandel, Todd L. 2015. *Brides on Sale: Taiwanese Cross-Border Marriages in a Globalizing Asia*. New York, NY: Peter Lang.

Sanjek, Roger. 1994. "Intermarriage and the Future of Races in the United States." Pp. 103–30 in *Race*, edited by S. Gregory and R. Sanjek. New Brunswick, NJ: Rutgers University Press.

Schachter, Ariela. 2016. "From 'Different' to 'Similar': An Experimental Approach to Understanding Assimilation." *American Sociological Review*. 81 (5): 981–1013.

Shimizu, Celine Parrenas. 2012. *Straitjacket Sexualities: Unbinding Asian American Manhoods in the Movies*. Stanford, CA: Stanford University Press.

Shinagawa, Larry Hajime and Gin Yong Pang. 1996. "Asian American Panethnicity and Intermarriage." *Amerasia Journal*. 22 (2): 127–52.

Shinagawa, Larry Hajime and Gin Young Pang. 1988. "Intraethnic, Interethnic, and Interracial Marriages Among Asian Americans in California, 1980." *Berkeley Journal of Sociology*. 33: 95–114.

Sklair, Leslie. 1991. *Sociology of the Global System*. Baltimore, MD: Johns Hopkins University Press.

Smedley, Audrey. 1993. *Race in North America: Origin and Evolution of a Worldview.* Boulder, CO: Westview Press.

Smith, Anthony D. 1990. "Towards a Global Culture?" Pp. 171–91 in *Global Culture: Nationalism, Globalization and Modernity,* edited by M. Featherstone. London: Sage Publications.

Song, Miri. 2017. *Multiracial Parents: Mixed Families, Generational Change and the Future of Race.* New York, NY: New York University Press.

Song, Miri. 2009. "Is Intermarriage a Good Indicator of Integration?" *Journal of Ethnic and Migration Studies.* 35 (2): 331–48.

Song, Miri. 2003. *Choosing Ethnic Identity.* Cambridge, UK: Polity Press.

SoSuave. 2007. June 26. [www.sosuave.net/forum/threads/brutal-truth-dating-advice-to-asian-american-men-by-my-consultant.125925/. Retrieved May 10, 2017 (2:22 pm CST)]

Spickard, Paul. 1989a. "Injustices Compounded: Amerasians and Non-Japanese Americans in World War II Concentration Camps." *Journal of Ethnic History.* 5 (2): 5–22.

Spickard, Paul. 1989b. *Mixed Blood: Intermarriage and Ethnic Identity in Twentieth-Century America.* Madison, WI: The University of Wisconsin Press.

Spivak, Gayatri. 1988. "Can the Subaltern Speak?" Pp. 271–313 in *Marxism and the Interpretation of Culture.* Urbana, IL: University of Illinois Press.

Steinbugler, Amy C. 2012. *Beyond Loving: Intimate Racework in Lesbian, Gay, and Straight Interracial Relationships.* New York, NY: Oxford University Press.

Strauss, Anselm L. and Juliet Corbin. 1990. *Basics of Qualitative Research: Grounded Theory Procedures and Techniques.* Newbury Park, CA: Sage Publications.

Strmic-Pawl, Hephzibah V. 2016. *Multiculturalism and Its Discontents: A Comparative Analysis of Asian-White and Black-White Multiracials.* Lanham, MD: Lexington Books.

Suh, Stephen Cho. 2016. "Negotiating Masculinity Across Borders: A Transnational Examination of Korean American Masculinities." *Men and Masculinities.* 20 (3): 317–44.

Sung, Betty Lee. 1990. *Chinese American Intermarriage.* Staten Island, NY: Center for Migration Studies.

Swarns, Rachel. 2012. "For Asian-American Couples, a Tie That Binds." *New York Times.* March 30.

Tajima, R. 1989. "Lotus Blossoms Don't Bleed: Images of Asian Women." Pp. 308–17 in *Making Waves: An Anthology of Writing by and About Asian American Women,* edited by Asian Women United of California. Boston, MA: Beacon.

Takagi, Dana Y. 1994. "Post-Civil Rights Politics and Asian American Identity: Admission and Higher Education." Pp. 229–42 in *Race,* edited by Steven Gregory and Roger Sanjek. New Brunswick, NJ: Rutgers University Press.

Takaki, Ronald T. 1979. *Iron Cages: Race and Culture in Nineteenth-Century America.* New York, NY: Knopf.

Takezawa. 2000. *Contemporary Asian America: A Multidisciplinary Reader,* edited by Zhou, Min and James V. Gatewood. New York, NY: New York University Press.

Taylor, Charles. 1994. *Multiculturalism: Examining the Politics of Recognition.* Princeton, NJ: Princeton University Press.

Tells, Edward E. and Vilma Ortiz. 2008. *Generations of Exclusion: Mexican Americans, Assimilation, and Race.* New York, NY: Russell Sage Foundation.

Tinker, John H. 1982. "Intermarriage and Assimilation in a Plural Society: Japanese Americans in the U.S." In *Intermarriage in the U.S.,* edited by Gary A. Crester and Joseph L. Loen. New York, NY: Haworth Press.

Tomlinson, John. 1999. *Globalization and Culture*. Chicago: University of Chicago Press.

Tse, Lucy. (1999). "Finding a Place to Be: Ethnic Identity Exploration of Asian Americans." *Adolescence*. 34: 121–138.

Tuan, Mia. 1999. "Neither Real American nor Real Asians? Multigeneration Asian-Ethnics Navigating the Terrain of Authenticity." *Qualitative Sociology*. 22 (2): 105–25.

Tuan, Mia. 1998. *Forever Foreigners or Honorary Whites: The Asian Ethnic Experience Today*. New Brunswick, NJ: Rutgers University Press.

Twine, France Winddance and Charles Gallagher. 2008. "Introduction: The Future of Whiteness: A Map of the 'Third Wave'." *Ethnic and Racial Studies*. 31 (1): 4–24.

Vallejo, Jody Agius. 2012. *Barrios to Burbs: The Making of the Mexican American Middle Class*. Stanford, CA: Stanford University Press.

Vasquez, Jessica M. 2017. *Marriage Vows ad Racial Choices*. New York, NY: Russell Sage Foundation.

Vasquez, Jessica M. 2014. "The Whitening Thesis Challenged: Biculturalism in Latino and Non-Hispanic Intermarriage." *Sociological Forum*. 29 (2): 386–407.

Vasquez, Jessica M. 2011a. "The Bumpy Road of Assimilation: Gender, Phenotype, and Historical Era." *Sociological Spectrum*. 31 (6): 718–48.

Vasquez, Jessica M. 2011b. *Mexican Americans Across Generations: Immigrant Families, Racial Realities*. New York, NY: New York University Press.

Vasquez, Jessica M. 2010. "Blurred Borders for Some but Not 'Others': Racialization, 'Flexible Ethnicity,' Gender, and Third-Generation Mexican American Identity." *Sociological Perspectives*. 53 (1): 45–71.

Vo, Linda Trinh and Rick Bonus. 2002. *Contemporary Asian American Communities: Intersections and Divergences*. Philadelphia, PA: Temple University Press.

Volker, Thomas, Terri A. Karis, and Joseph L. Wetchler (eds.). 2003. *Clinical Issues with Interracial Couples: Theories and Research*. New York, NY: Haworth Press.

Volpp, Leti. 2007. "'Obnoxious to Their Very Nature': Asian Americans and Constitutional Citizenship." Pp. 526–41 in *Contemporary Asian America: A Multidisciplinary Reader*, edited by Min Zhou and James V. Gatewood, 2nd ed. New York, NY: New York University Press.

Warner, W. Lloyd and Leo Srole. 1945. *The Social Systems of American Ethnic Groups*. New Haven, CT: Yale University Press.

Waters, Mary C. 1990. *Ethnic Options: Choosing Identities in America*. Berkeley, CA: University of California Press.

Waters, Mary C. 1989. "The Everyday Use of Surname to Determine Ethnic Ancestry." *Qualitative Sociology*. 12: 303–24.

Waters, Mary C. and Tomás C. Jiménez. 2005. "Assessing Immigrant Assimilation: New Empirical and Theoretical Challenges." *Annual Review of Sociology*. 31: 105–25.

Wiegman, R. 1991. "Black Bodies/American Commodities: Gender, Race, and the Bourgeois Ideal in Contemporary Film." Pp. 308–28 in *Unspeakable Images: Ethnicity and the American Cinema*. Urbana: University of Illinois Press.

Wielding, Elizabeth. 2003. "Latin/a and White Marriages: A Pilot Study Investigating the Experiences of Interethnic Couples in the United States." Pp. 41–55 in *Clinical Issues with Interracial Couples: Theories and Research*, edited by Joseph L. Wetchler and Terri A. Karis. New York, NY: Haworth Press.

Williams, Lucy. 2010. *Global Marriage: Cross-Border Marriage Migration in Global Context*. New York, NY: Palgrave Macmillan.

Williams, Patrick and Laura Christman. 1994. *Colonial Discourse and Postcolonial Theory: A Reader*. New York, NY: Columbia University Press.

Wimmer, Andreas. 2008. "Elementary Strategies of Ethnic Boundary Making." *Ethnic and Racial Studies*. 31 (6): 1025–55.

Winant, Howard. 2001. *The World Is a Ghetto: Race and Democracy Since World War II*. New York, NY: Basic Books.

Wong, E.F. 1978. *On Visual Media Racism: Asians in the American Motion Pictures*. New York, NY: Arno.

Wu, Frank. 2003. *Yellow: Race in America: Beyond Black and White*. New Haven, CT: Yale University Press.

Xie, Yu and Kimberly Goyette. 2004. *A Demographic Portrait of Asian Americans*. New York, NY: Russell Sage Foundation and Population Reference Bureau.

Xie, Yu and Kimberly Goyette. 1997. "The Racial Identification of Biracial Children with One Asian Parent: Evidence from the 1990 Census." *Social Forces*. 76 (2): 547–70.

Yancey, George. 2003. *Who Is White? Latinos, Asians, and the New Black/Non-Black Divide*. Boulder, CO: Lynne Rienner Publishers.

Yancey, George and Richard Lewis, Jr. 2009. *Interracial Families: Current Concepts and Controversies*. New York, NY: Routledge.

Yancey, William, Richard Juliani, and Eugene Erikson. 1976. "Emergent Ethnicity: A Review and Formulation." *American Sociological Review*. 41 (3): 391–403.

Yang, Jeff. 2012. "They Real Reason Why Asian Americans Are Outmarrying Less." *Speakeasy, The Wall Street Journal*. (Online journal). April 16.

Yang, Wesley. 2011. "Paper Tigers: What Happens to All the Asian-American Overachievers When the Test-Taking Ends?" *New York Magazine*. May 8. [http://nymag.com/news/features/asian-americans-2011-5/]

Yip, Alethia. 1997. "Pan-Asian Bonds of Matrimony." *Asia Week*. February 14.

Young, Robert. 1995. *Colonial Desire: Hybridity in Theory, Culture and Race*. London: Routledge.

Yu, Henry. 2001. *Thinking Orientals: Migration, Contact, and Exoticism in Modern America*. New York, NY: Oxford University Press.

Yu, Henry. 1999. "Mixing Bodies and Cultures: The Meaning of America's Fascination with Sex Between 'Orientals' and 'Whites'." Pp. 444–93 in *Sex, Love, Race: Crossing Boundaries in North American History*, edited by Martha Hodes. New York, NY: New York University Press.

Yu, Ji-Yeon. 2002. *Beyond the Shadow of Camptown: Korean Military Brides in America*. New York, NY: New York University Press.

Yuen, Nancy Wang. 2017. *Reel Inequality: Hollywood Actors and Racism*. New Brunswick, NJ: Rutgers University Press.

Yuval-Davis, Nira. 1997. *Gender and Nation*. Thousand Oaks, CA: Sage.

Zhou, Min and Carl Bankston. 1998. *Growing Up American: How Vietnamese Children Adapt to Life in the United States*. New York, NY: Russell Sage Foundation.

Zhou, Min and James V. Gatewood. 2000. *Contemporary Asian America: A Multidisciplinary Reader*. New York, NY: New York University Press.

Zia, Helen. 2000. *Asian American Dreams: The Emergence of an American People*. New York, NY: Farrar, Straus and Giroux.

# INDEX

Made in the USA
Middletown, DE
29 March 2022

63336188R00137